# PRIVATE
# POLITICS
# AND
# PUBLIC
# VOICES

Nikki Brown

# Private Politics and Public Voices

Black Women's Activism
from World War I
to the New Deal

*Indiana University Press*
Bloomington and Indianapolis

This book is a publication of

Indiana University Press
601 North Morton Street
Bloomington, IN 47404-3797 USA

http://iupress.indiana.edu

*Telephone orders*　800-842-6796
*Fax orders*　812-855-7931
*Orders by e-mail*　iuporder@indiana.edu

The paper used in this publication meets the minimum
requirements of American National Standard for Information
Sciences—Permanence of Paper for Printed Library Materials,
ANSI Z39.48-1984.

Manufactured in the United States of America

**Library of Congress Cataloging-in-Publication Data**

Brown, Nikki.
　Private politics and public voices : Black women's activism from
World War I to the New Deal / Nikki Brown.
　　p. cm. — (Blacks in the diaspora)
　Includes bibliographical references and indexes.
　ISBN-13: 978-0-253-34804-3 (cloth : alk. paper)
　ISBN-10: 0-253-34804-8 (cloth : alk. paper) 1. African
American women—History—20th century. 2. Middle class
women—United States—History—20th century. 3. African
American women political activists—History—20th century. 4.
Patriotism—United States—History—20th century. 5. Social
service—United States—History—20th century. 6. World War,
1914–1918—African Americans. 7. World War, 1914–1918—
Women. 8. World War, 1914–1918—Social aspects—United
States. 9. United States—Social conditions—1918–1932. 10.
United States—Race relations—History—20th century. I. Title.
　E185.86.B6975 2006
　305.48'896073009041—dc22

　　　　　　　　　　　　　　　　　2006021426

1 2 3 4 5 11 10 09 08 07 06

# Contents

# Acknowledgments

This book would not have been possible without the support of friends, family, mentors, professors, librarians, and institutions. First and foremost, I thank James and Maxine, Scot and Kimberly, Thomasina and Annie Lou, Herbert and Bill Sr., Beverly, Carol, Bill Jr., Shirley, and Khaula for their enduring love and guidance. My exceptional cousins—Deon, Reginald, Adam, Abdul Khaliq, Ahmed, Abdullah, Yusef, Usama, and Thomasina—listened patiently and suggested new avenues of thought to pursue. Many thanks go to Michelle Wright for planting the seed of this idea and to Karen Pursell for giving the idea room to grow. I also thank Mary Thornton and Yasmin Degout for their sustaining friendship.

I am forever indebted to the Social Science Research Council and the Mellon Minority Undergraduate Fellowship (now Mellon Mays Undergraduate Fellowship) for imparting upon me the importance of rigorous research and study. Lydia English, Carma Van Allen, and Beverlee Bruce have been extraordinarily helpful from the initial stages to the end. I thank Oberlin College professors Geoffrey Blodgett and Gary Kornblith for instilling in me a lifelong love of history.

At Yale University, Glenda Gilmore, Cynthia Russett, Jay Winter, and Robert Johnston pushed me to higher levels of precision and concentration. Their sound advice and insightful observations for improvements to the manuscript were vital elements in the evolution of this project.

The Center for Black Studies at the University of California Santa Barbara and the Career Enhancement Fellowship of the Woodrow Wilson National Fellowship Foundation provided vital funds for the eventual completion of this project. I thank Claudine Michel of UCSB and Richard Hope, Bill Mitchell, and Sylvia Sheridan of the Woodrow Wilson National Fellowship Foundation for selecting this project to fund. Caroline Frost, David Brent Field, and Ken and Anne Warfield of the Santa Barbara Public Library supported me and this project in ways too numerous to mention.

At Kent State University, Elizabeth Smith-Pryor and Richard Pryor II lent their considerable talents to reading and commenting on the manuscript. I also thank Richard and Lisa Steigmann-Gall, John Jameson, Leone Hudson, and Kevin Floyd for their immense encouragement and assistance.

The helpful staff at several university libraries made the daunting task of researching this history enjoyable and enlightening. The Sophia Smith Collection at Smith College and the Oberlin College Archives of the Oberlin College Library also provided much-needed financial support for this book. I thank Dagmar Getz and Lara Friedman-Shedlov, who administer the Kautz Family Papers at the University of Minnesota, for keeping the library open an extra hour to accommodate last-minute finds. The Kent State University Library possesses the Tuskegee Institute News Clippings File, which became an invaluable addition to this project. The Beinecke Manuscript and Rare Book Library and the James Weldon Johnson Collection at Yale University provided significant archival material on black women's organizations. The Special Collections Library at the University of Delaware, the National Archives Research Administration II in College Park, the Schlesinger Library at the Radcliffe Institute for Advanced Study, and the Erie County Historical Society have important archival collections available for future research. The Africana Studies and Research Center granted me access to its considerable resources and space to write.

Bob Sloan and Jane Quinet at Indiana University Press supported this project from its earliest stages as a manuscript. Tera Hunter, at Carnegie Mellon University, and Barbara McCaskill, at the University of Georgia, provided invaluable guidance and advice.

And at Grambling State University, the faculty and staff in the Department of History have been wonderful. I would also like to thank Horace Judson, Robert Dixon, Brenda Wall, Hugh Wilson, and Chimeg Banzar for giving me the most important incentives to finish.

# Introduction

The following story of black women and World War I began with a brief note by Willie Mae King in an article about the war's impact on black women. In the July 1918 issue of the *A.M.E. Church Review,* King provocatively wrote, "This World War is destined to solve the problems of colored women just as it will solve other problems. . . . We colored women are in this great fight too, and we must prove our worth and ability because through this achievement over hate and oppression lies equal rights and opportunities not only for the colored men of America but colored women as well." King alluded to a national political agenda that revolved around key questions. How soon after the World War for Democracy could African Americans expect democracy in America? Might black participation in the war result in long overdue civil rights legislation? How much could African American patriotism counteract the institutionalized racism endemic throughout the country? Could the World War fulfill the promise of full citizenship for African American men and women, a promise made at the end of the Civil War?

Clearly, King thought so. Their individual writings were indicative of a larger trend among black clubwomen, who played crucial roles in African American enlistment in World War I. Similar to the efforts of middle-class white women supporting their doughboys, middle-class black clubwomen held fundraisers at local auxiliaries, knitted sweaters and mittens, petitioned their neighbors for donations, and encouraged the conservation of foodstuffs and household wares. In the course of researching the NACW and black clubwomen, I found that the National Association of Colored Women (NACW) embedded within its fundraising efforts the elements of an important political debate about the future of black America, and within black middle-class women's war work was a political discussion that went beyond the NACW's constituency of 50,000 women. In fact, if the NACW's volunteer work had not contained the political elements of a civil rights agenda, there would have been no need to expand on the story.

World War I also played a pivotal role in shaping the black female experience in the twentieth century, and the story of black women's politics, in the wake of the war, needs to be told. The black woman's experience has existed interdependently to the black man's experience; that is, they are linked symbiotically by race and racism yet divided by gender and sexism. In terms of national questions, such as the right to vote and the spread of Jim Crow, and in terms of individual experiences, such as work and the family, the black woman's experience has navigated complex political terrain by skillfully employing their private politics and public voices. Black women's politics prior to the outbreak of war were driven by the notions of uplift and service, evident in the structure of black women's organizations prior to the war. Still another theme within black women's political expressions was black identity and black representation, particularly important at the dawn of the New Negro Movement and the Harlem cultural renaissance.

Thus, understanding World War I and its aftermath is essential to recognizing the singularity of the black female experience in a time period dominated by masculine narratives and viewpoints. First off, the most important impact of World War I on African Americans was its stimulation of the Great Migration. The estimated numbers of migrants range from 250,000 to 500,000, but the numbers of migrants in the early years of the war are not as important as the geographical shift, as 90 percent of the nation's black residents lived in the southern states and 80 percent of those lived in the Deep South. From the southern states to the northern and Midwestern states, the Great Migration determined the type of work black women were most likely to be engaged in. For example, domestic work and agricultural labor were the most common types of jobs for black women, both married and single, prior to 1920. During the World War, the call of the North drew a small yet important population of black women northward into industrial jobs. But for most black women, the World War granted women more control over their work, working conditions, and pay. The empowerment of controlling one's future in work naturally evolved along political terms. As working-class black women formed labor unions and labor leagues to study the impact of new industrial jobs, southern legislation politics came under increased pressure to secure these new gains for women in the postwar period.

Then there were tensions from the public and private spheres. One of the prevailing myths about the tensions between public and private was that the public sphere, such as political work or labor outside the home, was so strenuous that most women avoided it in favor of maintaining a private life; conversely the private sphere, which included family life and church activity, was absent of political expression. In short, middle-class African American women in 1918 had little to do with their time, while working-class African American women in 1918 worked all the time, and neither group showed an interest in politics. All these assertions are untrue. If we redefine politics, so that it includes community development, as Stephanie Shaw writes, and social justice and social welfare, as Dorothy Salem argues, and national party politics, as Evelyn Brooks Higginbotham explores, then politics becomes a multifaceted enterprise in which women worked toward the goals of African American equality within the strictures of Jim Crow, gender inequity, and class limitations.

Black men's and black women's politics bridged the American entrance into the World War, anti-lynching bills, and the extension of political equality to black Americans. In fact, most black politicians and intellectuals were convinced that the World War for Democracy would reestablish the full citizenship of African Americans, a national priority abandoned after Reconstruction. Still, middle-class women offered a different approach to the civil rights agenda during World War I. They pursued an agenda of community development and social work. Middle-class African American women often broached the subjects of nurseries, daycares, parks, and old folks' homes in their political speech, and they emphasized that maintaining a respectable private sphere was critical to the advancement of black communities. One of the most important things to keep in mind about black women's politics in the early twentieth century is that private concerns, such as respectability and representation, deeply influenced political interests, such as the vote, education, and labor. The turning point in the struggle for civil rights came after the war, however, after race riots in large and small American cities infused the New Negro Movement with militant political defiance. In the course of the New Negro Movement, black women's politics faced new challenges to their mission and visibility. Other organizations, like the NAACP and the Universal Negro Improvement Association, were poised to lead black Americans in a direction of self-conscious and self-aware authentic blackness.

But, ultimately, World War I's influence on the black female experience was felt most deeply in the women's suffrage movement. World War I granted the women's suffrage movement in America the political leverage needed to ratify the vote for women in 1920. For white suffragists, the right to vote was a matter of equity and empowerment in politics. For black suffragists, who had been long estranged from the movement, the right to vote appeared to be the sword with which black women might cut through the Gordian knot of racism and sexism constraining their political voices. Black women also were excited about the prospect of universal suffrage. Not only were black women un-franchised in the states where blacks were highest in population, but black men were also disenfranchised in these same states. Voting rights and accessible politics for African American men were stymied time and again owing to fears of racial mixture and intermarriage, since many whites believed that black men might use their votes to codify social equality. The agitation for black women's suffrage heightened those fears, feeding cultural stereotypes of a general black menace. Middle-class African American men demanded that politics be accessible to them, but for African American women, the primary challenge was in convincing white legislators that black women would use the vote for themselves, and that they would not attempt to speak for their husbands, brothers, and sons. The right to vote granted black women a political legitimacy that engendered even greater political pursuits. Though their voices were undermined by Jim Crow legislation in the 1930s, black women's political voices triumphed in the 1920s by aligning to national party politics.

From the viewpoint of the twenty-first century, African American involvement in World War I seems disappointing, if not fruitless. But without World War I, there would have been no Harlem Renaissance and no New Negro Movement. The NAACP and Marcus Garvey still would have had a captive audience among African Americans, but without the war, neither the NAACP nor Garvey could have rallied African Americans to a more militant self-awareness that fueled a national movement of black peoples. There would have been no women's suffrage amendment, since Cary Chapman Catt, as president of the National American Woman Suffrage Association, would have had no patriotic sacrifices on which to base her argument for the recognition of women's right to vote. And for the leading figures among African American women's politics, like Mary Church Terrell, Mary B. Talbert, Alice Dunbar-Nelson, and a good many lesser-known women, a generation of political expertise and empowerment might have been lost between 1914 and 1930. World War I produced an alchemy of opportunity, agenda, and motivation that reinvigorated black women's politics, so that their lives and their experience entered a new phase after 1920. Thus *the black experience of the New Negro* could no longer be presumed to be a black male experience, but rather a female experience as well, shaped by gender, class, race, representation, and political motivation.

PRIVATE

POLITICS

AND

PUBLIC

VOICES

# 1

# Patriotism and Jim Crow

The twenty-four months between the summer of 1916 and the summer of 1918 marked the African American women's club movement at the height of its political influence. In the summer of 1916, the National Association of Colored Women (NACW) achieved a feat that no other organization, black or white, male or female, had accomplished: it had saved Frederick Douglass's historic home in Anacostia from ruin. Douglass was arguably the most important and most recognized figure in African American history in 1916, second, perhaps, only to Abraham Lincoln. In 1916 the intellectual leaders among black men, such as W. E. B. Du Bois or the recently deceased Booker T. Washington, still lived and worked in the shadow of Frederick Douglass, who was an escaped slave, three-time author, feminist, abolitionist, and international statesman. And no organization had been able to save his home from the brambles, bushes, creeping vines, and weeds of the Washington, D.C., suburb that threatened to reclaim it.

The property had been willed to the NACW in 1905 by Douglass's widow, Helen, and the NACW took up the charge to restore it at the organization's 1916 convention in Baltimore. With the help of a $1,000 donation from African American soldiers stationed in France, a $500 personal gift from millionaire Madam C. J. Walker, and a contribution of $400 from the Illinois Federation of Colored Women's Clubs, the clubwomen not only collected enough contributions to cover the cost of the mortgage but also raised an additional $30,000 for repairs. At the organization's 1918 Denver convention, Mary B. Talbert, president of the NACW, announced to her fellow clubwomen that the organization had rescued the property. Before an audience of cheering NACW delegates, Talbert ripped up and burned the bank mortgage, adding that with the renovations the property was now worth $65,000.[1] The Reverend Francis J. Grimke congratulated the women of the NACW on their victory in restoring the house and rescuing it from bankruptcy. "Hurrah! Hurrah! for the women of our race. Hurrah! Hurrah! for the National Association of Colored Women. . . . I have never felt prouder of the women of our race than at that moment. And, specially, when I remembered that we men for fourteen years had been struggling with the problem and failed, utterly failed of a solution."[2]

In the summer of 1917 the NACW marked a more solemn occasion, one that overshadowed the affirmation twelve months earlier. A silent march called several thousand African Americans to New York City's Fifth Avenue to protest a riot in East St. Louis, Illinois, in June 1917, which had claimed the lives of nearly one hundred blacks and destroyed the entire black district of the city. The march began at 57th Street and continued for thirty-four blocks to 23rd Street, past the New York Public Library, through midtown Manhattan, and ending at Madison Square Park.[3] The violence and brutality of the East St. Louis riot shocked Americans, and black Americans called on black leaders—intellectuals, politicians, clergymen, and businessmen—to bear witness to efforts by black East St. Louisans to protect their families and homes as rioters tore down the city.

Almost half of the marchers in New York were women, who all wore ankle-length white dresses, white hats, and Red Cross sashes. In front of the procession of women was a sizeable group of children, also dressed in white, and following the women were rows of black men, wearing black suits and black hats. One group of black women made a special banner reading, "Pray for the Lady Macbeth of East St. Louis," a reference to an alleged incident wherein at least two white women pulled black women off a streetcar, tore off one woman's clothing, and "then took off her shoes and beat her over the face and head with their shoe heels."[4] Soon after the riot, the Northeastern Federation of Colored Women sent a strongly worded letter of protest to President Woodrow Wilson, inveighing the violence and asking him to do the same. The Northeast Federation also reminded the president of his responsibilities to protect democracy for African Americans, continuing, "*you can never without them [African Americans] win this war for world democracy.* Neither can *you win it* unless you abolish lynchings, discrimination, disenfranchisement, jim crowism, and show that '[our] government is for the protection of all American citizens alike, and not for the destruction of rights.'"[5]

It was no coincidence that black clubwomen made their boldest political utterances—saving the Douglass home and protesting the East St. Louis riot—at the height of the World War. For the World War had created an unusual political space, where, for the first time in the twentieth century, middle-class African American women combined prowar sentiments and antiracist protests for the purpose of elevating African Americans to first-class citizenship. The organizational route that black clubwomen and the

NACW traveled after 1916 put black women's politics at the forefront of African American politics. Additionally, middle-class black women embedded gender politics in their wartime community activism, via uplift for black families. When middle-class club workers spoke to the health and welfare of black people during the war, they focused on black women's political voice at a time when black men's political attention was directed toward increasing the number of black soldiers in the armed services. Thus, middle-class clubwomen's politics formed around supporting black men's participation in the war and advocating black women's empowerment. The public politics of clubwork evolved in the often-suffocating political atmosphere of World War I and during a time when towering figures in black male leadership overshadowed women's work. Furthermore, black clubwomen tolerated, or cooperated, with Jim Crow, and they confronted it to its core in the same unusual political space of wartime. The World War accelerated the organizational dominance of the NACW, but the final two years of the war witnessed black clubwomen forming their political identity around an entrance into public, national politics.

In order to advance a progressive agenda of civic equality and civil rights, the organization's support of the World War revolved around several interconnected considerations: engaging in war work that also adhered to notions about the private sphere of family and home; maintaining Progressive Era gender relations; and tolerating but challenging racial segregation. All three considerations required substantial navigation. However, black clubwomen, and the larger number of black middle-class women, did not necessarily maneuver their war work in spite of these structures; that is, black clubwomen did not always seek to dispute unequal gender relations or to push gender reform on black leaders and intellectuals who were sure to reject it. Despite the NACW's political agility, the organization learned a number of hard lessons during the war that would help construct the New Negro Movement in the postwar period. This final struggle would last much longer than the end of the war, but it was also the driving conflict, in the form of the riotous summer of 1917, that would transform the grassroots politics of black clubwomen.

## Public Politics and the World War

Black clubwomen's politics crossed multiple domains as the Great War unfolded in the United States. By navigating their relationships with middle-class African American men, with middle-class white women, and with Jim

Crow, black clubwomen redirected their focus from the private sphere of home and family to the public sphere of public war work and military life. Some women considered the war and black participation in it as an opportunity for immense transformation. Others used the war as a springboard to indict the poor state of racial relations and the low quality of life endured by many African American families across the nation. To these ends, black clubwomen used their background in community work to give black soldiers their support, through offering goods and services and forming the social foundation for black families affected by the loss of a breadwinner. As a response to black involvement in the war, black clubwomen created networks of grassroots organization and engaged in war work that spoke to two interdependent discourses—the language of patriotism and the language of civil rights. Mary B. Talbert, who helped found the NAACP and was an expert public speaker, interwove the two strands of thought, saying, "The race will get out of this war just what it puts into it."[6]

In the United States, the federal government shut down nearly all forms of debate and dissent during the Great War, particularly among African Americans. Historian Theodore Kornweibel has found that the national debate on black participation in the war was closely watched by the federal authorities. "Dissent was unpopular, and, given fears that African Americans were susceptible to manipulation by enemy agents, black protest was widely distrusted," Kornweibel writes, commenting on the crackdown on political expression in black organizations and newspapers. Historian Mark Ellis has described also the motivations driving black organizations to encourage black enlistment and to positively report on the war's impact on African Americans. The NAACP and its outspoken magazine, *The Crisis,* were specifically targeted by the Bureau of Investigation, as the organization and other blacks "embraced various political ideologies and methods during and immediately after World War I, most of which entailed uncompromising opposition to discrimination." Under surveillance and threatened with censorship, black organizations and black newspapers were caught in a precarious situation. If they continued their work against the racial segregation and violence victimizing black people, then black organizations faced prosecution on charges of inciting disloyalty. But, if they actively campaigned for black involvement in the war to make the world safe for democracy, then they risked offending their black constituencies, who pressed for coverage of efforts to gain political rights and economic opportunities. With the exception of the National Equal Rights League and a handful of small churches and socialist groups, black leaders and black organizations shifted their political discourses to support the war for the short term and to continue their activism for black rights in the long term.[7]

The NACW was one of the organizations that took a pro-war stance, or rather, a pro–black involvement stance. As the nation's largest black organization—with 50,000 members and a reserve of millions of dollars and property worth over $100,000—the NACW focused its attention on the war's impact on black women and families, a subject that black male leaders had taken for granted. Prior to the war, the NACW had built its historical legacy on assisting black women to improve black homes and to uplift black communities. Shifting from the private sphere to public politics required an adept navigation of gender relations, as men not only dominated politics in the Progressive Era but also determined which issues were gendered and which were not. Politics were not open to gendered analysis among middle-class blacks, but the stereotypical images of black women were often woven into politics as a way to cut off women's political ambitions. Historian Deborah Gray White has argued that some race men believed in and shared harmful stereotypes of black women as coarse, lazy, and immodest that were no different than white stereotypes of African Americans. Though black clubwomen defended themselves in the pages of black newspapers and journals, the consequence was "a growing tendency to blame black women for every weakness of the race . . . which held them accountable for the progress of the race."[8]

Similarly, historian Stephanie Shaw has argued that middle-class black women wrestled with competing responsibilities in the private and public spheres, where they were raised and expected to be models of womanhood, black success, and middle-class refinement. Shaw has contended in an intriguing statement on gender relations, "Even if black women desired to work as professionals and were prepared to do so, they had to be *allowed* to."[9] Black clubwomen and professional workers invested much time and energy in supporting the middle class's embrace of the doctrine of superiority in the political arena. As scholar Glenda Gilmore has explored, well-to-do African Americans of the Progressive Era adhered to strict rules of gender and politics, and the image of the "Best Man" dominated the public and intellectual sphere—presenting the best and brightest black men to lead the race and to inspire loyal black enthusiasm. "For most black women, politics began at home, blending the public and the private," writes Gilmore, and as the World War gradually drew in the United States, middle-class black women created a movement of politics that employed notions of the home and family and "realized the practical importance of the group over the individual" in issues such as voting rights, education, and political leadership.[10] On top of the dynamics of gender relations, the NACW felt the pressure to encourage black participation in the same way it had supported black economic and social uplift, as its primary clubs and many of its members had come under federal surveillance for inciting disloyal acts.[11]

The World War had the effect of masculinizing gender relations within the African American middle class, reframing discussions from black participation to black male participation. Clubwomen found that the war for democracy, in Europe and in the United States, was a man's war. Among African American leaders and intellectuals who supported black participation in the war, social values such as duty, honor, and valor were oft-repeated phrases in their commentary. When their editorials turned to what women could give, the sacrifice of sons was invariably the answer. In December 1917, Ralph Tyler wrote in the African American *Cleveland Advocate,* "It is the mother upon whom falls heaviest this awful blood-steeped and death-charged cruel war. When she has to give up the son, just as he entered into manhood's estate—the son whose growth she has watched from the cradle up—her heart bleeds. . . . Who wouldn't love a mother?"[12] Black women's magazines shared the sentiment of mothers' duties in the war. The *Half-Century Magazine,* a popular journal for middle-class black women, urged its readers to prepare their sons to defend democracy, explaining, "Thousands of mothers and wives and sweethearts carry heavy, saddened hearts because of their absence from the fireside, but these men are for work and for war; these men are the saviors of democracy."[13] James Weldon Johnson, as editor of "Views and Reviews," the editorial section of the *New York Age,* concentrated principally on the economic benefits for black men in his articles advocating black participation. Commenting on the loss of European immigrant workers to American businesses, Johnson wrote in the *New York Age,* "These are happy days for the colored brethren. Higher pay is the sort of uplift most valued, and is the best proof of growing appreciation and revaluation of the negro's services to society."[14] A few months before the United States declared war on Germany, Johnson argued that it was black men's patriotic duty to fight, adding, "He [the African American man] should not let any of his rights go by default. . . .The enthusiasm with which black men have always sprung to the colors, and the loyalty and bravery with which they have fought for this country in all of its battles have become a tradition."[15] On the issue of black migration and northern assistance in the transition, Johnson reminded his readers, "It is a situation that should make us all remember and feel that we are our brothers' keeper."[16]

But one editorial exchange in "Views and Reviews" illustrated that questioning the war's consequences for women was neither an insignificant nor a facile matter, particularly as black participation and black women's sacrifices were foregone conclusions. In a 1916 letter to the *New York Age,* a "Colored Wife and Mother" wrote to oppose the participation of black men in the war in Europe, saying that with black men absent from the community, there would be no one left to protect black women and children from hostile whites. "And let me say right here that there is not one white woman in this country who fears the black brute one-half as much as the colored woman fears the white brute. Our fear is double, for ourselves and for our natural protectors who are at every disadvantage in the community and in the courts when they protect their women. . . . No one can know a colored woman's predicament unless they live her life." The woman also voiced feminist concerns. She believed that African American involvement in the Great War would have precipitated a reversal in the quality of black life, particularly black women's lives. "Feeling thus, yet knowing that we must bow to circumstances because we have no alternative and if the need arises, we women must bravely send out our loved ones, though it rends our very souls, and must try to inspire them with hope so that they may fight bravely and thus make their task easier. Even though we may do this, still our real selves fiercely protest."[17] The idea that the Colored Wife and Mother had to hide her real self, or real social and political consciousness, reveals dissatisfaction with the male-centered and male-dominated politics of the period.

In his response, Johnson recognized the author's passionate argument, but he thought her claims were impractical. "Our correspondent makes no pretense of setting up a logical argument on why colored men should not enlist to fight; she is speaking not for her head, but from her heart; and possibly, she is speaking for the hearts of thousands of other colored wives and mothers." Johnson answered the Colored Wife and Mother by musing on the loss of black women's support for enlisted men, speculating, "The letter is disquieting because it makes us pause and consider what the result would be if the women of the race lost heart," though he did acknowledge "how bravely they [African American women] have struggled, in spite of the double burden which they bear."[18] But Johnson had not mentioned in his editorial, or in later writings, that black working women, as well as black working men, had benefited from the labor shortage in factories, agriculture, and domestic work. Black women were as poised as black men to earn higher wages and empower their political voices through migration. But while Johnson had supported women's suffrage and had given publicity to black women's war work circles in the pages of the *Age,* the progress of communities, homes, and families had little resonance in his "Views and Reviews" column. The Colored Wife and Mother's gendered views of the war were so incongruous to the male perspective that when she asked, "What will happen to the women? And what will happen to our families? Who will protect us?" her concerns were summarily dismissed.

"Views and Reviews" rarely mentioned the impact of the war on African American women, and Johnson had assumed that as black men's fortunes improved, black women's fates would follow. Though economists and social workers had reported that black working women were increasingly productive and gainfully employed, their work was not given the same recognition as black men's, particularly in the pages of gender-conservative newspapers like the *New York Age.* For instance, Addie Hunton, a graduate of the University of Strasbourg, an accomplished writer, and a longtime clubwoman, recognized black women's economic contributions during the war in 1916. Hunton found that of all black women in the United States, two million, or nearly half, were wage earners, and nearly one million of those were agricultural laborers. Black women held dual roles in their farm labor, found Hunton, explaining, "Many of the farms managed by colored men are managed entirely by the women of the family while these men give themselves to other employment." Hunton also reported that 800,000 black women labored as domestic workers nationally, in addition to the several thousand black women working in professional industries like nursing, dressmaking, teaching, and "displaying surprising genius in conducting successful business enterprises."[19]

Similarly, in 1917 the Women's Wage Earner's Association of Washington, a wartime employer relations liaison and uplift organization, argued that, "Our women wage-earners are a large factor in the life of the race. They are becoming more so every day as the business interests of the race expand and the demand for intelligent workers grows with the expansion."[20] While African American women made important contributions to black economic progress during the war, Johnson's editorials rarely moved past the belief that black women's chief contribution was in encouraging their sons to enlist. Traditional notions of gender were not upset by the war in Europe. Rather, most black clubwomen found that if they pursued their political goals without challenging the authority of black men in the political realm, war work and community service were generously applauded.

The war also assisted the NACW in perfecting its political voice. The NACW was the largest of the black organizations that offered protection to women in the form of war work, financial assistance, and institutional guidance. It also answered the rhetoric of the sacrifice of sons by shifting the dialogue to sacrifice of foodstuffs, merging the public sphere of politics with the private sphere of the home. Mary Burnett Talbert, president of the NACW from 1916 to 1920, urged the delegates at the biennial NACW conference to save their food in support of the war. She continued, "I shall urge the women to help in Red Cross and relief work. I shall urge them to do their best in food production and conservation, realizing that the bulk of conserving lies in the kitchens where a million of our women are called to duty. I shall urge them to buy as many Liberty bonds as possible."[21]

Talbert was the perfect woman for the job of heading the NACW during the war. A founding member of the NAACP and the NACW, she had enjoyed success in fundraising for both organizations. Yet, her influence among white organizations opened the door for the NACW and allowed black clubwomen to embark on wartime activism with the blessing of powerful white women leaders. A graduate of Oberlin College, a school principal of an all-black high school, and a founder of the Empire State Federation of Colored Women, Talbert was well versed in the ideology of educational and political uplift for African Americans. But she also knew how to work with wealthy white philanthropists, and she knew how to assuage white fears of black disloyalty during the war. She had formed a close professional relationship with John Shillady, the president of the NAACP, and had become the organization's primary fundraiser. During the war, Talbert also cultivated a professional association with the co-president of the National American Woman Suffrage Association, Anna Howard Shaw, a political friendship that would be tested in the postwar period. From her home base of Buffalo, New York, Talbert ushered the NACW, as well as millions of black clubwomen in the membership, through the perilous waters supporting the war while challenging Jim Crow.[22]

The organization enjoyed success in galvanizing black women for war work that began in the home, specifically in the kitchen. At the turn of the century, the NACW described the private sphere as the sphere of women's work. Maintaining a clean home and preparing healthy meals became the foundation of a well-bred, successful black family. During the war, the kitchen was the new battleground. Black clubwomen urged each other, as well as working-class women, to conserve foodstuffs and to learn to can fruits and vegetables in order to assist the war effort. Martha E. Williams, president of the Kentucky Federation of Colored Women's Clubs in 1917, rallied an audience of African American clubwomen, reminding them of the necessary sacrifices from their kitchens. "Our government has called the women of the great commonwealth to arms to do her fighting with the knife and fork, by eliminating all waste and using less wheat, beef, pork, mutton, lard, sugar and milk, may the women of the Federation of Kentucky not be slackers but measure up on the foremost line with the women of the world in this battle. We can win and come off the field with flying colors and we must win."[23]

Though the NACW expertly organized volunteer work in other arenas as well, focusing on the black kitchen, and thus the black home, carried more political weight. By situating war work at the intersection of community service and homemaking, the NACW empowered black clubwomen to express their political beliefs in broader political movements and debates. Georgia A. Nugent, the NACW's corresponding secretary in 1917 and 1918, urged clubwomen to join other movements as the war extended from black homes to other war service organizations: "The great World's War, which in we have been so deeply plunged and one that has no parallel in history, has been the means of a closer cooperation . . . . [We will] cooperate in every way from conservation of food, Red Cross work, and buying of Baby Bonds and Liberty Bonds."[24] Red Cross work and food conservation were critical issues in African American politics, as they would later indicate that institutionalized racism had permeated the American war effort.

## Patriotic Activism and the Black Middle Class

From the kitchen and the home, the NACW moved into a wider political arena. The organization's biennial convention in Denver in 1918 provided a number of opportunities for the NACW's public figures to instruct their colleagues on wartime adjustments. Some women educated their eager listeners in the science of home economics and food substitution. Fannie Turner and Eliza Holliday, clubwomen from Chicago, led demonstrations on replacing fats, flour, and butter with potatoes and other substitutes. Mrs. S. H. Carry, of Guthrie, Oklahoma, successfully handled the subject of maintaining a sound budget, suggesting that clubwomen "help the war widows to manage their money and spend some in an economical way." Mary F. Waring, one of the most eminent doctors in the country, led a symposium on "Health, Hygiene, and War Foods," which attracted the highest attendance at the conference. Broaching the uncomfortable subject of sexual health, Waring adjourned her symposium by handing out circulars on venereal diseases and tuberculosis.[25]

The Denver convention also showcased the activities of the smaller city-wide clubs across the country. Significantly, these clubs formed the backbone of the NACW's cooperation with the Allied war effort. The individual reports from the local NACW clubs detailed the clubwomen's wartime labors, especially the creation of handmade materials given to African American soldiers and their families. Women from the Pennsylvania State Federation reported that the Civic Club of Wilkes-Barre had assembled and sent comfort kits for African American soldiers in the European trenches. Also in Pennsylvania, the black women of Chester raised $352.70 for the Red Cross and packed 210 comfort bags for the soldiers. A few weeks later the women donated a Victrola phonograph, forty records, and several bulk packs of chewing gum. In California, the Sewing Circle and the Fanny J. Coppin Club of Oakland had met twice a week since April 1917 to assist the Red Cross in collecting bandages and knitted materials. The Colored Ladies Circle of Portland, Oregon, assembled more than 800 packages and sent them to soldiers at black training camps. Mrs. E. D. Cannady joined the Colored Ladies Circle, and on behalf of the Red Cross, she organized a 900-member knitting class, whose members then donated their projects to the relief organization. In the South, African American women relied on their extensive network among clubwomen to tend to the needy in both rural and urban areas. Coordinating organizations in the cities of St. Louis, Kansas City, and Columbia, the African American clubwomen of Missouri fashioned 300 surgical dressings and laundered 450 hospital sheets for the Red Cross. Around the same time in Nashville, Tennessee, and in Daytona Beach, Florida, women's auxiliaries knitted hundreds of pairs of bed socks and made bunches of bed shirts, and they also established local units of the Emergency Circle of Negro War Relief.[26]

The work of the NACW did not escape the War Department or its special assistant for Negro affairs, Emmett J. Scott. In a telegram to Mary Talbert, Scott proclaimed, "Your federation represents the highest aspirations, the loftiest ideals and the most practical achievements of the womanhood of our race . . . . Your patriotism is of the purest quality and your service is willing, prompt, and sympathetic."[27] Scott's message carried great inspiration to the clubwomen, as it was one of the few open acknowledgements of the clubwomen's work. The validation from Scott and also the secretary of war, Newton D. Baker, renewed the vigor of the conference and of black women's war work till the end of the war. The last day of the conference brought resolutions from the clubwomen to redouble their efforts in helping the United States win the war, as well as to increase their pressure on the federal government to enact a federal statute against lynching and mob violence.[28]

Independent black women's war work, or work by groups loosely affiliated with the NACW, also flourished in American urban centers with large African American populations. Segregated by tradition if not by law, this individual work coalesced around local African American regiments and soldiers. For example, Chicago was home to the 8th Regiment of the National Guard, later known as the 370th Infantry Unit of Illinois in the 93rd Division. The 370th enjoyed great success in France, quickly becoming the pride of African Americans in the Midwest. The African American women of the Phyllis Wheatley Club of Chicago adopted the soldiers of the 8th Regiment and presented them with "forty-eight sweaters and one hundred and fifty wash rags, one for each of its 'sons.'" The Phyllis Wheatley Club was later joined by the Fortnightly Ten Club, a social organization, which sent 125 Christmas boxes to the unit. Chicago's Kit and Comfort Club, in association with the Auxiliary No. 295 of the American Red Cross, also sent donations to African American soldiers of the 8th Regiment, many of them handmade gifts, including "one hundred and fifty pairs of socks, sixty winter convalescent garments, thirty hospital bed shirts, twenty five pairs of pajamas, twelve trench caps, twelve pairs of mittens, and one hundred reclamation garments."[29]

In Washington, D.C., African American women of the Women's Volunteer Aid Society gathered to aid the 372nd Infantry Regiment by making garments and bandages for the base hospital serving the regiment. The World War was "causing the colored women to work with much enthusiasm," one volunteer observed. The black women–led Volunteer Aid Society worked with the African American YWCA of Washington, D.C., on a number of comfort and medical programs for the soldiers. Likewise in Boston, Melnea Cass, a clubwoman, explained the various forms of war work between single men and women as "similar to the U.S.O.," the organization famous for entertaining soldiers during World War II. Attending a YWCA Hostess House for African American troops, Cass remembered, "[They] had us there, young girls, to dance with them and to be hostesses with them and all. And they used to knit all the time, make gloves and mittens . . . and sweaters and all, and send them across as gifts, to the fellows from Boston." Boston also hosted the Soldier's Comfort Unit, whose list of duties included hospitality and entertainment, and a Junior Comfort Unit, to "cooperate with us in the patriotic service we are trying to render to the race."[30]

The most exciting war work in the country took place in New York City between 1917 and 1918. War service got off to a rousing start when the

Woman's Loyal Union, the oldest African American woman's club in the city, pledged its support to the 369th Infantry Unit. Originally the 15th National Guard Unit of New York City, the 369th joined the 93rd Division of the American Expeditionary Forces soon after the United States declared war on Germany in April 1917. The "old" 15th held the distinction as New York's first African American regiment, as well as one of the first American units to arrive in France. Susan Elizabeth Frazier, a graduate of Hunter College and the first African American teacher at an interracial school in New York, revamped the Woman's Loyal Union in April 1917 as an Auxiliary to the 15th Regiment. Hailed by Hallie Q. Brown as a homespun heroine and a woman of distinction, Frazier was a native New Yorker whose ancestors fought in the Revolutionary War. Along with her work as a schoolteacher, Frazier also worked as an activist for women's rights and civil rights.[31] Rallying African American women to the cause, Frazier pledged "to arouse women to a sense of duty, pride, and honor . . . to render any possible service to the 15th Regiment, National Guard." Frazier intended that the Woman's Loyal Union should inspire a general patriotic movement of African American women of New York. Her efforts caught the attention of the *New York Age* in late April 1917, and the group's efforts were frequently chronicled by the newspaper.[32]

In fact, the *Age* and the Woman's Loyal Union formed a symbiotic relationship early during the war. As it attracted more volunteers, the Woman's Loyal Union appealed "through the press to all patriotic women to join this committee, in order that the organization may be perfected as soon as possible." The *New York Age* publicized the Woman's Loyal Union, hoping that the group would set an example of active patriotism and encourage more women to help the Allies. An article about the group appeared on the front page of the *Age* in May 1917, "the greatest and most ambitious effort to mobilize colored women of Greater New York for National service in the Nation's crisis." The newspaper also featured an official commendation from President Wilson, thanking the group for its pledge of loyalty to the nation.[33] The *Age* published personal narratives about the group and other stories from volunteers throughout its service. Eventually, the newspaper became the chief source of information about the women's activities. Soon after the 369th Regiment left for training camp, the Woman's Loyal Union mobilized for service as the Woman's Auxiliary to the 15th Regiment, New York Infantry, and took on "accelerated interest and additional volunteers . . . at every meeting," reported the *Age*. Martha Venable, who wrote the *Age* urging African American women to action, attended a meeting of the Woman's Auxiliary and judged it the best type of war work for African

American women. She continued, "I have attended three meetings since the declaration of war and each time I have called for the women who were willing to place themselves at the service of the 15th Regiment, to assist their wives and families . . . four-fifths of the women pledged themselves to do whatever they could."[34]

Frazier directed the Woman's Auxiliary to meet specific and simple goals for the 369th Infantry. Officially registered as a volunteer body on 2 May 1917 and servicing some 1,300 soldiers, the Woman's Auxiliary primarily worked on assembling comfort kits for the enlisted men. These kits included pencils and paper, a collapsible aluminum cup, soap, toothbrushes and toothpaste, handkerchiefs, cigarettes, and a chocolate bar. The occasional care package also contained a knitted sweater, scarf, socks, or mittens, magazines, and pulp fiction for reading. The Woman's Auxiliary endeavored to place these kits in the soldiers' hands while the units were stationed at training camps or just before they left for the European front. The group's work became a regular feature of the *New York Age,* appearing in nearly every issue of the newspaper from late April 1917 through the end of the war in November 1918. In early 1918, the Woman's Loyal Union became affiliated with the National League of Women's Service, thus boosting African American women's war work in New York by providing a well-tuned, thriving organization to join.[35] After the official recognition from a national organization, the Woman's Loyal Union of New York City continued to compile comfort bags and to produce and send knitted goods to training camps in the area. They corresponded with enlisted men and provided financial assistance to families left without a principal wage earner. The Woman's Auxiliary joined the growing ranks of small and local organizations run by African American women.

Tolerating the indignities of Jim Crow comprised the most challenging task facing black clubwomen and their war work, given the inherent conflict between the war for democracy abroad and the war for democracy at home. By 1917, black clubwomen had devoted nearly three decades of organizational resources to turning back, if not altogether defeating, racial segregation and discrimination. With the outbreak of war in Europe, middle-class black clubwomen articulated optimistic expectations for further transformation in American race relations. But the structures of white supremacy and the institutionalization of racial segregation had nearly paralyzed an emergent civil rights movement among African Americans during the war. Despite the 368,000 black soldiers who served in the war, the War Department had not granted black men opportunities for advancement. In the army, blacks rarely moved past the rank of private, and in the navy, black recruits were usually assigned duty as messmen and cooks. Middle-class black women also encountered segregation, usually in war work organizations. In wartime employment, educated black women with high-school diplomas and college degrees found it difficult to obtain civil service positions in predominantly white offices and departments.

Still, the long thread of African American participation in past American wars was deeply interwoven with the wartime rhetoric of black women's wartime volunteerism. And middle-class African American women, in the early months of American involvement, described black participation in the war as a patriotic responsibility. Ruth Bennett, president of the Pennsylvania State Negro Women's Convention, described black patriotic commitment in clear terms, declaring "that the negro race is patriotic to the last, and that within its bounds will be found no slackers."[36]

The key element in maneuvering Jim Crow during the war was promoting black patriotism in the face of racial segregation. Martha Venable, a resident of New York City and a longtime reader of the *New York Age,* not only defended the Allied war effort to African Americans but also urged black women of New York to support their local African American military auxiliaries. "We must teach our children that after having lived in America for three hundred years we are full fledged Americans," wrote Venable in a letter to the "Views and Reviews" column of the *New York Age* in 1917. Venable stressed putting aside African Americans' "special grievances" until after the war, deftly weaving the subject of African American progress since the Civil War into a mandate for African American participation in the Great War. "The progress made by the race in the past fifty-two years proves that we must have been given an opportunity. And for that we are indebted to our country. Let us prove our worth now and demand our rights at the proper time." Her letter supporting the war, which appeared in the *New York Age's* op-ed column, "Views and Reviews," joined a growing chorus of voices from the African American intellectual elite, who considered the war an opportunity for progress in a march toward racial equality. At this stage of official American involvement, black intellectuals contemplated the Great War's impact on black life, optimistically viewing African American participation as a keystone in their bid for full citizenship. Venable's primary concern focused on maintaining and extending the tradition of African American loyalty to the United States. She confronted African American women, taking them to task for not showing more patriotism during this critical period. "I feel our women are losing time and not acting as quickly as need be," she feared. "We want to arouse our people to the proper spirit of patriotism. This is not the time for the grumblers to nurse race grievances or present them to the country to right wrongs."[37]

When black war work sought to conciliate racial segregation, it did so by turning to black patriotic booster clubs. Working to counteract the segregated facilities, African American women formed wartime institutions dedicated to supplying financial services, clothing, emotional support, and pleasant facilities for black soldiers. Nannie H. Burroughs offered a telling example of black women's organizational response to the war. At the time of the American entrance into the war, Burroughs was the renowned president of the National Training School for Women and Girls of Washington, D.C., and a longtime clubwoman. In 1918, Burroughs came up with the idea of training 1,000,000 African American women for war service. Beginning with the training of 200 volunteers in August 1918, Burroughs endeavored to attract African American women as volunteers for local patriotic groups. In a statement of her proposal, Burroughs declared, "We must not lose sight of the fact that the colored woman is a most valuable ally. Her power and influence reach from the kitchen to the castle—from desk to ditch. She handles the food for 10,000,000 of her own race, as well as millions of tons for other Americans. The country needs her intelligent co-operation in its food conservation and other war activities. America needs every woman, white or black, to help win this war."[38] But Burroughs also saw in the war an opportunity to educate white Americans about patriotic service necessitating full recognition of African American citizenship. Burroughs's essay, "Lynching and Negro Unrest," written during the early months of the war, remarked, "Nothing remains to be done but to make and administer adequate laws, and begin at the fireside to teach white children to respect the laws of our land and to have a correct estimate of the value of human life . . . . Let all Americans remember that one race cannot hate another without itself returning to savagery."[39]

Other booster clubs flourished around the country. Largely overseen by the Council of National Defense (CND), middle-class black women were employed to encourage black support across the United States, particularly in the South, where the majority of African American women lived and worked. The CND praised the efforts of the Amelia Current Opinion Club of Amelia, Maryland, for teaching food conservation and for sending comfort kits to black draftees from the area. In Louisville, the CND asked colored women to put on a food conservation parade, "in recognition of their already faithful work in handling regimental work."[40] Similarly, the Welfare League, which was connected to the 367th Infantry, called all women to service to help supply the regiment with amusements and recreation, and

Lad of 4 Wants to Fight Kaiser

PORTLAND OPE EVE TELEGR UP,
JANUARY 3, 1918

SURRENDER!

Figure 1. The original headline for this photo was "Lad of 4 Wants to Fight Kaiser." George Edward Cannady's parents were also the owners of the black newspaper the *Portland Evening Telegram*. Middle-class black women used the language of patriotism—duty, honor, and sacrifice—to form their politics of uplift and political equality during World War I. The brief article accompanying this photograph explains that George Cannady gave up candy and toys to help with the conservation efforts, popular wartime activism among middle-class African Americans. *Courtesy of the Tuskegee Institute News Clipping Files, reel 9, "Soldiers."*

"to create and foster pride in the history of the colored race, and in the traditions of our country, thereby stimulating their patriotism and increasing their Americanism, and thus making of them better citizens."[41] In Baltimore, prominent middle-class black women formed the Women's Patriotic League on 23 April 1917, just three weeks after the United States declared war on Germany. The Women's Patriotic League put on a patriotic pageant in late 1917, and invited a guest speaker from the CND to give an encouraging talk on "Patriotism as It Stands in America for Democracy."[42] Patriotic encouragement had also touched the home of George Edward Cannady, a four-year-old boy, who told the *Portland Evening Telegram* that he wanted to be a real soldier in the World War and was "going to eat less candy so the soldiers could have all the sugar they want." A half-page photograph accompanied the article and pictured George in a dress uniform, complete with a hat of army insignia, spats, and an Allied button on his lapel, all fashioned by his mother. To the left of the photograph was a cartoon featuring an animated George aiming his gun and cannon at a mustached German soldier, with the caption "Surrender!" George's parents, Mr. and Mrs. E. D. Cannady, were the owners of the *Portland Advocate,* the largest newspaper for blacks in the city, which drummed up support for the war by printing several articles sympathetic to the Allied cause.[43]

Patriotic boosting could also be found in black prose and literature during the war, and within these works, middle-class values associated with African American military participation—duty, honor, sacrifice—undergirded much of the language. An intriguing example of the melding of patriotic duty with black uplift was offered by Alice Dunbar-Nelson in her play, *Mine Eyes Have Seen.* An essayist, poet, author, and former wife of Paul Laurence Dunbar, Alice Dunbar-Nelson told a story of a black family of siblings, who have been beset by tragedy in the waning months of the World War. Set in a cramped apartment in New York, the play's principal characters were a brother and sister, Dan and Lucy. Severely wounded in fighting on the Western Front, Dan was confined to a wheelchair with a spinal cord injury, while Lucy tended to him and worked outside the apartment to make ends meet. In the play's stage notes, Dunbar-Nelson described Dan as a world-weary man, his "face thin, pinched, bearing traces of suffering. His hair is prematurely grey; nose finely chiseled; eyes wide, as if seeing BEYOND." Similarly, Lucy was "slight, frail, brown-skinned, with a pathetic face. She walks with a limp." The rest of the cast was comprised of Chris, the youngest brother who has just been drafted; Jake, a Jewish socialist who opposes the war; Mrs. O'Neill, their Irish neighbor; and Cornelia Lewis, a settlement house worker who supports the war.[44]

At just over four pages long, the play is too short to comfortably elaborate on its main theme, which was African American loyalty and patriotism to a segregationist nation during the World War. But the play's primary exchange is between Chris, who considers dodging the draft, because his parents have been murdered by a white mob, and his older brother, Dan, who has lost the use of his legs fighting for the United States in France. Though Dan deeply laments that he has been "maimed for life in a factory of hell; useless—useless broken on the wheel," he also urges his brother to fight because he could not stand to be "the excuse, the woman's skirts for a slacker to hide behind." Chris answers Dan with dissent, posing his questions:

"Must I go and fight for the nation that let my father's murder [in a race riot] go unpunished? That killed my mother—that took away my chances for making a map out for myself?" Chris resolves to claim exemption, in order to support his brother and sister, but Dan, as head of the family, will have no part of that, and he reminds Chris of his duty to his race and to his country. "Ours is the glorious inheritance; ours the price of achievement. And you, too, Chris, smouldering in youthful wrath, you, too, are proud to be numbered with the darker ones, soon to come into their heritance." Lucy, their sister, agrees, and she has the last word in the play. "Yes, we do need you Chris, but your country needs you more . . . . We'll get on, never fear. I'm proud! *Proud!*"[45] Dunbar-Nelson would later work for the federal government to investigate the state of black women's patriotic support in the South. In this theatrical piece, she offered much critique, with a bitter-sweet resolution. The middle-class values of loyalty, honor, and sacrifice trumped the other characters' arguments for dissent and could eventually outwit Jim Crow. The moral to the story, when viewed through the lens of middle-class black political discourse, was that race pride and black loyalty would triumph, and it was a race lesson that resonated with black women's political consciousness.

## Challenging Segregation in Wartime

Black women's patriotism between 1916 and 1918 also coincided with several lawsuits and other protests launched by middle-class black women, challenges aimed at halting the spread of Jim Crow or dismantling it altogether. The history of the legal challenges illustrates a growing confusion among middle-class black women about the outcome of the war. Many black women found the daily indignities of racial segregation intolerable, and they decided to confront the issue head-on through appealing to the courts or to local race organizations. Historians of the Progressive Era have explored, for example, the impact of segregated public transportation and workplaces in the nation's capital. August Meier and Elliot Rudwick have argued that segregation in the civil service sector of Washington, D.C., which had begun under the Taft administration, had spread to the level where "most government departments hired few colored clerks, and the majority of Negro white collar workers were concentrated in the Treasury, Interior, and Post Office Departments." The policies of segregating continued through the World War, when the War and Navy Departments, as well as the War Trade Commission, mandated segregated restrooms in their facilities.[46] In a recent exploration of Jim Crow in federal workplaces, Nicholas Patler has described the spread of racial segregation through federal bureaucracy in the early years of the war. The World War was to have a chilling effect on race relations in the national capital, as Jim Crow took hold during a national emergency and froze African Americans out of the civil service. "The NAACP's protest against federal Jim Crow also seems to have fizzled out after summer 1914 because of the war as well," writes Patler, but the individual and collective humiliations incurred in the following years resulted in a mounting hostility toward the poor state of American race relations.[47]

In the last two years of the war, which were critical to an emergent civil rights movement, African American women challenged segregation by filing individual lawsuits. For instance, Carrie Hill, a black resident of Atlanta, sued the Georgia Railway and Power Company for $5,000 after a white rider pulled her from her seat and threw her to the floor for not giving her seat to two young white passengers.[48] In black urban areas across the country, middle-class black women challenged racial segregation primarily in the service sector, usually in department stores or restaurants. In Louisville, the Sellmann's women's clothing store, after years of integrated restrooms, declared in 1917 that its public restrooms were for white customers only. The Kaufman-Strauss store, also in Louisville, soon followed suit by refusing to fit corsets on its black patrons. One of the regular black customers of Kaufman-Strauss told her story to the *Louisville News,* adding "that when they insulted her they insulted every self-respecting Colored woman in Louisville."[49] In Springfield, Massachusetts, Nannette Howe and Annie West sued the S. S. Kresge Five and Dime Store (the future K-Mart stores) for discrimination. The lunch counter waitresses made the women wait for forty-five minutes for service and then refused them service when they complained, as the *Chicago Defender* reported. The jury found the Kresge store guilty and awarded the women $25 each, below the $1,000 the women sought in damages. But the judge offered his opinion that "racial discrimination would not be tolerated in any public place in the city or the state."[50] In 1916, a famous case in New York City centered on Frances Johnson and Harriet Beckett of Harlem. The women sued the Otto Pfaeffle Bakery for discrimination, after they waited for nearly thirty minutes in a near-empty restaurant for their orders of coffee and tea. The verdict initially favored Johnson and Beckett, and they were awarded $117 each. But their case was overturned on appeal when the presiding judge, Judge Cowan, found that there was insufficient evidence to prove racial discrimination. Judge Cowan ruled in favor of Pfaeffle, and ordered the women to pay Pfaeffle $35 each.[51]

Some of the cases were resolved in favor of the African American litigants, but at great personal cost. Jane Bosfield, for instance, encountered several rejections for jobs as a medical clerk in Medfield, Massachusetts. In an interview with the *Boston Traveler and Evening Herald,* Bosfield recounted her employment woes. Most of the potential employers did not specify why they did not select her, but Bosfield occasionally received an explanation for her rejection. "It would always be because of my race; in every other way I would have passed the requirements," Bosfield told the *Traveler and Evening Herald.* Bosfield appealed to the former governor of Massachusetts, David Walsh, whom she met at a public address at Symphony Hall in Boston. Walsh secured for her another interview with the Medfield State Hospital.[52] Bosfield was eminently qualified for the position, as she explained in her own words: "I am a graduate of the Cambridge Latin and High School. I studied bookkeeping and stenography in the evening after I graduated. In 1912 I passed the Civil Service Examination for the first time, and later tried for a position. I have been certified for almost every position in the clerical departments of Boston. From 1912 to 1915, I tried for a position, desperately hard, and always I was refused."[53] By the time Bosfield was hired at the Medfield State Hospital in October 1916, she had been out of work for three years, with the exception of a brief factory job that paid her less than half of her expected wage as a clerical worker.

However, her job at Medfield State Hospital as a medical stenographer and file clerk was disrupted when she refused to eat her lunch alone in her office and, instead, joined her white coworkers in the hospital cafeteria. In the first few months of work, Bosfield's supervisor, Dr. Edward French, advised Bosfield that she would have to eat her lunch at her desk. Bosfield considered this policy inconvenient, as, while she was eating, "errand boys would be passing through continually. The girls would rush in to look at my tray and see what they would be served, a little later, in the dining room."[54] After months of eating at her desk, Bosfield ate three full meals in the cafeteria with other workers. Dr. French fired her the next day with no reason given. Bosfield's lawyers sued Dr. French and the Medfield State Hospital for racial discrimination, and the case made headlines in Boston and New York. The unfavorable publicity forced a public hearing before Governor Samuel McCall and the Executive Council. The body ruled that Bosfield be reinstated at her position, and it considered dismissing Dr.

French. Bosfield accepted her old position, but she did not believe that her working environment would be pleasant. The uproar surrounding her dismissal lasted nearly four weeks, but after the position was again secured for her, she was physically and emotionally exhausted. Speaking to the white readers of the *Traveler and Evening Herald,* Bosfield concluded, "In the North, you fought hard for us not very long ago, but you aren't living up to the contract you made. We pay equal taxes—we do not have equal rights."[55]

The most significant challenge to racial discrimination and segregation came as a response to the East St. Louis Riot of 1917, a watershed moment in middle-class black women's politics and the wartime civil rights movement. In East St. Louis, the immediate goals of black participation in the present war were melded to a postwar agenda for eliminating racial discrimination and racial violence. In the aftermath of the riot, African American clubwomen and many black leaders posed the problems of racism and lynching as an embarrassment to the United States. East St. Louis was the deadliest riot in America up to that period, but it also stands out for its peculiarly disturbing timing and its harbinger of American race relations.

The riot erupted in early July 1917, almost four months to the day after the United States declared war on Germany. It was one of the most widely covered events in the summer of 1917, and the ferocity with which the white residents of East St. Louis set upon the black residents made front-page headlines in both black and white newspapers. In the days and weeks following the riot, the specific causes remained unknown, an uncertainty that contributed to the lingering outrage. Without knowing what caused the riot, it was difficult to determine which factors played the largest role. Black migration northward was blamed, as were labor unions, alcohol, foreign immigrants, and police dereliction of duty. For instance, the *Chicago Defender,* the most widely circulated black newspaper, argued that the mayor of East St. Louis exacerbated the unrest, though "seeing the trouble arising Sunday [July 1], he failed to order the saloons closed."[56] Labor disputes and long-simmering racial tensions were the common themes in most of the narratives that emerged. The *Atlanta Constitution* reported that an earlier conflagration in June 1917, caused by "the importation of large numbers of negro laborers from the south," led to the second, more violent riot in July.[57] The *St. Louis Democrat* called the rioters callous and "matter of fact" when most of its white interviewees justified their actions by saying that "the niggers started it."[58] In a variation on that theme, Congressman Pat Harrison of Mississippi offered that the riot in East St. Louis was

Figure 2. One of the most famous political cartoons of the World War was printed in the *New York Age* during the aftermath of the East St. Louis riot. The eruption of violence in the midst of largely positive black participation in the World War quickly eroded black patriotic support. Middle-class black club-women urged their legislative representatives to convene hearings on the riot's causes. Also, the anti-lynching movement took on new urgency and carried black women's politics into a more critical and determined postwar agenda. *Courtesy of the Tuskegee Institute News Clipping Files, reel 6, "Riots."*

caused by the migration of blacks northward, who found employment "instead of white men in the factories of that city, and the first difficulty so aroused and incensed the feelings of the white people that they did not confine their feelings against the Negro to the offending individual, but vented their spleen against the Negro as a race."[59] The *New York Times* offered an account that combined several factors, including white anxieties about decreasing employment, previous disturbances over strikes, and the problem of "labor agents [who] induced the negroes to come here from the South."[60]

After a two-week investigation, W. E. B. Du Bois and Martha Gruening, writing for the *Crisis* magazine, concluded that the riot started on 1 July, when a car full of white joyriders rode into the African American district and opened fire on the houses in the neighborhood. A car of plain-clothes policemen pursued the joyriders, but it was the police car that was caught in the return fire from the black residents, killing two policemen. On 2 July, mobs of angry whites set upon the black residents of East St. Louis, when at least forty African Americans and eight whites were killed.[61] Some African Americans were burned to death, and others were kicked and shot to death in the street as they tried to flee. In one case, a group of white women chased down an African American woman, pelting her with rocks and beating her with a broom handle. In another account, a woman testified to witnessing a white mob throw an African American child into a fire set from the ruins of the School for Negroes.[62] Just days after the riot, Ida B. Wells-Barnett, the most seasoned and forceful anti-lynching activist of the twentieth century, traveled to East St. Louis to conduct interviews of blacks caught in the riot and collect them for one of her signature pamphlets, *The East St. Louis Massacre: The Greatest Outrage of the Century*. As historian Linda McMurry explains, Wells-Barnett "sought to maintain the role of reporter by providing victims' stories and white accounts of the riot," especially the stories of black working women.[63] Some of the most poignant narratives in Wells-Barnett's collection came from African American women who had resided in East St. Louis for several years, many of whom had migrated to the city before the beginning of the war. Several of the women had escaped with their lives, but had lost all of their personal belongings or their homes and had seen African Americans perish in front of their eyes. When black families were forced out of East St. Louis, they left with no money, with no property, and with few hopes of finding gainful employment. This was the case of Emma Ballard, who said, in an interview with Wells-Barnett, that she was forced from her home at the height of the riot, but she was able to shield her children from the worst and flee with the clothes on her back. When she returned to her burned-out house, she found "the windows broken, bedding and clothing thrown on the floor, all wet with much of it scorched. After getting together a few wearing clothes, she went out and closed the door, leaving furniture and mattresses that must have cost five hundred dollars. After a day of uncertainty she found her husband who had already found a home in St. Louis and they were going to stay there."[64] In the end, thousands of dollars worth of white- and black-owned property was lost and nearly all of the black residents of East St. Louis left the area for good.

Black protests to the riot came in quick succession. The NAACP organized a silent protest march down Fifth Avenue in New York, which attracted African Americans across the country to participate. African American clubwomen also were sharp in their critique. The College Alumnae Club, a national group of black women college graduates, appealed to President Wilson to use the war as an occasion to end the segregation in the armed services. "Yours is the opportunity, Mr. President. . . . A word from you, courageous, unequivocal, would bind to you and your cause, the faithful, undivided service of twelve million Americans who would go to the death for their country. . . . You have the chance before the world to show your belief in democracy by striking a blow at its enemy in America—the American government's denial of the rights of citizens to one-tenth of the American people."[65] The Empire State Federation of Colored Women wrote to President Wilson directly, urging "him in the name of justice to put a stop to these innumerable horrors."[66] The Citizens' Committee of the Negro Fellowship League and the Bethel A.M.E. Church of Chicago condemned the riot and, in a petition to the U.S. Congress, urged the United States to recognize that "as American citizens, our lives are subject to the nation's call, and at no call have we faltered or failed. As American citizens we call to the Nation to save our lives; to that call will the Nation falter or fail?"[67] Wells-Barnett also convened a special meeting of the Illinois State Federation of Women's Clubs to raise money for the victims and to draft a resolution denouncing the rioters.[68]

Along with the action from the Citizens' Committee, the NACW organized one of the most popular forms of protest, the prayer meeting. Mary B. Talbert directed her club sisters in a nationwide "Call to Prayer" on 11 July 1917, a week after the riot, writing, "We propose to fight for our country to help against foes at home and abroad to conserve its food and fuel supplies, and we believe that this fight for 'Democracy' must begin at Jerusalem (at home)."[69] Talbert appealed for every available woman and girl to spend one hour in prayer at the Metropolitan Baptist Church in New York City, repeating the meeting once a week for the rest of the summer. Talbert's request traveled across the country and many state organizations joined the prayer meeting, including, for example, the Minnesota State Federation of Colored Women, whose president personally informed every member in the state.[70] Similarly, Susan Frazier, the president of the patriotic Woman's Auxiliary to the 367th Infantry, announced prayer protest meetings in the *New York Age,* writing, "The Woman's Auxiliary, Fifteenth Regiment, requests all women to attend their 'Hour of Prayer' of their headquarters . . . August 6, 1917 from 6am to 8am to make a special appeal to Almighty God for His loving mercy and to deliver us by His power from the terrible hardships and crimes of murder in its many wicked forms committed upon our people in the country, and to beseech Him that mob violence may cease at His command. [And that] all discrimination, segregation, jim crowism and the like may be abolished." The appeal brought nearly seventy women to the headquarters, with several more stopping in on their way to work. Moreover, the prayer meetings linked the war to abolishing institutionalized racism, as the Woman's Auxiliary showed when it asked the participants to "muster all women that can be reached into a regiment of war prayer, like that which God heard, from our forefathers, in the dark days of slavery."[71]

While the nationwide prayer meetings were an immediate and active response to riots and violence, they also foretold an organizational transformation. Protesting the East St. Louis riot, through marches, telegrams to President Wilson, and prayer meetings, formed the most visible challenge to Jim Crow that the NACW had made since the beginning of the war. After the summer of 1917, the NACW turned its efforts to identifying wartime inequality in the treatment of black troops and providing relief to them, in conjunction with other organizations, such as the Circle for Negro War Relief, the YWCA, and the YMCA. There were other riots that summer that had garnered much attention. The Houston riot of August 1917, which pitted black soldiers against white residents of Houston, ended with twelve whites and two blacks dead. Seventy-four black soldiers were court-martialed, thirteen of whom were hung without the benefit of an appeal.[72] Black clubwomen had protested that riot as well, and many state federations drafted resolutions condemning the violence, such as the Illinois State Federation of Colored Women. But the shocking brutality of the East St. Louis riot put African American uplift organizations, particularly the NACW, on a new path in activism. East St. Louis was the turning point, and the NACW moved from tolerating most aspects of Jim Crow to challenging all aspects of racial discrimination during the war. The East St.

Louis riot had granted the NACW an activist agenda that, in the years after the war, would put the organization at the forefront of another civil rights movement.

In the winter of 1917, Lelia Walker (who later changed her name to A'Lelia), daughter of wealthy businesswoman Madam C. J. Walker and a resident of New York City, penned an editorial to the *New York Age* opposing black participation in the World War. Walker wrote, "America claims she is striving to gain a more democratic government, but she will never accomplish this until she gives up her hatred against the color of a race and cease striving to trample that race underfoot."[73] Unafraid of reprisal, she did not hide her identity, and confident in her social and economic standing, she spoke to a growing number of dissenting African Americans who were frustrated by the events of the previous summer. Unlike the letter from a Colored Wife and Mother in April 1916, editor James Weldon Johnson had no pithy commentary for Walker's letter, and he did not challenge Walker's analysis of the war or of black involvement. African Americans had already fought in every previous American war, Walker wrote, so fighting in the current war would not improve their already unassailable record of loyalty. In attesting African American patriotism, she asked, "Why should not the government protect these citizens as much as another? Are they less law-abiding than any other race of people in America? Are they a menace to the Government?" Instead of arguing that black participation would make a case for full citizenship later, Walker reasoned that the opposite had been the case. As the riots of 1917 had indicated, African Americans needed American protection from the terrors of lynching and mob violence far more than England needed American protection from Germany. Walker could not offer a compelling reason for blacks to contribute to the American cause. Doubting the war's capacity to do away with racial prejudice in the United States, Walker forecast, "America will never form a true democracy until she is able to show justice to all her subjects."[74]

In the five months after the East St. Louis and Houston riots, much had happened in African American life. The migration of southern blacks who followed job opportunities to northern urban areas continued unabated, and white communities, northern and southern, continued to resist the demographic shifts. After putting pressure on the War Department, the NAACP had won a black officer's training camp at Camp Dodge in Des Moines, Iowa. The training camp would allow black enlisted men to seek and gain promotion through the military ranks, an important development in the wartime civil rights movement.[75] Black soldiers, headed for the Western Front and supply routes in Europe, had landed in France in December 1917, and they continued to be the pride of African American military history. In response to the East St. Louis riot, Congress held several investigative hearings in October and November 1917. As Elliot Rudwick has explained, the congressional hearings found the city of East St. Louis culpable for the "community's mores, clearly showing how the activities of employers, labor organizers, and politicians created a milieu which made the riot possible."[76]

African American support for black participation did not wane after the riot in East St. Louis nor after the explosion of black fury in the Houston riot of August. The timing seemed to be right for a mass defection from the war and a mass rejection of capitalism. The Socialist Party suggested that blacks bolt from the Democratic and Republican parties, and claimed, "All the sickening babble of 'patriotism,' 'liberty,' 'human rights' (to starve), ad infinitum, will be marshaled to heap odium on those . . . union men and maintain the labor standard of freedom to starve in America. . . . And he [the Negro] takes to Socialism like a duck to water."[77] But, instead of discouraging black participation in the war, middle-class African Americans, including African American clubwomen, held fast to the notion that the war would improve black life in the long term. Achieving the benefits of full citizenship remained the most significant objective in African American wartime endeavors. Lelia Walker, though her most strident criticism of the United States came in the wake of the East St. Louis riot, still considered herself an American patriot. Both Lelia and her mother, Madam C. J. Walker, made substantial individual contributions to the war effort in the winter and spring of 1918. Both she and her mother belonged to the Circle for Negro War Relief, the Navy League, and the 367th Infantry Welfare League, and they made large personal donations for knitted goods and comfort materials for soldiers.[78] Lelia Walker also enlisted the opera talent of Enrico Caruso, the renowned tenor, for a musical benefit on behalf of black soldiers in New York City.[79]

In the same way, the NACW's efforts after the summer of 1917 shifted from supporting the war to supporting black soldiers and their families. It resolved to protest and combat mob violence at its 1918 Denver biennial, adding, in blunt language, that "the continuance of mob violence is the worst reproach that can be charged against us by those at war with us." The explicit resolution against mob violence had not appeared at its 1916 meeting or at earlier meetings. Furthermore, the organization extended its commitment to abolishing lynching, requesting widespread support for "the enactment of a federal statute against lynch law with severe penalties for the violation thereof and that in case of violation in any section of our beloved country that such status be enforced if need be by the military power of the Government."[80] The NACW worked closely with the Council of National Defense to coordinate black women's patriotic activity across the country, though it had a self-consciously separate agenda from the predominantly white federal agency. The resources that the organization had marshaled during the war created a system of grassroots politics that addressed the issues of segregation, lynching, and Jim Crow after a series of race riots in 1919. African American clubwomen embraced patriotic activity in the two years between 1916 and 1918, asking themselves and their country, "What is to be done?" African American women responded with vigorous war work activity. As for the question, "What is to be done for us?" African American women were poised to politicize their civic and cultural agenda.

African American clubwomen also took notice of the gains made by working-class black women, particularly black working women in the South. In the latter half of the war, working-class black women had sought and found economic autonomy, and they had formed a political discourse that shared the same aspirations as middle-class women's discourse. What differed were working-class women's motivations and, just as important, their treatment by government policies and by middle-class Americans. The grassroots political movement among working-class women formed the counterpart to middle-class women's politics. As working-class women contemplated other issues during the war, primarily earning a higher wage, contributing to the family payroll, and forming labor unions, the development of black women's political consciousness evolved to include working-class black women in a groundswell of war-related activism.

# 2

## Investigations of the Southern Black Working Class

"Occupied the pulpit in the largest colored church in the city (Baptist) this morning. Preached a *sermon*," dashed off Alice Dunbar-Nelson in a hurried letter to Hannah Patterson in September 1918. Dunbar-Nelson hardly had enough time to finish her lecture before her next engagement. The listeners were a captive audience in Jacksonville, Florida, earlier that morning, but by mid-afternoon, Dunbar-Nelson had to break away to speak to the black soldiers stationed at Camp Johnston. Immediately afterward she headed north to survey the conditions in the neighboring counties. The day before, Dunbar-Nelson, with the help of Sister Carlotta, an Episcopalian nun, convened a meeting of African American women in Jacksonville, where they discussed the prospect of a playground for African American children and a Mutual Protection League for working African American women and girls.[1]

As soon as she completed her work in Florida, Dunbar-Nelson boarded a train for Atlanta and started her routine once again, addressing the interested public, visiting base camps, and planning community projects for urban African American women. Before she left, she wrote, "The situation in Florida is very gratifying and the work is moving on. . . . Best arrangements I've seen yet."[2] By the time she reached Georgia, Dunbar-Nelson had been working for four weeks, but already had stopped in Jackson, Como, Sardis, and Vicksburg, Mississippi, as well as Selma, Mobile, and Birmingham, Alabama.

Dunbar-Nelson's rushed lectures in the southern United States had little to do with religion, however. Rather, Dunbar-Nelson preached secular sermons to African American audiences on the subject of the Great World War and how the Allies must win it. Stressing the urgency of wartime conservation and volunteer registration in the name of the Allied cause, Dunbar-

Nelson, an authorized field representative of the Committee on Woman's Defense Work of the Council of National Defense (the "Woman's Committee"), served as an intermediary between the federal Woman's Committee and African American women.[3] For her narrative, Dunbar-Nelson embarked on a six-week trip discussing topics such as: "the meaning of the war to the Negro," "what Germany's victory will mean to the Negro," "what the Negro can do to help win the war," and, finally, "the need of combined forces of colored women to help make the country a lovable place for the race."[4] Dunbar-Nelson's special assignment centered on organizing black women and black communities to combine their war work with the efforts of local white organizations. Her greatest challenge was convincing racially segregated communities to cooperate with each other, particularly those that insisted on maintaining their separate spheres.

For American women generally, the immense selection of ways "to do one's bit" fell into roughly two categories: federal agencies or privately funded organizations. The Red Cross, the YWCA, and the YMCA, who were the most visible and best-funded organizations, provided a laundry list of programs devoted to hospital assistance, canteen service, Hostess Houses, and financial contributions. If, instead, an American woman preferred to work with a federal agency or one of its state chapters, she could look no further than the Woman's Committee, the National Liberty Loan Campaign, or the United War Savings Stamps Program.[5] On the surface, these programs strove to afford American women equal opportunities for patriotic service.

A closer analysis of southern black women and World War I finds that staunch, racist opposition met black war work activity. The Woman's Committee, joined later by the War Camp Community Service (WCCS), hesitated in creating war work programs where blacks and whites worked in allegiance across the color line. The Jim Crow laws in some southern cities restricted equal levels of assistance and material support for black and white residents. The option most open to African American women was, in fact, to blaze their own trails and institute their own programs in local communities. Working-class and middle-class African American women worked on their own, more often than not, and directed their efforts for predominantly black programs. In almost every occasion, all-white executive councils led the national groups, overseeing the widest range of war work programs. But as long as black women demonstrated that they had not engaged in disruptive activity, federal agencies, like the Woman's Committee, supported or funded black war work activities, but they also distanced themselves from

African American women and their labors. When federal programs called on black clubwomen to help in organizing war work activity, middle-class African American women relied on their own wartime networks, but they turned to the federal programs for monetary support and professional recognition.

Thus, a key pattern emerged that frames African American women's war work in the South. When black women were excluded from war work activity, they initiated and led political and economic movements outside of mainstream political views. These movements gave African American women a voice that had been denied in patriotic work, and in turn, black women changed the political landscape at the highpoint of the war for democracy. For instance, very troubling to the Woman's Committee was the growth of unions throughout the South. Alice Dunbar-Nelson's investigations in Alabama and Louisiana revealed an active labor movement among domestic workers, particularly in New Orleans. Domestic workers in Louisiana were threatened with heavy fines and jail time under the "Work or Fight" laws, which local governments used to force black women who had left their jobs back into employment. The burgeoning labor movement sidestepped prosecution by urging the domestics to keep their jobs and continue with organizing. Throughout much of the South, three competing visions of black women's work became apparent. At the federal level, the Woman's Committee considered the domestic labor unions patriotic and subversive. Alice Dunbar-Nelson thought the unions were treading uncertain ground, but she admired the progressive steps toward securing higher wages and better working conditions for black working women. The leaders of the domestic unions believed that their work counteracted years of employer control and gave black domestics a much-needed, long-awaited upper hand in labor negotiations.

The primary narrators witnessing the unfolding story of African American women's war work in the South were Alice Dunbar-Nelson and Mary Church Terrell. They conducted investigations for two federal ad hoc organizations of World War I, the Woman's Committee and the WCCS, respectively. The Woman's Committee and the WCCS operated as federal agencies and addressed specific matters relating to the World War and urban American communities. After the war, the groups condensed their operations and were defunct by May 1919. Despite their individual analyses, Dunbar-Nelson and Terrell shared similar backgrounds in upbringing, education, professional outlook, and social affiliations with the NACW. As representatives of predominantly white organizations, Dunbar-Nelson and

Terrell manifested the spirit of double consciousness, a notion described by W. E. B. Du Bois in his polemic *The Souls of Black Folk*. They wore one facade for their white employers, another for the white southerners offering hospitality and contacts, and still another for the African American women whose wartime activities were the subject of investigation. Dunbar-Nelson and Terrell launched their war research wearing several interdependent masks of perception at once: African American and white, institutional and public, middle class and working class, secular and religious, and marginalized and patriotic. Their explorations uncovered a greater labyrinth of illusion, where expectations for better race relations formed an unequal partnership with short-lived opportunities for interracial cooperation, an association that proved unsustainable after the war.

But this story would not be complete without the voices of the black working-class women who challenged white supremacy and their white employers in the southern urban areas. Historian William J. Breen has argued that southern black women saw possibilities for social reform offered by the war, though their war aims differed significantly from the states' and the nation's objectives.[6] The federal war work machine had little idea of what black women were doing for the nation, which was why Dunbar-Nelson and Terrell were sent on investigations of black communities in the South. Still, the labors of working-class women defied almost all expectations, including those of the investigators. Mary Jackson, a labor expert employed by the YWCA, noticed the change as well. "Patriotism among Colored girls and labor conditions that have shown them that the possibilities for their service outside of domestic work have been the prime factors in the new movement. The shortage of men workers and the falling off in immigration have given them their chance, and they are taking it."[7] As a labor movement figured into the social reform efforts, black women's political aims had more to do with securing better jobs and challenging Jim Crow rather than fighting a far-off enemy. The challenge for Dunbar-Nelson and Terrell was to show their black constituents the link between the far-off enemy and social reform during the war.

## Alice Dunbar-Nelson and the Woman's Committee of the Council of National Defense

Before Alice Dunbar-Nelson embarked on her journey for the Woman's Committee, she was already primed for debate on the war and the prospect of a transformation in the political status of African Americans. In January 1918, she attended a colloquium on the preparedness of the American forces, and it piqued her professional interest. A local professor, who chaired the discussion, had prepared a test measuring the intelligence quotient of enlisted servicemen. Proclaiming the day "of sentimental consideration in education was past!" the professor concluded that black soldiers rated lowest on his test, lower than the "ignorant sturdy mountaineer" or the newly arrived immigrant, although both were declared "much below par."[8] To no one's surprise, middle-class, educated, native-born white men scored best on the exam. Dunbar-Nelson became indignant when the professor announced his results, though she let him finish his presentation. When he claimed that for the first time in history, human nature was scientifically studied, Dunbar-Nelson had had enough. She shot back immediately, "Good Lord, Professor, it has been studied since the world began!"[9]

Dunbar-Nelson then launched into her own critique. The test was not based in actual science, nor did it reveal much of anything besides the professor's own racial bias, she corrected. The professor responded that caste systems existed in all other countries, and that a racial caste system had become the American way of separating groups based on merit and ability. Dunbar-Nelson replied, "[This] is nothing in the world but the old-time aristocratic landholding class trying to grab for power, and using this time, not theological argument but the kind of science learned from German universities (where it has, as everyone knows, been a howling success on moral character)." If a racial caste system endured in the United States after the war, Dunbar-Nelson sardonically concluded, "I'd rather take my chances in England."[10]

While the professor remains nameless in Dunbar-Nelson's memoirs, the content of the argument represented two significant problems confronting African Americans during the World War. When dealing with the federal government and the Department of War, the fates of black women's war work and black men's military service were closely linked. For African American men, aptitude tests given by the armed forces reinforced widespread assumptions of black men's low intelligence and inability to cope with the pressures of service. The army's reliance on scientific racism was just another step in its self-fulfilling prophecy. Since the American armed forces considered black men suited only for low levels of responsibility, the military balked at extending to *all* black soldiers the same opportunities and services that were available to white recruits, which led to black men's low test scores in knowledge of military doctrine and codes of conduct. Secondly, the remaining responsibilities for soldier care that the army partly shouldered fell on black women and charitable institutions. In defense of their servicemen, northern and southern African American women summoned their resources, or asked for help, when trying to meet the needs of black soldiers. A Crispus Attucks Circle of the Circle for Negro War Relief in Philadelphia, for instance, rallied public support for a hospital for black soldiers and insisted that black doctors and nurses be hired to meet the demand. "They have given their best boys. They have bought bonds, and are buying thrift stamps," said the white newspaper, the *Philadelphia Inquirer*. "They have given to the Red Cross, the Y.M.C.A. and to all other war funds, and have volunteers to help nurse the sick and do whatever the country demands or suggests."[11] When charitable donations fell short, black women filled in the blanks and picked up the slack by forming their own groups on the local and state levels.

The idea for an African American woman to travel in the southeastern United States and to investigate war work in African American communities originated with Emmett Scott, the special assistant to the Department of War. Appointed in October 1917 as a liaison between African Americans and the Department of War, Scott oversaw all matters, military and domestic, relating to African American service and the American effort during the Great War. Scott took notice of the increasingly tense relationship between the Red Cross and African American nurses nationwide. In spring 1918, the Red Cross issued a national call for 25,000 experienced nurses to join the armed forces. At the same time, the agency denied admittance to all African American registered and graduate nurses, on the grounds that building separate living facilities for them had stretched the Red Cross's budget beyond its limit. By summer 1918 the disenchantment and anger among African American women had become acute.

At an 8 July 1918 meeting of the executive board of the Woman's Committee, Scott relayed his fear that African American women were in a state of unrest. Due to the Red Cross situation, Scott recommended to his colleagues that "a woman be employed to organize the colored women in the States."[12] Hannah Patterson, resident director of the Woman's Committee, knew Alice Dunbar-Nelson from her previous efforts in war work, and suggested her for the position. Under the Woman's Committee plan, Dunbar-Nelson visited eight states to organize African American women under the direction of each State Council of Defense. The committee also intended Dunbar-Nelson to monitor the level of anti-American sentiment in African American communities. The executive board determined that Dunbar-Nelson "will confer with the leaders among her own people and report to the Woman's Committee their opinion as to conditions among colored people."[13] The executive committee approved the measure, and Hannah Patterson wrote Alice Dunbar-Nelson about the position. On 12 August 1918, Patterson formally authorized Dunbar-Nelson as a field representative of the Woman's Committee.[14]

Dunbar-Nelson was born Alice Ruth Moore in 1875 to Joseph and Patricia (Wright) Moore. She had gained national recognition as an essayist and poet before her thirtieth birthday. Her parents afforded her every educational opportunity available to them, insisting that Moore finish high school before sending her to Straight College (now Dillard University) in New Orleans in 1889. Moore's twenties witnessed a period of immense productivity, particularly in her educational and professional development. The Straight College teaching program prepared her for a career in education, and after graduating she taught in New Orleans for two years. A few years later, Moore relocated to Philadelphia, where she began her studies at the University of Pennsylvania in Philadelphia, then at the School of Industrial Art in Philadelphia and Cornell University. Moore extended her social and professional network when she attended the first National Association of Colored Women (NACW) convention in 1896, and presented a paper on "The Afro-American Child and Patriotism." When she moved again, this time to New York City, she taught at a high school in Brooklyn, and helped establish the White Rose Mission, the rescue home and settlement house for working-class black girls.[15]

Moore also displayed an early talent for writing, publishing in 1899 her first book of poetry and fiction, *Goodness of St. Rocque, Short Stories,* when she was barely twenty-five years old. A year earlier, she had married Paul Laurence Dunbar, who had achieved critical acclaim as the foremost African American poet and literary figure. By all accounts, their marriage was stormy, and they separated just four years later in 1902.[16] Paul Laurence Dunbar died in Atlanta of tuberculosis in 1906, but Alice Moore Dunbar was already on her way to Wilmington, Delaware. Deciding to make Wilmington her home, she returned to teaching, and expanded her career as a journalist, editing the *A.M.E. Church Review* and the *Wilmington Advocate.* In 1916 Alice Dunbar married Robert Nelson, and from Wilmington, she devoted herself to a number of activities: secondary-school education, the NACW, regional politics, the NAACP, and the women's suffrage movement.[17]

Throughout the winter and spring of 1918, Alice Dunbar-Nelson made selective attempts to engage in war work. She corresponded regularly with Private Ernest Jones, a friend and colleague from Wilmington, who was stationed at Camp Chillicothe in Ohio. The exchange brought her fresh news about life in the black training camps. Jones took pains to explain to Dunbar-Nelson that army life was, at times, difficult, and he urged her to dissuade her friends and students from enlisting only for the chance to go abroad. "It's more than putting on a uniform and walking around," Jones confided in a letter. His duties ranged from manual labor—"I've shoveled coal and snow, patched boilers, lain bricks, and mixed mortar"—to working in the quartermaster's office as a radio operator. When the outbreak of spinal meningitis put the entire camp under quarantine, Jones and other enlisted men endured weekly injections of antibiotics from large hypodermic needles. On a happier note, the Colored YMCA Hostess House, "a very fine building and very cozy," showed great hospitality to the black soldiers. "It is our only chance to enjoy the real life and see colored civilians." The 200 African American recruits were also treated well, and received accommodations comparable to those of the 5,000 white recruits. "It is a rather hard life," he decided, "but there is no reason for complaining, the food is good and plenty of it. We sleep fairly warm, and we have pretty fair washing quarters if there wasn't so much ice on the floor." Ultimately, the things that Jones requested to make his life at Camp Chillicothe more pleasant were books, magazines, and news from his friends back in Wilmington.[18]

Dunbar-Nelson was gratified by Jones's correspondence, but she sought an established organization that made use of her professional experience. The Circle for Negro War Relief fit just the type of work she desired. As its name implied, the Circle dedicated its work to bringing material relief to African American soldiers and aiding their families who, in the absence of a head of household, had fallen on hard times. Established in August 1917, the Circle for Negro War Relief was begun by Emilie Bigelow Hapgood, a white reformer in New York who had sought to develop an organization that offered more than "fashionable" charity. The *New York Times* accentuated Hapgood's gentility and aristocracy as it explained the birth of the idea of the Circle for Negro War Relief.

> Mrs. Emilie Bigelow Hapgood of 12 West Twelfth Street, that quiet refined old section of New York City where they still have winding staircases and where every stocking is blue, determined to launch a novel charity—relief for the negro soldier and his family. . . .
> 'How did you come to start it?' was asked of Mrs. Hapgood.
> 'In just the same way,' she replied, 'that all of those other leaders came to take up war relief. It was quite apparent to me that the real sufferers among

our soldiers would be the colored soldiers, and that the ones left behind who would first feel the pinch of hunger would be the families of our negroes who go to France. I know that the negroes are in a more helpless condition in times of such emergencies as war than our white families. It occurred to me that when a negro joined the army, or was drafted in, the ones left at home were indeed stripped of the dependence, and that unless there were enough members of the family who could work for their own living, they were going to need help.'"[19]

Emphasizing the differences in class and background between the wealthy white northerners and black soldiers, the *New York Times* also stressed for its elite, conservative readers the willingness and compassion whites showed for cooperating with the *right* black cause. Notwithstanding Hapgood's good intentions, the *Times* article also sought to avoid the appearance that the wealthy whites had favored their war-stricken cousins abroad and turned away destitute African American soldiers at home. The article gave the Circle for Negro War Relief a dual boost, in publicizing the good works of New York's upper class and the honorable intentions of the interracial committee governing the Circle.

The Circle assembled a coterie of African American and white American activists, including on the executive board W. E. B. Du Bois, James Weldon Johnson, Colonel Charles Young, George Foster Peabody, and Arthur Spingarn. "In all cases," the Circle's advertising pamphlet read, "the negro soldier's absence will be felt more keenly than can possibly result from the service of any other soldiers in ranks, for it must be admitted that the colored troops represent the most impoverished class in the United States. . . . 'The Circle for Negro War Relief, Inc.' was formed out of the minds of its founders as a most needed war measure."[20] Concerned that other national agencies overlooked the immediate needs of black soldiers, the Circle followed a proactive formula by contacting black base camps directly to ascertain what the soldiers needed most, then turning to local African American churches and schools asking them to send the materials.

The Circle's executive secretary, Caroline S. Bond, made a personal appeal to Alice Dunbar-Nelson at the end of January 1918. Hoping to establish a Unit of the Circle in Wilmington, Bond wrote Dunbar-Nelson, "I am especially happy to have this offer coming from you because I know just what influence you have and what you can do. Won't you start a Unit there? We already have twenty Units started and are anxious for the work to spread over the country as rapidly as possible."[21] From the beginning, the Circle offered Dunbar-Nelson autonomy to conduct war work in Wilmington the way she saw best. Beyond the $10 fees for new Unit members, Dunbar-Nelson was free to raise funds using various methods, including benefit dinners and concerts, selling buttons, and passing a collection box at local Wilmington churches. Bond acknowledged Dunbar-Nelson's experience in club work, a compliment not often paid to African American women by predominantly white organizations.

Bond then sent Dunbar-Nelson a list of different camps that required special attention. The Midwestern black base camps needed assistance most urgently, so Dunbar-Nelson's efforts focused on providing sweaters, earmuffs, wool socks, scarves, gloves, Bibles, and songbooks for the servicemen at Camp Grant in Rockford, Illinois.[22] While Dunbar-Nelson awaited word from the YMCA or YWCA about a chance to serve on the wars fronts in Western Europe, she found satisfying labor and attainable objectives at the Wilmington Unit. "I note what you say about being interested in going 'Over There' and really before many moons we may need someone for just that sort of thing," Bond assured Dunbar-Nelson, who had requested early on to be sent to France.[23] For the time being, the Circle was content with Dunbar-Nelson's help to "keep the home fires burning and the fires of patriotism burning in the cabin homes of the negro soldiers."[24]

African American clubwomen thrived on the Circle's structure. The agency provided a platform for clubwomen to link the labors of their own local groups to a national organization, one that had African American men and women on its executive board. The *New York Age* joined the chorus of supporters for the organization, heralding the work of the Circle as "a laudable undertaking." The Circle also enjoyed public endorsements from former president Theodore Roosevelt, Mary McLeod Bethune, New York Governor Charles Whitman, and Grace Nail Johnson, clubwoman and wife of James Weldon Johnson. "Colored women throughout the country are showing more than a casual interest in the work of the Circle for Negro War Relief," declared the *Age*, adding that Units had been founded in New York, New Jersey, Connecticut, Pennsylvania, Ohio, and Washington, D.C. Well-known clubwomen, such as Margaret Murray Washington, Beverly K. Bruce, Madam C. J. Walker, and her daughter Lelia Walker Robinson joined the list of volunteers.[25] By mid-1918, the Circle counted among its members over fifty Units in twenty-five states.[26] The Circle stood among a few other organizations dedicated to sending equipment and supplies to black troops, including the National Colored Soldiers Comfort Committee, based in Washington, D.C., and the Soldiers Comfort Unit, located in Boston.

Acting as a clearinghouse of clubs and groups, the Circle's most impressive financial achievement was the purchase of an ambulance for black servicemen in August 1918, at a cost of $2,146.[27] The ambulance was donated to the Department of War, who sent it to France to aid black troops in need of medical materiel. The Circle found great success in gathering together African Americans who wanted to contribute to the war but had little idea of where to make donations or of how much to give. The *Crisis* magazine reported that women of the Circle helped to make and distribute 500 knitted garments for soldiers. Caroline Bond wrote Dunbar-Nelson in March 1918 and applauded the Wilmington Unit so far, adding, "I feel sure that we can count on the interest and efforts there."[28] For Dunbar-Nelson personally, the Circle filled a niche that had opened up in her professional life. She supplemented her work in the Circle with writing fiction and war poems for the *A.M.E. Church Review* and *The Crisis* magazine.[29] Dunbar-Nelson continued her work with the Circle until July 1918, when the Woman's Committee approached her about an investigative tour of war work through the southeastern United States.

The organization Dunbar-Nelson joined was theoretically a federal body overseeing the war work of all American women. The Woman's Committee aimed to get every American woman functionally performing in the American war machine. "It is generally recognized that the greatest duty of women in war times is to keep social conditions as normal as possible . . . : to keep the home fires going, while the men fight for the country's defense," wrote Emily Newell Blair, the Woman's Committee's wartime historian.[30] The Council of National Defense and its subordinate committees coordinated the women's preparedness movement and organized the women of the nation. An executive committee comprised of politically active American women governed the Woman's Committee, including Anna Howard Shaw as director and Carrie Chapman Catt as an executive board member, both representatives of the National American Woman Suffrage Association. As for general areas of interest, the members of the executive board were assigned to investigate and encourage American women's activities in organization, finance, registration, food, educational propaganda, industry and labor, morale in training and base camps, patriotism, democracy, and special training for service.[31] On all matters relating to women, the Woman's Committee took the recommendations of the Department of War and the Council of National Defense, and issued its own set of instructions to the State Councils. Following the directions of each State Council, county chairmen and civic leaders oversaw the actual implementation of national policy.

As for the internal structure of the Woman's Committee, the executive board oversaw the agency's activities, aided by the presidents of nearly one hundred national women's organizations, all of whom sat on an honorary committee. While the honorary committee added more prominence to the Woman's Committee, logistically, an executive office committee of fifteen women carried out the directives of the executive board. Hannah Patterson, a white woman, served on both the executive board and as the resident director of the executive office committee, as well as personally administering the state and territorial Divisions of the Woman's Committee. Patterson focused much of her attention on the southeastern United States and the war work of African American women. However, Dunbar-Nelson was often the first and only representative from the Woman's Committee to contact African American women of the South, due to the inconsistencies in relationships between local Units and the State Councils in the South. In some cities, local Units worked closely with their governing State Councils, but in others, the State Councils had little control over the activities of the local Units. While Dunbar-Nelson traveled as an individual field representative for the Woman's Committee, standing low on the political totem pole and possessing less autonomy than the state chairmen and regional directors, she alone was responsible for forming a cohesive investigation of southern African American women's work for the Woman's Committee.

The NACW joined the Woman's Committee in August 1917. Mary Burnett Talbert, then-president of the NACW, not only held a seat on the general board but also was the de facto chairman of black women's war work. In this capacity, Talbert pledged the full participation of African American women. "When Congress declared that a state of war existed between Germany and the United States, I knew that every colored woman would gladly come forward and offer her service to our government," Talbert assured in a letter to her fellow clubwomen.[32] A tireless fundraiser and an adept networker, Talbert's professional contacts extended into the National Association for the Advancement of Colored People (NAACP) and the National American Woman Suffrage Association (NAWSA). She assured Clarinda Lamar, the Woman's Committee's executive secretary, that the Woman's Committee could count on the NACW for a full contribution. Talbert offered the same assurance to Anna Howard Shaw, president of NAWSA, declaring, "Our women . . . were particularly interested in food conservation, and when we realize that the greatest conservation of food is in the kitchen, where so many of our colored women are employed as cooks, you will readily agree with me that they are playing a very important part in this war. . . . You may rely upon me, as president of the National Association of Colored Women, to keep them keyed up to their responsibility as long as this war lasts."[33] As historian Anne Meis Knupfer has argued, African American clubwomen considered themselves ambassadors of the race, and, in turn, saw their duty as representing millions of black women's voices.[34] Though the notion of a small group of middle-class women appointing themselves as ambassadors for all black women was problematic, black clubwomen considered their war work as a representative answer to the call of duty as Americans.

But if African American women's war work typically fell within the province of the NACW, why did the Woman's Committee enlist a special field representative to survey African American women? The answer lies in the NACW's standing as a national, autonomous organization. It operated as an independent agency, external to the management of the Woman's Committee. In 1918, alongside the war in Europe, the NACW considered other substantive matters affecting African Americans: the renovation of the Frederick Douglass Home, which clubwomen had saved recently from bankruptcy; women's suffrage; mob violence and lynching; Jim Crow; and organizing war work among its own member clubs.[35] Regarding African American women's community service, the NACW's primary goal was to present a united front of its club members during the war. Alternatively, the Woman's Committee needed an African American representative who felt little pull from other organizations. Dunbar-Nelson remained a long-standing member of the NACW, but the black women's organization was left out of the loop concerning her appointment. So distant from the NACW was the Woman's Committee that it chose not to inform the NACW of Alice Dunbar-Nelson's wartime employment until six weeks after she had concluded her survey. When Talbert found out about Dunbar-Nelson's appointment, much after the fact, she sharply criticized the Woman's Committee's executive board: "As a matter of fact, we were not asked to endorse her [Alice Dunbar-Nelson] by the National Council, a thing which perhaps should have been done, as we represented the largest body of organized colored women actually engaged in all branches of war work."[36]

Instead the regional directors of the State Councils of Defense reported black women's wartime service to the Woman's Committee. Florida found success in establishing a special "Colored Women's" section of the Woman's Committee in every county of the state.[37] The Missouri State Council reported that black women had organized themselves already, meeting in the state's large cities and creating different topical divisions.[38] In Alabama, African American women established six new units, each one with food conservation, food production, child welfare, and home service committees.[39] The eventual arrangement between Dunbar-Nelson, the Woman's Committee, and the NACW served as a fitting metaphor for the wide gap separating African American women's war work and the federal government during the war. Dunbar-Nelson's primary obligation was to work as a mediator between a federal agency and southern African American communities. Her research revealed that southern African American women maintained a high level of political activism, despite the exigencies of the war and of racial segregation. The racial politics of World War I held that black and white women kept the appearance of unified patriotic activity, but the racial etiquette of the period demanded that black women and white women undertake their war work in separate racial spheres.

Alice Dunbar-Nelson boarded a train in Washington, D.C., on 12 August 1918 bound for her home of New Orleans, the first stop in her tour. The Woman's Committee gave her vague instructions about the nature of her work, although it stressed she should interview African American women with their respective State Councils of National Defense. Her first destination proved the most revealing. When she arrived on 14 August in New Orleans, Dunbar-Nelson found that 20,000 African American women had registered with the Louisiana Council of National Defense. Infant-weighing and baby-measurement stations were the most popular programs, all guided by Mrs. William Porteour, the special city chairman of the Louisiana State Council. "The colored women have been lovely and have co-operated in every way possible and the feeling between the races is ideal—no need of anxiety at all," wrote Dunbar-Nelson in her first letter to Hannah Patterson, her supervisor. All that was missing, Dunbar-Nelson felt, was a community spirit of war work for the nation. "There isn't any organization," she added, "just a lovely co-operation, and general foggy feeling of goodwill and sisterly love."[40]

Upon further investigation, Dunbar-Nelson discovered that in densely African American areas of Louisiana, there had been no organization whatever. No one from the Louisiana State Council had made a trip to Baton Rouge, Shreveport, or Alexandria, cities where African Americans numbered at least half of the total population. Dunbar-Nelson made an address before an audience of African American women in New Orleans to ascertain the extent of the problem. At the end of the meeting, she offered her opinion: "We really don't know what the colored women are doing in this war and I am going from one part of the country to the other to find out. . . . This is the biggest opportunity that has ever come to any race in the world—this opportunity that the colored race has today to show its patriotism and loyalty, and I hope that every man and woman is going to seize it." Her exploration of activities in Louisiana signaled a pattern of black women's participation with the Woman's Committee. After a few days in her hometown, Dunbar-Nelson was frustrated by the lack of cooperation between black women and white women. Her sharpest criticism was reserved for the black audience: "We really don't know what the colored women are doing in this war, and I am going from one part of the country to the other to find out. . . . This war will be either better or worse, and it is for us to decide."[41]

What captured Dunbar-Nelson's attention next were the intense labor negotiations of a union of black domestic workers. The workers called for higher wages, shorter hours, and greater personal freedom, radical requests from a group that had been rendered nearly invisible in the years leading up to the war. But news of a domestics' union led to an anxious reaction by the white employers of New Orleans. They asked for letters of reference from all applicants for positions as cooks, maids, laundresses, and housecleaners, as "a self-defensive measure." Reflecting a growing consternation for black domestics' claims for better compensation, white employers wanted to know if the domestics would challenge the rules of the house. "Will they work regularly, or will they stay at home when it pleases them?" asked an unnamed employer in the *New Orleans Times-Picayune.* "Will they work properly, or in a slovenly manner?" Letters of reference were not the only ways to solve the servant problem. The anonymous employer concluded that the only way to keep black domestics in line was to end pantoting, the practice where domestics took home leftovers and extra materials that the employers would have otherwise thrown away.[42]

Requiring reference letters was hardly the answer to the problem of a shortage of domestics, but the demand indicated that white employers were losing their control over the domestic labor market. The union movement in New Orleans became the latest cause for concern, but the domestics forged ahead. Similar to black farmers' acts of resistance, as described in Robin D. G. Kelley's groundbreaking study of the growth of communism in Alabama, the domestics of New Orleans were primed to turn their daily experiences into political expressions, in this case, for more money and shorter hours.[43] The movement had gained momentum by the time Dunbar-Nelson arrived in New Orleans.

In May 1918, Ella Pete founded the Colored Domestic Union of New Orleans, and she became the union's first president. Ella Pete was also the wife of Sylvester Pete, the president of the black freight handlers' union of

New Orleans. Gathering some 300 laundresses, cooks, maids, and nurse-girls at the mass meeting, the organization voted to apply for a charter from a national labor organization. In August 1918, the Colored Domestic Union allied itself with the nurses' labor union in New Orleans. When Dunbar-Nelson took a moment to speak with them, they explained to her the difficulties of domestic work in New Orleans. For instance, white families often hired domestics, but had little money to pay for them, and then withheld the agreed-upon wages from the domestics. Even with the low pay, "women who get $12 or $15 a month" were required to stay late into the evening, leaving them little time to spend with their own families "or for recreation and at a wage which is not a living one." One memorable incident was reprinted in the *New Orleans States,* when the white employers accused the union members of spying for the German government. The Colored Domestic Union denied any connection to the Germans, and it kept its promise not to strike. The domestics also told Dunbar-Nelson that segregation in the Red Cross and the federal government deeply troubled African American women of the area. They attempted to gain employment with the government in its war work campaign, but, instead, they were assigned to domestic and janitorial positions, even as "potential scrubwomen, no matter how educated or refined the girl may be."[44] Still, the Colored Domestic Union held firm in its demands for "fair wages and reasonable hours," and eventually reached an agreement with the employers.[45]

As a federal representative, the best Dunbar-Nelson could do at this point was to listen and report. She promised to follow up the case, if time permitted. Her intention was to ask the Woman's Committee if it would lend its official endorsement to the Colored Domestic Union. Dunbar-Nelson wrote Hannah Patterson of the racial troubles in New Orleans. Patterson responded with a firm rebuke, primarily on the circumstance of the domestic workers' union. The Woman's Committee would not recognize the efforts of the domestics' union, or any labor union, Patterson declared. The domestics' labor union of New Orleans represented highly suspicious activity during the war. The Russian Bolshevik Revolution in the previous summer of 1917 had ignited American fears of labor unrest in the United States. Patterson added, "The New Orleans Unit of the Woman's Committee would be entirely right in . . . not giving [the domestics' union] any assistance." In contrast, the women's suffrage movement had given itself over to war work, and in Patterson's opinion, the National American Woman Suffrage Association provided the perfect model of nonpartisan, organizational cooperation.[46] Patterson directed Dunbar-Nelson to limit her survey to war work alone. Dunbar-Nelson left New Orleans on 18 August, but not before asking another Louisiana State Council war worker why there had been such a "labored effort to emphasize good will and cooperation," where clearly none existed.[47]

What Alice Dunbar-Nelson did not know, or rather did not comprehend, was that southern black women struggled for recognition of their patriotic activity. The accusations of disloyalty and the refusals to cross the color line for the sake of war work effectively counteracted working-class black women's enthusiasm for war work. The battle lines had already been drawn by the time Dunbar-Nelson arrived in the summer of 1918. On one side were white employers, many of whom were local government officials, who suggested that the black women of their states were unpatriotic at best or potential spies for Germany at worst. On the other side were black war volunteers, many of whom were middle-class clubwomen, who had placed patriotic activity ahead of civil rights. The rise in African American women's political movements, such as union organizing and anti-lynching efforts, gained strength and membership at about the same time that segregated white agencies denied black women equal access to key war work organizations.

Nor did Dunbar-Nelson fully understand early in her journey the complexities of race and class in her investigation and employment. She miscalculated the impact of Jim Crow on turning southern black women away from war work. At several points in the beginning of her survey, she referred to working-class black women as the "ignorant classes," while her classist views led her to assume that the "lower classes" had caused trouble with the domestic union. She assured the white war workers she met that "it was the lower classes of servants who had organized; the better class had nothing to do with it, nor did they wish to co-operate with their sisters in such a union."[48] She eventually changed her views, but only after she found the same problem of segregated, unequal, and disparate war work throughout the South.

The next state was Mississippi, a state that offered well-meaning, but uneven, interracial war work. On 18 August Dunbar-Nelson was greeted warmly in Como by Mrs. Edward McGehee, the white chairman of the Mississippi State Council of Defense. "The colored women are alive and anxious to work—Mrs. McGehee has seen to that," boasted Dunbar-Nelson in a letter to Patterson.[49] McGehee vowed to assist her in her travels through Como, Sardis, Jackson, and Meridian. McGehee had splendidly organized the women of the state, even going as far as "financing the salary and expenses of the colored organizer out of her own pocket." She also recognized that more had to be done in the area of African American women's work. In Sardis, McGehee had appointed a state worker to oversee the organization of clubs among black women. Jackie Green, the appointee and a former Hampton Institute student, traveled from county to county organizing African American women, forming canning clubs for food conservation and cooperating with the white county chairman.[50]

Dunbar-Nelson found the same strained interracial relations in Mississippi as she had in Louisiana. In private meetings with the African American residents, Dunbar-Nelson heard that segregation in war work, combined with the poor attention paid to the contributions of blacks in the city, pushed black Mississippians to their limits. "The colored people, even the most ignorant, are doing a lot better thinking. . . . It isn't German propaganda, either, it's American propaganda, that is working harm among the people."[51] Mississippi had been the site of several episodes of mob violence during the war. One terrible incident took place in Vicksburg, where a number of blacks from the city had been tarred and feathered, including one woman whose husband was fighting in France.[52] In response, the African American brass band of Vicksburg refused to accompany draftees marching to the station. The Mississippi chapter of the Red Cross had refused to allow black women to wear its canteen uniforms and denied them membership in the organization.[53] In Jackson, registration for the Council of National Defense had been a failure among white women, and barely initiated among black women. In a final insult, the Negro Patriotic League of Mississippi was denied membership in the Mississippi State Council of National Defense, and in response, the group launched a statewide protest. In the meantime, the League held its own meetings and clubs, and sent its representatives to organize African Americans living in Vicksburg.[54] The tense interaction between whites and African Americans undid the pleasant association begun by Mrs. McGehee at the beginning of Dunbar-Nelson's Mississippi trip. Despite her suggestions that African Americans "align themselves as far as possible with the Woman's Committee and work with them," Dunbar-Nelson left Mississippi sensing that African Americans had already embarked on independent work, external to white agencies.[55]

Encouraged that African American women continued to gather for war work, but concerned about the growing distance between white and black women, Dunbar-Nelson arrived in Selma, Alabama. She found the same hopeful but disconnected efforts in some parts of the state. She also continued to misread the extent of the segregation. On 25 August, she spoke before a crowd of African Americans in the largest black church in the city. She argued that the World War would improve the current social conditions and increase economic opportunities, but first African Americans should participate with enthusiasm. Black soldiers must do their best in military service, while black wives and mothers must encourage their loved ones to enlist. Everyone had a duty to join the Red Cross, to work in food conservation, to knit, or to send comfort bags.[56] A German victory in Europe would never advance African American citizenship, Dunbar-Nelson added, because it would crush white America and, along with it, black America. In the meeting after her speech, nearly one hundred black women informed Dunbar-Nelson that a war work organization of black women had failed to materialize so far. Some women directed themselves, selling war savings stamps and knitting scarves, but the Alabama State Council generally had not approached them, much less organized Units for them. From that group of women, an executive committee for colored war work was formed, and Dunbar-Nelson instructed it to familiarize itself with state activities, then to meet regularly to develop the organization. It is doubtful that an organization for African American women of Selma formed in time to engage in war work by the end of the war in November 1918.

In Mobile, Alabama, however, African American laundresses had launched a new union and challenged race relations in the town with a strike. Nine African American women were at the center of the labor unrest, when they confronted other black washerwomen with pickets at American Laundry, which was owned by G. U. Potter. The picketers tried to prevent the other laundresses from gaining entrance to the laundry, and finally the police were called in, the *Mobile Advertiser* reported. The original nine strikers were threatened with a $10 fine or a twenty-day imprisonment before they dispersed. This was not the end of the incident, however. The next day, several hundred African American men and women returned and joined the strike. An entire squad of police officers were on the scene again, "and succeeded in breaking up the assembly by arresting ten persons for not moving on, all of them negroes."[57] While the *Mobile Advertiser* did not follow up on the fates of the strikers, the growth of unions typified the pattern of segregated war work among black women in the South. By the time Alice Dunbar-Nelson arrived in Mobile, black women had all but opted out of war altogether. "There is no Council of Defense, Woman's Committee, so called for Mobile county for colored women, but a 'War Service Club' operating in the same manner. . . . I talked with the chairman and the other members of the War Service Club, but was unable to elicit any definite information as to their activities. I fear their work is [yet] to be done, not [already] accomplished."[58]

However, the city of Birmingham and its industrial neighbor, Bessemer, had a better partnership. Jefferson County, the seat of both Birmingham and Bessemer, constructed a war work program "more thriving, active, and alert than any that I have come across anywhere thus far," Dunbar-Nelson wrote to Patterson.[59] Under the guidance of the Jefferson County chairman and Mrs. H. C. Davenport, who led African American women's efforts, African American women ran elevators in department stores, while in the factories, women replaced men at the machines. At Acipco, an industrial plant making light materials in Birmingham, the welfare manager vowed to make the workspace as pleasant for African American female workers as he had for the men, with "YWCA buildings, swimming pools, a woman director, etc."[60] War work in Jefferson County, Alabama, provided the best model yet of cooperation and spirit between African American women and white women.

In the city of Bessemer, the African American residents joined a thriving Council of National Defense Unit, one that worked in conjunction with the Colored Community House of Bessemer. The Bessemer Unit was responsible for the ever-popular comfort kits, filled with chocolate, cigarettes, magazines, and Bibles. The ladies made their own service flag, decorated with 500 stars, and the wives of soldiers knitted layettes for expectant mothers. When Dunbar-Nelson visited, a food conservation drive was under way, amassing over 1,000 quarts of canned food. For the children of the area, the Unit built its own playground and hired a teacher in the industrial arts to oversee it. The high level of productivity led to the development of a Council of National Defense Unit in Brighton, another industrial town a few miles away. Dunbar-Nelson happily reported that the "work of the Council of National Defense among colored women in Alabama is quite active."[61] Though African American women in Birmingham and Bessemer worked within the confines of segregated war activity, their patriotic labors thrived when they were given ample attention and resources. Some black women criticized or actively opposed Jim Crow, Dunbar-Nelson discovered in Birmingham. "There is some feeling among the colored women of Montgomery against war work, owing to the action of the local Red Cross as to the canteen service, similar to the action in Vicksburg, Mississippi."[62] But it seemed that many black women accepted the intransigence of Jim Crow in war work, as long as the predominantly white war work agencies reached out to black women and recognized their labor.

Nineteen hours after leaving Selma—"trains slow, distances tremendous, state chairman importunate"—Dunbar-Nelson arrived in Jacksonville, Florida. Patterson told Dunbar-Nelson to expect Florida to have the best-organized units through the South. Florida lived up to its reputation. She first met with Eartha White, a colleague from the Woman's Committee and chair of the Florida Colored Woman's Committee of the Council of National Defense. From the beginning of her stay, the Florida State Council and White's efforts in gathering African American and white women together impressed Dunbar-Nelson greatly. "Florida is so well organized I told them they hardly need me at all. . . . The colored men are organized as completely as the women, and co-operated not only with the white women, but the colored women."[63] The Jacksonville Unit formed a partnership with the Mutual Protection League, which oversaw African American women working in previously unheard-of positions as elevator operators, bellhops, and chauffeurs. Dunbar-Nelson also met with a newly formed union of domestic workers, who had allied themselves with the Council "in the way I had dreamed the New Orleans unit would do."[64] African American audiences greeted her warmly in St. Augustine and Jacksonville, and she preached the power of organized war work at the largest African American churches in both cities. Hannah Patterson shared this opinion of Florida's leaders, especially of Eartha White, who had encouraged African American women of Florida to expand their community activities. "The spirit and co-operation of our colored citizens has been most gratifying since our entrance into the war—and Eartha White with her kindly spirit and level head has had a great deal to do with the cordial understanding which exists between white and colored people of Jacksonville."[65] In Florida generally, the only thing that stood in Dunbar-Nelson's way were the gasoline-free Sundays, which forced her to rely on public trolleys.[66]

So far, Dunbar-Nelson's tour had covered nine cities, and she had journeyed nearly 500 miles. Generally, Dunbar-Nelson found African American women following a self-made course in their war work. Like their northern counterparts, southern black women formed groups and circles, which had originated in their local churches, or created their own regional agencies. "Most Units have concentrated on comfort kits for soldiers and the care of soldiers' families," reported Dunbar-Nelson to the Woman's Committee in Washington.[67] For instance the Milk and Ice Fund of Jackson, Mississippi, brought aid to many black families hard-hit by the loss of a male wage-earner, now soldier in the armed forces, during the war.[68] Notwithstanding the occasional exceptions, African American women's war work focused on home and family, and remained within the province of African American communities. The Council of National Defense made less of an impact on African American communities than it expected. Furthermore, Dunbar-Nelson found herself in the awkward position of attempting to establish common ground between white and black women's war work when class and racial boundaries had divided the women for generations before the war. Mrs. McGehee, of the Mississippi State Council, was the notable exception to the shaky state of affairs in southeastern war work. McGehee worked to include African American women within the sphere of the Council of National Defense, yet she also observed that much more had to be done to make the effort truly interracial. For Alice Dunbar-Nelson, her personal, middle-class visions continued to reconcile the patriotic, long-term vision of African American women's work with the short-term objectives of white-led organizations.

In the last two weeks of her journey, Dunbar-Nelson's survey nearly unraveled, due to the lack of interest shown in Georgia, North Carolina, South Carolina, and Tennessee. In Georgia, the next state in her survey, there had been a miscommunication with the State Council chairman, Mrs. Inman, about the travel arrangements. After twenty-two hours on the train, Dunbar-Nelson stood alone at the Atlanta train station, without a place to stay in a city where she was a stranger. She looked at several places the first evening, but, as an African American woman traveling alone, her options were limited. Finally she found a room and immediately scheduled a meeting with Alice Dugged Cary, the Georgia State chairman of the Colored Woman's Committee and president of the Georgia State Federation of Colored Women. Cary was a woman of considerable power in Georgia, particularly in the war work movement. She had been employed by the Department of Labor to travel through Georgia and talk with African American women about labor conditions. Urging women to buy thrift stamps and war bonds, as well as "to continue to work and not use up extra money they may have from allotments," Cary counseled the hundreds of black women she met to stay the course and remain cautious with their economic resources.[69] Based on her series of speeches, Cary gave Dunbar-Nelson an optimistic report of events in Atlanta and around the state, including the affiliation of several organizations, the two playgrounds established for black children, Red Cross rooms in operation, four district nurses seeing to African American neighborhoods, and labor conditions under supervision.[70]

Dunbar-Nelson was not convinced, given that interracial cooperation in war work was the exception, not the rule. She thought the situation too good to be true, suspecting the report from Atlanta "too roseate and indefinite."[71] For a fuller picture, she consulted Lucy Laney, the African American principal of the Haines Institute, "a woman whose veracity is unquestioned and whose influence is far-reaching, and information wide."[72] Laney set Dunbar-Nelson straight on the state of war work in Georgia. There was no organized committee for African American women in Georgia, only sporadic work. Nothing had been established along the lines of the Woman's Committee, not even a black YWCA. Laney joined Dunbar-Nelson in a meeting with Mrs. Harrington, the chairman of Woman's Work in Richmond County. She corroborated Laney's assessment, explaining that the "work among colored women was at a standstill, and that all that had been done was done by Miss Laney." Dunbar-Nelson stayed long enough to relay this information to Patterson and then take a train to South Carolina.[73]

One likely explanation of the low turnout among African American women in war work was the rising tide of the anti-black women's suffrage movement in Georgia. Though the anti-suffragists would reach the peak of their activities in the summer of 1919, during Dunbar-Nelson's investigation, anti-black suffragists had launched a campaign that drew on fears of the vote for black women and, by extension, the re-enfranchisement of black men. For instance, the Writers' Club, a group of white students from South Georgia State Normal College in Valdosta, was comprised of pro-suffrage white supremacists. In the *Pine Branch,* the student newspaper, the Writers' Club argued for new disenfranchisement laws on the pretext that black women were the true heads of African American households. Their suspicions about the ambitions of black women led to even greater anxieties about the intentions of black men, though "they are shiftless, [and] some of the men were excluded from the polls on a purely educational ground." The solution was in imposing an educational test for black women. The test could exclude white women from the polls as well, but the Writers' Club was willing to take that chance. "If we do not exclude the undesirable Negro woman voter but allow all to have the suffrage, we might as well allow the men to vote too, because their influence will be felt in the way she casts her vote." A competing black newspaper, the *Christian Recorder,* answered the *Pine Branch* editorial by linking women's suffrage to the sacrifices black women made on account of the war. "One feels a sense of deep regret that in a time like this when mothers are called upon to give up their sons to war, black sons as well as white sons." The *Christian Recorder*'s solution was for black women to quit their jobs and move northward if they were denied the vote.[74] Historian Rosalyn Terborg-Penn has explored the political expediency in the women's suffrage movement, at the cost of sisterhood between the races.[75] The opinions expressed by the Writers' Club demonstrated a uniform rejection of African American women's political voices or labors.

Unfortunately, war work in South Carolina and North Carolina closely resembled the situation in Georgia. In fact, the further north Dunbar-Nelson traveled, the greater distance she found between African American women and white women in the war work they pursued. Regarding their ideological outlooks or actual war work, African American women and white women remained as far apart in Columbia and Charlotte as they had in New Orleans or Vicksburg. Once again, the Council of National Defense had barely organized white women, and had done nothing for black women.[76] During her travels through North Carolina, Dunbar-Nelson found that war work activities among black women fell on the shoulders of Mamie McCullough and the programs she headed in Charlotte. McCullough, an African American teacher, led all of the service-related events in Charlotte for black women, leaving Dunbar-Nelson to conclude that McCullough's efforts, "with that of one or two other women, working on their own responsibility, constitutes all that has been done."[77] War work among African American women showed no signs of unrest or disorder, but it fit the pattern that Dunbar-Nelson encountered on her tour. "These last three states, Georgia, South and North Carolina, are rather discouraging, but by no means hopeless."[78]

On 8 September Dunbar-Nelson pulled into Tennessee, the last state on her survey. She expected Tennessee to be well organized. According to the information provided by the Council of National Defense for a January 1918 article in the *Beaumont Journal,* the African American women of Tennessee had flocked to war work activities, directing "work under their leaders and often [having] their own units. Tennessee is planning to organize the entire state in separate units and to encourage them to train for nursing."[79] But war work in Tennessee followed the same pattern as in Georgia, North Carolina, and South Carolina. "Women eager, interested, but not sure of their ground," Dunbar-Nelson added. War work activity had come together in Knoxville, Nashville, and Memphis among African American women, along the usual lines of canteen service and comfort kits. Beyond these three cities, the Woman's Committee had not reached rural white and black women.[80] The Woman's Committee had also launched a food conservation campaign in Tennessee in the months leading up to Dunbar-Nelson's visit, but the tactics it used to reach the black working class, especially black domestics, relied on appealing to racial stereotypes. For instance, the Woman's Committee was certain that black domestics would always remain close to their employers, since in "the South the household domestics are loyal to start with," but the main "obstacles to conservation that principally needs to be overcome among them is their tendency to respect what is lavish and to consider all saving as 'stingy.'" The Woman's Committee also employed two brief films to publicize its message. "One of these portrays the need of conserving food and the use of substitutes. The other shows the troubles of an old darkey cook in learning food conservation."[81] There was not much evidence that the films went over well with their African American audiences, since Dunbar-Nelson left Tennessee with a long list of people to convince and improvements to make. But she was confident that black women would create another organization that best served their needs.

By mid-October 1918, Alice Dunbar-Nelson had been at work for nearly six weeks. After she wrapped up her Tennessee visit, she continued on to a few states in the upper South and then returned to Wilmington, Delaware. Upon arrival, she was greeted with the news that the Woman's Committee had abruptly disbanded nearly a week earlier. The organization no longer existed as a federal body, nor did it retain any employees except the executive board members. Instead, a newly created field division of the Council of National Defense replaced the Woman's Committee, although the Woman's Committee maintained an advisory role to the field division to meet any emergencies that arose regarding women's war work.[82] Dunbar-Nelson received a letter from Hannah Patterson further explaining the dissolution of the Woman's Committee, as well as informing Dunbar-Nelson that she had been laid off.[83] The field division chose not to continue the survey, a decision that left Dunbar-Nelson suddenly without a job. With an Allied victory secured by September 1918, the field division considered the situation "inadvisable to send out a representative from headquarters for work among Negro women," and set aside all the past and future work among southern African American women.[84] "We know that you will appreciate the conditions which make this change necessary," Patterson concluded in her letter. In the course of the changeover, Patterson had been promoted to associate director of the field division.

Dunbar-Nelson's split with the Woman's Committee freed her to co-edit and publish the *Wilmington Advocate* and share her traveling experiences with her friends in Wilmington. She also considered leaving for Chicago in December 1918 to help organize the African American stockyard workers, a major personal transformation for her, given that she initially dismissed the domestic workers union in New Orleans in August 1918.[85] Emmett Scott, who recommended Dunbar-Nelson to the Woman's Committee, also suggested that she join the WCCS. On the advice of Scott, who wrote another supportive reference letter, Dunbar-Nelson signed on as an official of the WCCS in its Wilmington Unit until mid-1919, and then resumed her teaching and editing duties.[86] She continued her profession as a writer of short stories and poetry, a career that brought her success during the Harlem Renaissance.

Alice Dunbar-Nelson's narrative would have ended with the abrupt dissolution of the Woman's Committee had she not been given an opportunity to reflect on her findings and publish them. Early in 1919, Scott approached her again, this time about writing an essay about black women and the World War. She set to work assembling her data, then submitted an article, "Negro Women in War Work," which appeared in Scott's *The Official History of the American Negro in the World War.*[87] She painted a heroic picture of African American women during the war. In contrast, her description of interracial war work had not been altogether optimistic, and she explained the association between black and white women as uneven and lukewarm. "The problem of the women of the Negro race was a peculiar one," Dunbar-Nelson wrote. "There were separate regiments of Negro soldiers; should there be separate organizations for relief work among Negro women? Could she be sure that when she offered her services she would be understood as desiring to be a help, and not wishing to be an associate?"[88] In fact, a loose partnership bound by few lasting commitments was the best association African American women and white women could expect, Dunbar-Nelson concluded.

Despite vigorous patriotic activity on both sides, cooperation between the races was hampered by a general suspicion of black women's allegiance, evident as a reluctance to fully include black women in national war efforts. In a few northern cities, Dunbar-Nelson reported that black and white women merged their organizations. But across the country, black and white women were more likely to maintain separate units, often with a Negro auxiliary or an independent colored unit associated with an established national organization. Even the Woman's Committee preferred not to strenuously press the issue of interracial war work.[89] William J. Breen has argued that the Woman's Committee attempted at least to use interracial units to bridge the gulf separating southern black and white women in their patriotic pursuits.[90] However, Dunbar-Nelson found that southern black women were left to their own devices, despite statewide and federal programs aimed at uniting the work of black and white women. She was disappointed with national organizations like the Red Cross because they perpetuated racial discrimination. But she applauded black women for transcending the problem of color. "Local conditions, racial antipathies, ancient prejudices militated sadly against her usefulness in [Red Cross] work. To the everlasting eternal credit of the colored woman it could be said that, in spite of what might have been absolute deterrents, she persisted in her service and was not downcast in the face of difficulties."[91] She gave credit to African American women for lending their support, but she repudiated the partnership that came to nothing.

As for the fear of African American women's unrest—the reason Dunbar-Nelson was sent to the South to investigate—the difficulty of engendering war work within a system ruled by Jim Crow begs for a reexamination. To anxious southern whites, black disloyalty took many forms and lurked around every corner. Lack of interest, strikes, and unions were interpreted as disloyal and revolutionary. In that environment, African American women were expected to express a kind of super-patriotism, one that was passionate and unflinching. White Americans also presumed that African American women would render their support with few resources and limited cooperation. The paradox frustrated both sides. While the Woman's Committee inched toward interracial war work, progress was made in places where the women already committed themselves to bridging the divide. Still, the organization could not compel white women to work with black women, nor could it advocate the goal of civic equality to women who would not have it. White anxieties about race conflict extended beyond the Woman's Committee into other federal agencies, and for black women, it threatened to scuttle any substantive transformation in race relations as a mandate after the war.

## Mary Church Terrell and the War Camp Community Service

Mary Church Terrell's similar study of the southern United States represents an organizational bookend to Dunbar-Nelson's investigation. The War Camp Community Service (WCCS), similar to the Woman's Committee, also envisioned a close cooperation between white and African American communities. Arranging for recreational services to neighborhoods around war camps, the Department of War established the WCCS to mobilize resources among residents and business owners. However, unlike the Woman's Committee, which had achieved partial success in interracial war work in the southeastern United States, the WCCS amounted to a complete failure in its wartime efforts. Terrell documented the WCCS as it attempted to provide recreational programs for African American women and soldiers, and what she found was that the WCCS hardly noticed the distress of the people it was trying to assist. Furthermore, the breakdown of WCCS programs was not apparent to African Americans until the war was long over.

Established as a branch of the Commission on Training Camp Activities in July 1918, the WCCS's primary duties were to organize recreational activities in war camp communities for officers and soldiers.[92] The agency also coordinated the activities of other groups, usually by bringing together volunteers from other national organizations, such as the YMCA/YWCA, the Red Cross, the Knights of Columbus, and the Salvation Army, and supplementing their war work as well.[93] Operating with a pyramid-like structure in its internal hierarchy, the WCCS comprised its workforce of community organizers, district representatives, and an administrative staff at the National Headquarters in Washington, D.C. The community organizers had the most direct contact with residents in local areas, working on behalf of and with all soldiers, "going where they are sent and acting under orders from Headquarters."[94] The district representatives supervised the community organizers, helping them to resolve any difficulties arising from community work, as well as keeping them in touch with activities in other areas. The district representatives, in turn, reported to the WCCS's National Headquarters in New York City, which worked in conjunction with the district directors for the Departments of War and Navy. Beyond these high-level relationships with public and private institutions, the WCCS built the core of its partnerships with the support of local law enforcement, landlords, camp song leaders, camp athletic directors, theater managers and drama directors, local business owners, and local libraries.[95] In an effort to make local neighborhoods more accessible to officers and soldiers, the WCCS linked the resources of the community to the training camp so that each area would operate more efficiently.

While recreational assistance implied an abstract association between the federal government and the local communities, in fact, the WCCS articulated in its handbook that its primary goals were to distribute information to soldiers about places to go, stay, eat, and relax when the soldiers stepped off the base. The WCCS investigated the state of living accommodations, physical recreation facilities, and local hospitality clubs, and then passed their findings onto the soldiers. It also hired local men and women to form a cadre of community organizers and chaperones. This key group of WCCS representatives organized the social gatherings—dances, concerts, pageants, and community songs—which were designed to "stimulate, co-ordinate, or supplement the social and recreational activities of the camp sites."[96] In its assistance to black and white soldiers, the WCCS envisioned recreation activities that equally served both constituencies. Its handbook stated, "Every effort should be made to provide leisure time activities for the colored troops in the same general way as is being done for the white soldiers and sailors."[97] Representatives and chaperones of both races were hired, as they linked the base camp to the local residents. The number of representatives most readily determined the success of the WCCS in base camp communities, especially the African American representatives, since many of the black base camps were in hostile white territories, and black soldiers needed assistance in navigating the social and racial surroundings.

From the first, serving African American soldiers and communities was a daunting task. Soon after the declaration of war, the organization admitted that no facilities existed for African American soldiers, nor were the cities around African American training camps prepared to handle the influx of black soldiers. Another WCCS publication, *The War Camp Community Service and the Negro Soldier,* found that in cities near African American training camps, as many as 40,000 black soldiers had no comfort stations or canteens, no movie theaters, hotels, or clubs, "not even a place where a colored soldier might sit down and write a letter, as a white soldier could do in any hotel or city. And this condition existed in practically all the smaller cities and towns."[98] Enlisting the aid of its Red Circle Clubs, which were volunteer groups initiated by the WCCS, the organization was able to develop activities in large cities like Philadelphia, Louisville, Baltimore, and New York. In smaller cities, such as Knoxville, Macon, Raleigh, and Charleston, local groups, such as Negro Red Crosses, picked up the slack. The WCCS hired local women to arrange dances, socials, and Bible study classes, and it sent its community organizers to chaperone mixed-gender outings. The chaste activities had to compete with illicit attractions, since prostitution, gambling houses, pool halls, and saloons flourished around the training camps. "Even in the larger communities only the forces of evil voluntarily made efforts to receive and entertain colored soldiers," the WCCS recognized.[99]

Mary Church Terrell, who maintained an active political life with club duties during the war, joined the WCCS after the Armistice was signed in November 1918. Terrell held the position of director of the Colored Girls and Women's Work Program, a separate division within the WCCS. Reporting directly to WCCS headquarters, Terrell held more autonomy than Dunbar-Nelson, yet Terrell's work focused on the same issues and carried the same responsibility for investigating the wartime community service of

African American women. As the supervisor of colored work of the Girls' Division, her job had two objectives: (1) attracting black women to serve as community organizers for the Girls' Division and (2) visiting cities with large black populations to investigate the WCCS's activities. Interviewing and hiring black women as community organizers was a relatively easy task, given the high experience level of the applicant pool and the considerable resources the WCCS brought to bear as a federal program. Just fifteen days after beginning her position, Terrell had spoken with almost thirty women across the country, and after hiring "as fine, capable, and progressive a group of colored women as could be collected in the United States," she arranged for them to attend a training school for WCCS volunteers in Hampton, Virginia.[100]

The second task, the southern survey, proved more difficult, partly due to its extensive itinerary throughout the southeastern United States in a brief period of time. Covering nearly the same ground as Dunbar-Nelson's survey, Terrell started with Virginia and North Carolina, moved westward to Mississippi and Louisiana, and then traveled northward through Tennessee on her way back to New York. Similar to Dunbar-Nelson, Terrell focused on collecting information on the implementation of WCCS initiatives in several cities. She visited northeastern and southeastern states, stopping in areas that either had a large African American population or bordered an African American training camp. Unlike Dunbar-Nelson's investigation, which lasted a continuous six weeks before she returned to Washington, D.C., Terrell completed trips over a three-month period, traveling between New York and the designated southern cities. Beginning in late December 1918 and ending in late March 1919, Terrell stopped in twenty-eight cities and consulted with over a hundred community organizers working for the WCCS.

Terrell's first meeting as a WCCS director started ominously and signaled the impossibility of her position ahead. In Biloxi, Mississippi a banker associated with the WCCS apparently thought Terrell was a white woman, and advised her that whites had to exercise great caution when engaging in uplift work for African Americans. Professing that northern blacks misunderstood the need for uplifting southern blacks, the banker, Mr. Tonsmire, claimed that the presence of northern blacks caused disruption and strife. Tonsmire continued, "If a nigger woman came down here she would probably have her nose in the air and give a great deal of trouble. The nigger woman who came here would to come to this bank, sit down in that chair where you are and talk to me as you are doing."[101] As a fair-skinned black woman who often was mistaken for white, Terrell's African American identity frequently escaped the people she interviewed, which, ironically, led to Terrell's success in uncovering the WCCS's failure to African Americans. At another point in the interview, Tonsmire clarified his position on African American achievement. "Remember that whenever you try to do something for niggers, you have to exercise great care to keep them from harming themselves. They can't live and be useful, unless they stay in their place . . . Southern people have fed and clothed and taken care of niggers for years. Just as soon as they get something done for them they get sassy."[102] At another point during her trip, Terrell met a transplanted northerner, Mr. Gordan, living in Gulfport, Mississippi, who boasted that his father-in-law owned thirty-five slaves and lost them all after the Civil War. "I want you to spread the propaganda that both my wife and I are Southerners," Gordan insisted in his interview. Instead, Terrell concluded that Gordan's efforts at persuasion were "one of the most striking and pathetic illustrations of a Northern man's complete surrender to the cruel tradition of the South," and left the meeting.[103]

However, Tonsmire and Gordan had been hired by the WCCS to use their influence as community organizers in African American social programs. When she reported these two accounts to the WCCS headquarters in New York, the executive board filed her complaints but took no further action. The fateful meeting with Tonsmire most clearly revealed the wide gulf separating African Americans and whites during the war. "It is not asking too much, I think, to request those whose mission is to do good to everybody in a community not willfully and wantingly to wound the spirit and crush the pride of even its most humblest and most helpless groups," she offered in her report to the WCCS headquarters.[104] Terrell expected that southern whites would acknowledge economic and social disparity between themselves and African Americans, and she hoped whites would cooperate with blacks to help the entire community thrive. She was mistaken. Terrell only later found that as long as white Americans denied that there was a race problem, African Americans would never receive the federal services and funds they needed and deserved during the war. Moreover, her goals for race uplift, a campaign that she undertook in the 1890s, could not be realized in the socially and economically oppressive environments in which African Americans were mired.

Equally troubling for Terrell was the level of institutional neglect African American communities faced during the war. In the month of February 1919, Terrell focused her attention on four southern states, Tennessee, Alabama, Mississippi, and Florida, visiting eight of their cities with large African American communities. In Chattanooga, Tennessee, her interview with Mr. Stacy Bowing revealed that although there were about 25,000 African Americans living in the city, there were only two YWCA workers for the entire black population.[105] Of the living conditions in Chattanooga, Bowing described it as the worst he had ever seen, adding "there are no hotel accommodations here for colored people. There is no house of detention and there is no orphanage." Bowing informed Terrell that "there are so many colored girls in Chattanooga that the Y.W.C.A. could only scratch the surface," while the WCCS did nothing for the black girls of Chattanooga, leaving a sizeable element that would not be reached at all. The recently demobilized soldiers had organized their own Red Circle Club, but the general African American community lacked a library, an orphanage, a playground for black children, and any supervision at the local dance halls. Terrell described the situation as a "very serious condition existing among the colored people from the standpoint of recreation, living conditions and education. There is almost nothing done for the colored girl." The report she filed with WCCS headquarters gave uniformly poor marks to the state of Tennessee.[106]

In Chattanooga, however, a grassroots effort formed among the African American residents to meet some of the specific needs of the community. The residents approached Terrell to enlist the aid from the WCCS. For instance, black residents had clamored for another high school for teenagers. The black youth of Chattanooga were forbidden from attending white high schools, and "the old one now used is inadequate in every particular—old and situated in the red light district." Mr. Singleton, the principal at the African American high school, and Mattie Jackson, a longtime teacher in the public schools, approached Terrell for an interview. Singleton and Jackson believed that pressure from the WCCS would compel the city and county to relent. Of particular importance to Jackson was an after-school program for school-age black girls who were left alone at home when their mothers worked outside the home. "If the War Camp Community Service can provide ways and means of protecting these school girls of tender age, it would render the greatest possible service to the city and the race," Jackson told Terrell in an interview. Another specific project undertaken by the African American citizens of Chattanooga was the construction of an orphanage for black children. Black women had already raised $1,600 to buy the property, but the city and county had gone back on their promises to donate $5,000 each for the orphanage. The success of these programs necessitated the intervention of the WCCS. Terrell wrote immediately to the WCCS about these initiatives, and requested that a full-time recreational worker be sent to Chattanooga to help implement these plans.[107]

In Florida, Alabama, and Mississippi, Terrell encountered similar situations. "Nothing is being done for the Colored girls of Pensacola, by the Y.W.C.A. or any other organization," Terrell wrote in her March communication to WCCS headquarters. "There is no recreation center either for Colored boys or for the girls, no playground for the children, no public park."[108] The white-controlled town council, however, firmly opposed the addition of a black WCCS worker. Terrell theorized that the all-white executive committee of Pensacola would consent eventually to WCCS assistance for African American women, but only under certain conditions—the WCCS worker had to open up a cooking school as soon as she arrived, "in their zeal to get good servants."[109] Terrell also learned a bitter lesson, namely that white residents expected the WCCS to provide its resources to them immediately, then to black residents later, regardless of the need or the urgency. This was the case for Montgomery, Alabama, when the WCCS community organizer told Terrell that he would be "severely criticized if a worker were sent for colored girls," but not for white girls.[110] Although the YWCA already posted two workers for white girls, Mr. Elges, the community organizer, still insisted that no colored worker be sent to aid the African American community there, since nothing had been done for whites. Ultimately, of the eight cities Terrell visited in February 1919, all of them needed an African American worker for girls' work for the WCCS, but situations like the ones in Chattanooga, Pensacola, and Montgomery prevented the development of adequate services.

The African American residents of Pensacola, however, took the situation into their own hands and spoke to Terrell directly. As in Chattanooga, the black citizens in Pensacola urged Terrell to bring in a WCCS representative for the black girls there. A persistent problem in Pensacola was the condition of the educational facilities for school-age African American children. "I found little, old, dilapidated buildings with plastering falling from the walls inside and unsightliness everywhere," Terrell reported to the executive committee of the WCCS. Terrell recommended that the WCCS immediately address the level of inadequacy in Pensacola. But her correspondence to the executive committee began to show signs of frustration and impatience at the slow pace of intervention. "It seems to me that if the Executive Committee consented to having a Colored woman come to Pensacola, it is worth while to make the experiment for the sake of the Colored girls who so sorely need our help." Terrell's future recommendations included a clear demand that the WCCS regard the development of black communities as a form of war work, as well as quelling southern white hostility to black uplift.[111]

Yet, gaining the support of her white colleagues to improve WCCS programs in northern cities and around black base camps was also surprisingly difficult. In New York City during the last month of her investigation, Terrell spoke to Mrs. Aime, the WCCS director of girls for New York City, about starting up a program for the 125,000 black residents of New York. Mrs. Aime refused to consider the proposal outright, claiming "no matter what they know, or may have achieved, the fact is well-known that nobody is willing to receive colored girls, and it will be a long time before they are received into the sisterhood of American women."[112] Certainly, not all white women felt the same way. Yet, Mrs. Aime's response immediately sunk any possibility of WCCS funding for a black community organizer in New York City. Terrell reminded Mrs. Aime that African Americans had fought in the World War for democracy to gain the rights of citizenship. "The world is not ready for democracy, Mrs. Terrell," Mrs. Aime responded.[113] Terrell was warned of the same sentiment in Pittsburgh. "You might not get the support of the people," Terrell's friend Gertrude Mossell gently counseled her, and Terrell decided to forgo any further trips through the northern states.[114]

The final meeting in New York City left Terrell emotionally and physically drained. At the end of the three-month survey, in which she visited nearly fifteen states, Terrell requested a leave of absence from the WCCS in March 1919, and returned to her husband and two children in Washington, D.C. She still believed the federal program might work, as she continued to recommend the WCCS send workers to assist neglected areas until May 1919. At the same the WCCS program officially was closing down in the spring of 1919, race riots peppered the nation with increasing frequency. After her experience with the WCCS, coupled with the rising racial tension spreading across the nation, Terrell reconsidered her original expectations. Twenty years later in her autobiography, *A Colored Woman in a White World,* she reflected, "Before I engaged in this work, if anybody had related to me the opinions I heard expressed about colored people by well-educated, presumably fair-minded people both North and South, it would have been hard for me to believe them."[115]

With the war's end in November 1918 and the Woman's Committee and WCCS defunct by the end of spring 1919, the experiments at investigating black women's patriotic work yielded key lessons. One lesson was that the war for democracy was no competition for the institutional structures of Jim Crow and white supremacy. The troubling irony about the predominantly white agencies administering African American war work was that the national objective of American victory at its core contradicted African American causes of full equality and citizenship. Although the two federal agencies intended to provide comprehensive activities for African American women, their failure was primarily due to allowing segregationist and white supremacist structures to resist cooperation. The war work of white and black women barely materialized, and when it did, it mirrored segregation before the war. For Mary Church Terrell and Alice Dunbar-Nelson, the WCCS and the Woman's Committee respectively lost a prime opportunity to lead a national discussion in both war work and improved race relations. Furthermore, and perhaps more discouragingly, the Woman's Committee and the WCCS acted in complicity with Jim Crow, reserving their resources for white communities and preserving the status quo of suspicion and racial hostility.

Yet, Dunbar-Nelson and Terrell, while promoting the benefits of black participation in the war, had little conceptualization of either the strictures of segregation between 1917 and 1918, or of its impact on black war work in the southern states. Not until she wrote for Emmett J. Scott's *The Official History of the American Negro in the World War* did Dunbar-Nelson admit that Jim Crow posed too large a problem to overcome. "Local conditions, racial antipathies, and ancient prejudices, militated sadly against her usefulness of this work."[116] Similarly, Terrell wrote in her autobiography over twenty years after the war ended, "it had never occurred to me that it would be possible to find so many of its 'best citizens' who where unalterably opposed to giving their consent to permit competent workers to lift colored women and girls to a higher plane, even though they were not called upon to defray the expense themselves."[117] As middle-class northern black women, Dunbar-Nelson and Terrell arrived in the South encouraged by the patriotic rhetoric that the war in Europe would improve the lives of African Americans. By the summer of 1919, the shared experiences of Dunbar-Nelson and Terrell symbolized the larger trend—middle-class black women had abandoned their belief that the federal government had the power to compel states and white peoples to recognize the labors and the humanity of African Americans.

When compared to the conviction that both women had for a favorable outcome in the war for African Americans, their disappointment and frustration becomes more poignant. Their different narratives stressed a common vision for black women's war work—the institutionalization of interracial cooperation would defeat the institutionalization of Jim Crow in the South. War work in the South, as far as Mary Church Terrell and Alice Dunbar-Nelson knew, amounted to convincing African Americans to pledge their support for democracy and against the far-off enemy, the Central Powers and its allies. Enjoying a measure of freedom that class and education afforded them, their narratives, like their backgrounds, were linked by admirable intentions and a belief in the worthiness of their cause. Not only did they make a persuasive case for democracy for their southern black audiences, they also witnessed, and assisted, the growth of grass roots political and economic movements. Navigating the hostile terrain of white southern politics, the women were determined to achieve a measure of success in the South, as they had in the North. Their most gratifying interaction came at the local stage, where they worked most closely with other African American women, through knitting circles and fund-raising clubs, and African American men, through Hostess Houses, women's auxiliaries, and the canteen service.

Black women turned to organizations like the Woman's Committee and the WCCS for empowerment, so that they might grant their political expressions a greater voice. The pursuit for a better life after the war—higher wages, a recognition of civil rights, better schools, economic stability—invigorated patriotic activity among African Americans. Yet, the personal and political banners under which African American women worked formed barriers between black women and the white women with whom they worked. When war work within white organizations failed to live up to black women's expectations, black women turned inward, to create programs that met the immediate needs of families during war time or provided materials support for soldiers without hospitals or bandages. This was too important a time to opt out, and few black women did. The grass roots organizations, union activity, and suffrage movements reclaimed voices that had been excluded from the larger discussion of how black women would fit into a postwar America. What appeared to be a state of unrest to the imaginations of white war work agencies was legitimate political expression among African American women.

# 3

# Volunteering with the Red Cross and the YWCA

Aileen Cole had studied for some time to earn a registered nursing degree. She began her career as a young, eager, and hardworking student of nursing at the Freedmen's Hospital and Training School in Washington, D.C. "I was one of the stout-hearted probationers who survived the rigorous three-month testing period," Cole remembered. The probation period amounted to a proving ground of sorts, where the nurses-in-training cleaned toilets, gave baths and rubdowns, prepared meals, and changed beds. Cole's perseverance in the program was rewarded with entrance into the Howard University Medical School in 1917, where she received her official uniform, made of blue cotton, a white collar, white cuffs, and a blue cap. The cap was the most important part of the uniform, since its color denoted the level of responsibility and progress through the program. If a nurse-in-training had her cap taken away, it was usually due to an affair or inappropriate relationship with one of the doctors, interns, or hospital personnel, "the hardest rule to keep and the one most often broken." Imagine Aileen Cole, a young African American woman with high ambitions in 1918, dressed in a crisp blue training uniform and a starched blue cap, overseeing a hospital ward of thirty patients, working the night shift at Howard University Hospital, and studying for her exams, because night duty "did not excuse us from day-class lectures."[1] Cole was about to embark on a dispiriting journey navigating the American Red Cross, one of the country's leading segregated charitable institutions.

Other charitable agencies, in the waning months of the war, tried to avoid making the same mistake. The Woman's Committee of the Council of National Defense, for example, convened a number of meetings about the Red Cross in the spring of 1918. The Woman's Committee, as it came to be known, concluded that racial discrimination in private charities hampered the war effort among African Americans across the country.[2] In response, other organizations, such as the Circle for Negro War Relief or the Liberty Loan campaigns, invited African American women to join and contribute to the war effort. Many public and private charitable organizations, including the Woman's Committee, sought to controvert accusations that African Americans were denied democracy or deprived of opportunities to prove their patriotism, by hiring black volunteers to survey black communities and to hold patriotic meetings for black residents. But reaching out to black constituencies and allowing equal access for black war workers were two different matters entirely. The latter lesson would be reserved for African American women and men in the later months of the war, as they enrolled in two other charitable agencies, the YMCA and the YWCA.

Despite her optimism that the war would elevate African Americans to first-class citizenship, Aileen Cole, along with many African American women, found that internal and institutionalized racism were widespread and commonplace in predominantly white volunteer organizations during the war. The system of unequal and racially divided charitable systems neglected black populations affected by the war. Some charities withheld their services to black communities, while only a few black nurses were called up into the Red Cross, leading to even greater resentment among African American women. As this narrative unfolded in the waning months of the war, the Red Cross's mistreatment of black nurses might have served as an object lesson to other charities, primarily the YWCA. But neither the Red Cross nor the YWCA were inspired to dismantle their own structures of discrimination during the war, and the story that emerged was of one black woman managing with few resources, though a prima facie examination appeared to show good cooperation between the white charities and black women. Black women eventually worked out a professional wartime relationship with the Red Cross and YWCA, but it was a lukewarm partnership at best. In fact black women had begun to plan their departure from these politically conservative organizations long before the war had concluded.

## African American Nurses and the Red Cross

Aileen Cole entered nursing partly out of duty and partly out of confidence that her credentials as a registered nurse would attract a good, steady job. That she pursued a nursing degree just as the World War broke was an unfortunate coincidence, but one that would give her an opportunity to serve in the army or with the American Red Cross, both of which had asked registered nurses to volunteer for enlistment. The American Red Cross was a popular destination for African American women who wanted to engage in patriotic service in the medical corps in the opening months of the war. Its international stature as a nonpartisan, wide-ranging, and philanthropic organization attracted African American nurses, who, in turn, expected the Red Cross to welcome their participation. As historian Darlene Clark Hine has found, black women volunteered their aid and services to the Red Cross without special encouragement, and the outbreak of the World War "helped to raise their expectations and excite their professional dreams."[3] In early spring 1918, the surgeon general of the United States and the American Red Cross issued a call for the enrollment of 5,000 graduate and registered nurses by 1 June 1918, with another petition for 25,000 to 50,000 to join by January 1919. Eventually 22,331 white nurses enrolled between the spring and winter of 1918.[4]

Aileen Cole and other African American nurses were deeply disappointed when the American Red Cross, in the summer of 1918, rejected the offers from black nurses to join, particularly, as Cole said, "when the need was so great." But at a time when the blood plasma of black patients and white patients was separated to prevent contamination, as some thought would happen when whites were given the blood from black donors, the indignities and humiliations of Jim Crow were present in almost all facets of black life. Instead of hiring black nurses, the Red Cross requested that black nurses apply at a later date, preferably after the organization acquired the necessary resources to accommodate the nurses. Jane Delano, chairman of the American National Red Cross Nursing Service, defended the agency's position. She claimed that there were no working facilities for African American nurses, nor were there separate housing quarters for African American nurses, and the agency did not have the money to build them.[5] The U.S. surgeon general of the army, Dr. Victor Vaughan, had also not officially approved the applications of the black nurses, Delano asserted, but the American Red Cross was awaiting his approval. Dr. Vaughan shifted responsibility back onto the American Red Cross, countering that he was willing to enroll African American nurses as soon as the American Red Cross made the appropriate accommodations.[6] Delano responded that after the Red Cross approved the black nurses' applications, the nurses should be "organized for colored troops alone," not for white troops in the United States nor for any troops, white or black, in Europe.[7]

Racial or ethnic background was the sticking point for the American Red Cross, since being black or of African descent were the reasons given to black nurses for their rejection or dismissal. For instance, Ethel Browne, the African American superintendent of nurses at Frederick Douglass Memorial Hospital in Washington, D.C., was asked to fill out a questionnaire after the American Red Cross requested her to volunteer for field service. In her completed questionnaire, when she made note of her race the offer was rescinded and a second application ignored. In another incident, a fair-skinned black nurse, working at Camp Dix, a segregated training camp in New Jersey, was discharged after her white colleagues found her talking to her darker-skinned African American brother, since her white colleagues apparently thought the nurse was white. By adopting its own internal structure of segregation, the American Red Cross further complicated the problem of the color line. Institutionalized Jim Crow cheated black nurses out of their opportunities to engage in patriotic, philanthropic war work. Of these matters, Dr. Nathan Mossell, superintendent of the Frederick Douglass Memorial Hospital, remarked, "prejudice is sapping the whole-hearted loyalty of the colored race."[8]

Adah Thoms, the president of the National Association of Colored Graduate Nurses (NACGN), was particularly disturbed at the turn of events. Thoms's experience with training black nurses and doctors extended back to her direction of the Lincoln School for Nurses in New York City, and she had traveled widely to national and international conferences as the representative for the NACGN.[9] In August 1917, four months after the American declaration of war on Germany, Thoms stood before the National Medical Association, the largest medical body of black doctors since 1908, and promised the group that black nurses would assist in any way they could. She also proposed a national registry of black graduate nurses to help with the selection and placement process during the war. Thoms was especially hopeful that the Red Cross would request volunteers in the coming months of 1917 and 1918, as she had received a letter from the national headquarters of the American Red Cross asking "for one hundred and fifty nurses to serve in the government hospitals that will in all probability be established at Des Moines," the site of the first black officers' training camp. In her address to the black doctors, Thoms presumed that the primary difficulty would be for the doctors to behave professionally with the ambitious and diligent African American nurses. She urged the doctors to lend the nurses their moral support, "treat them as you would your wives, sweethearts, and sisters, and keep up the standard of nursing among our people."[10]

Thoms responded to the Red Cross's delay in 1918 with a series of sharp letters to Delano, pressing the Red Cross to reconsider its position. She gave a brief interview to the *New York Post* about the Red Cross, asserting, "We have no space in which to recognize the war work being done by the women of our churches, in the W.C.T.U. [Women's Christian Temperance Union], and kindred organizations."[11] Other interested parties lodged their complaints with the Red Cross. Marie Cross Newhaus, chairman of the Women's Civic Committee of Justice, bluntly accused the American Red Cross of racism in the pages of the *New York Sun,* declaring "there are now in the United States between 500 and 600 registered colored nurses who are waiting and eager to enlist as such. Why, I ask, are 600 registered nurses kept from national service because their skin is not white?'[12] Fred Moore, editor of the *New York Age,* was similarly outraged. Moore personally mounted a publicity campaign to compel the American Red Cross and the War Department to aggressively recruit black nurses. Moore told an audience at a mass patriotic meeting in May 1918, "We have trained colored nurses who are ready to go to the front and minister to the wounded. . . . Our nurses are no longer content to stay here, and the American Red Cross must stop 'passing the buck' to the War Department whenever our nurses ask to be sent to the front."[13] Joined by James Weldon Johnson, Moore also blasted the agency in the op-ed section of the *New York Age:*

> The Red Cross is calling for 25,000 nurses, saying that they must be secured if our soldiers are to receive proper attention. It seems improbable that so large a number of nurses can immediately be had; yet the colored trained nurses of New York and of other cities have been constantly offering their services for a year, and are constantly refused. They are being refused on the ground that there is no place to put them, which seems to mean that there are white nurses who object to being housed with or working side by side with colored nurses.

Moore concluded his editorial as Marie Cross Newhaus had in the pages of the *New York Sun:* "**Does anyone mean to say that it will not be a form of treason to allow any of our soldiers at the front to suffer for lack of nurses, because of such a prejudice as that?**" (emphasis in text).[14] But racial and ethnic segregation was not a treasonous offense. During the spring and summer months of 1918, black nurses waited for a change of policy. "Resentment is felt by the colored people of this city and elsewhere, because of the apparent exclusion of colored nurses from the nursing service of the American Red Cross," reported the *Philadelphia Telegraph.*[15] A year of direct appeals to the agency had begun to exhaust the black nurses' patience. "It was paradoxical that qualified Negro nurses were available but not assigned to duty, when the need was so great. But being young and optimistic, we hoped a solution would be worked out even though we were hurt," remarked Aileen Cole.[16]

After four months of delays, resolution came in the form of the influenza pandemic, raging through the United States and much of the world in the late summer of 1918. Nicknamed the "Spanish influenza," the virus struck down 500,000 Americans, but it was responsible for some twenty million deaths around the world. In the face of the growing tragedy, the American Red Cross relented. Two thousand black nurses were called into the Red Cross active nursing service in September 1918. Adah Thoms relayed the news to her colleagues in nursing at the annual convention of the NACGN in mid-summer 1918. Thoms also received a personal letter of congratulations from Theodore Roosevelt, the former president who would later take an interest in black working women in the YWCA. He wrote Thoms, "The Surgeon General has promised that as speedily as possible [the nurses] will be assigned to duty. I am pleased as possible from every standpoint."[17] At the NACGN convention, Thoms impressed upon her audience the importance of service, and admonished them to "not stop now for the adjustment of racial grievances." Instead, she asked her colleagues to embrace their duties and render excellent service to black soldiers, with the expectation that in making their contributions to democracy, they would "surely one day enjoy the privilege of equality of opportunity."[18] A few months later, in December 1918, the spirits of the black nurses were further lifted when the surgeon general called eighteen African American nurses into service in the Armed Forces Nurses Corps in the United States.[19]

Aileen Cole spent the autumn of 1918 administering medical care in coal-mining towns in West Virginia, which had been hit hard by influenza. She was greeted warmly by the residents of the region, as "'Red Cross nurses' proved to be a magic password to courtesy, respect, and friendliness." Joined by her two colleagues, Clara Rollins and Sue Boulding, in Charleston, Cole assisted Dr. Watts in his rounds through three adjacent counties. Together, Cole and Watts checked temperatures, looked for symptoms of exposure, and left "spiritus frumenti [diluted whiskey], aspirin, and a cough mixture" for patients strong enough to resist the flu. For patients with very high temperatures, Cole and Watts recommended hospitalization. Cole worked in West Virginia until 13 November, two days after the war ended, when she received formal notice from the Red Cross that she was one of the eighteen black nurses called into service with the Army Forces Nurses Corps. She concluded her brief memoir to the *American Journal of Nursing* saying that her story as an African American nurse in World War I was unremarkable. But, she added, "[E]ach one of us, in the course of our professional relations, did contribute quietly and with dignity to the idea that justice demands professional equality for all qualified nurses."[20]

Cole's modesty nearly obscured the actual significance of her contribution to the narrative of African American women and the Great War. In 1918 the matter of the Red Cross and black nurses left many African Americans questioning the extent to which the country was committed to extending democracy to all its citizens. Other federal departments, including the U.S. army and the Department of War, resisted offering equal services and materials to black soldiers, and these same agencies also faltered in admitting black women to their medical corps or training camps. A few weeks after the surgeon general issued a general call to African American nurses to enroll in the Armed Forces Nurses Corps, the Department of War canceled the request and determined that no black nurses were needed in Europe for active duty. Fred Moore, who had campaigned earlier in 1918 for the admission of black nurses to the Red Cross, personally contacted the secretary of war, Newton Baker, for an explanation. "There is a feeling that we are discriminated against," Moore wrote. He reminded Baker that the federal government had been presented with an important opportunity to place democracy above the color line in its wartime agenda.[21] The petitions for more African American secretaries was partly answered when, in April 1919, sixteen African American nurses were sent abroad to attend to the black soldiers closing base camps on the Western Front in France.

## YMCA Hostess House Network

African American women maintained their memberships in uplift organizations during the war, but they traversed the minefield of institutionalized racism in the organizations for which they worked. Eva Bowles, the director of the Colored Work Department for the YWCA, knew the difficulties well. While at work at the Denver YWCA, Arthur Brooks Baker, a newspaper columnist from the *Denver Post,* sat with her for an interview. During the interview, Bowles explained that the YWCA was engaged in worthwhile activities for black women. "The YWCA has a total fund of $5,000,000, of which $200,000 is being spent for the protection of colored girls in war camps and industrial centers." She later added that as the largest organization of women in the world, "the YWCA simply represents organized friendship." However, when Baker arrived at the YWCA earlier that morning before the interview, Bowles had just stepped away for lunch refreshments. Baker asked a cafeteria assistant when Bowles might return, and the young woman admitted, "Unfortunately, it is rather difficult for her to be served with food in Denver," even in the YWCA cafeteria that Bowles helped to run.[22]

Despite her high level of accomplishment, Eva Bowles's assessment of the YWCA was not overly charitable, and neither was her reception in Denver particularly unusual. Blacks all over the country found it difficult to get service at public cafeterias, restaurants, and hotels, and in some regions, it was impossible. But the incongruity of patriotic work in partnership with racially segregated institutions would not be challenged during the World War, at least not by the blacks who worked for these institutions. African American women accepted the limited budgets and access to facilities. In fact, in his interview with Bowles, Baker was more outraged than Bowles was, perhaps due to the relative security of his position as a newspaperman. But he added, "No patron of the cheaper restaurants in Canada and New England would refuse to eat because a colored woman was being served in the same room; but those same people who are willing for Aunt Mandy to do the cooking would starve for days before they would eat at the same lunch counter with Mandy's Boston niece."[23]

The YWCA had a complex history with African American women. Black women had joined the YWCA to participate in the organization's purposeful mission to uphold Christian morality and uplift. Scholar Cynthia Neverdon-Morton has written that the YWCA pursued two divergent paths regarding black women and war work, attempting to reconcile its claims for interracial cooperation on one hand, while segregating African American women and war work on the other.[24] Similarly, Judith Weisenfeld's study of the growth of New York City's black YWCA argues that African American women sought autonomy and respectability in their work for the YWCA, and they viewed the YWCA's racially segregated Committee of Colored Women as a viable, important institution. But in the first decade of the twentieth century, the YWCA's National Board required all new YWCAs, especially black YWCAs, to register their membership first with existing, local branch YWCAs. The effect of the 1907 policy, writes Weisenfeld, "meant that African American YWCA organizations had to subordinate themselves and become branches of white city associations in order to receive recognition at the national level." [25] The agency desired African American involvement, but it also limited the scope of that involvement primarily by minimizing financial support of black women's work. For instance, a deeper interest in the welfare of African American women of urban populations led the National Board of the YWCA to appoint Eva Bowles as its first African American national secretary, the Secretary of Colored Work in the Cities, in 1913. With additional support from Addie Hunton, Elizabeth Ross, and Mary Jackson, this committee worked toward the religious training, industrial conditions, and recreational activities of African American women and girls.[26] Yet, the YWCA allotted the Committee on Colored Work few resources with which to conduct its war work. The Committee on Colored Work also enjoyed less autonomy in its decisions, as much of the committee's policies on recreation and industrial work were debated and approved first by the National Board. Despite the unevenness, black women's labors with the YWCA afforded a number of opportunities to perform uplift work among African American working women and girls. When the World War erupted in Europe, Weisenfeld finds that black women viewed themselves as "national assets in order to make a stronger claim to the rights of citizenship."[27]

African American women also drew from a nationwide network of African American women's clubs and societies to supplement their work. For instance, due to their ongoing affiliation with the National Association of Colored Women (NACW), the YWCA and the NACW shared members and sent delegates to the same social welfare conferences. Black clubwomen and Y women occupied the highest positions in community service around the country. Lugenia Burns Hope, Addie Hunton, and Eva Bowles were three prominent members of both organizations, and in Hunton's case, her work with the YWCA predated her membership in the NACW. Helen Curtis worked at the New York YWCA briefly before taking a position as a YMCA worker in France. Some field workers and field supervisors of the YWCA, such as Mary Belcher and Josephine Pinyon, also made reports at NACW conferences.

The interorganizational cooperation between the NACW and the YWCA served a multitude of functions during the war. What the NACW could not achieve, the YWCA could as an internationally respected social welfare agency, and vice versa. For example, the NACW was loosely organized enough to make a national network of Hostess and Greeting Houses very difficult to establish and maintain. However, the YWCA, through its War Work Committee and its connections to the armed forces around the nation, put together the Hostess Houses at the black army camps to better serve the needs of African American soldiers and their families. The NACW had immediate access to talented and resourceful African American women committed to war work, a feat the racially striated system of the YWCA/YMCA was unable to trump. Since African American women comprised the entire constituency of the NACW, with a few honorary memberships for a select group of white women, the organization became the primary avenue white organizations used to reach African American women. Each state had an NACW federation, and each community could reach the NACW through their field workers, national organizers, and corresponding secretaries. African American women's war work found its beginnings in the clubwork and local organizations.

The YWCA's official war work campaign began just after the U.S. declaration of war in April 1917. On the recommendation of the War Work Council, Eva Bowles was named Executive of the Committee on Colored Work, also known as the Colored Work Committee, in autumn 1917, and she immediately implemented plans and programs for the newly formed African American war work agency. Born in 1875 to a middle-class black family, Bowles had a distinguished career in social work, first as a student at the New York School of Philanthropy, then as a secretary at YWCA's Harlem Branch in New York City. Moving up though the ranks of the YWCA, Bowles urged the YWCA to assist black working women and girls. At her insistence, the YWCA founded an Industrial Department to help black women find gainful employment, but she was concerned that a separate Colored Work Committee worked against the ideals of the organization. Throughout her career with the YMCA she urged the organization at its national conferences to repudiate racial segregation and integrate its departments. Still, the Colored Work Committee reported to the War Work Council in a supervisory relationship. "The country, both colored and white, is looking to the Y.W.C.A. for leadership. . . . However, we do wish most heartily to develop a work among colored girls and women that would be of the same quality and texture as a whole," Bowles remarked.[28]

The programs of the Colored Work Committee were boosted by the YWCA's allotment of $200,000 in March 1918 to establish recreation centers. In November 1918, another $200,000 was added to the budget for the purpose of establishing a national center in Washington, D.C., for African American girls. Bowles, along with sixty African American YWCA secretaries, established the Colored Hostess House network, the most far-reaching social welfare agency to involve African Americans during the war.[29] The Colored Work Committee sought to establish Hostess Houses in areas in the United States that lacked a YWCA, YMCA, or recreational/industrial center for African American laborers. The initial drive was to find recreational places for African American working women and girls, given the increased demand for labor in industrial centers. The work of African American women in the Hostess Houses also was invested with enormous pressure on African American women to speak for the race. Bowles, along with other African American clubwomen and war workers, saw the Hostess Houses as a demonstration of African American women's responsibility in holding executive positions. On the high level of achievement of black war workers, Bowles remarked, "Negro women just now are being given the chance to show the world what they are capable of doing, not because of, but in spite of, apparently insurmountable obstacles."[30]

Similarly, the time had come in late 1917 for a reassessment of recreational activities for black soldiers. In autumn 1917, black soldiers stationed at base camps had few alternatives or outlets for their interests. The army rarely granted black soldiers leave to travel off the base, or base camps were often located in rural, predominantly white towns where local bars, hotels, and theaters were strictly enforced "whites only" businesses. In Yaphank, New York, for instance, various news reports agreed that black soldiers from Camp Upton got into a fistfight with a group of white policemen in the neighboring city of Sayville. The *New York Times* described the altercation as a near-riot resulting from a late night of drinking and dancing. Two of the soldiers were ejected from a local hotel: "The proprietor stated that the trouble was due to his refusal to sell liquor to men in uniform, while the negroes say food was refused them at the lunch counter." The *Brooklyn Eagle,* an African American newspaper, faulted the white officers for beginning the fistfight, but more importantly, the *Eagle's* headline highlighted the black soldiers' mood, when it blared "Negroes Tired of Abuse."[31] The situation was quickly defused when the soldiers' commanding officer interceded in the fistfight before it ended in disaster. The same elements that put the soldiers of Camp Upton at risk—a hostile police force, segregated services, insulting behavior, and a white backlash to the black soldiers' presence— had already led to a race riot in Houston in August 1917.

Consequently, African Americans across the country became increasingly sensitive to black soldiers' frustration, seeking to resolve difficult situations before they exploded. Better recreational facilities for black soldiers appeared to be the solution. Some of the recreation might be athletic in nature, argued middle-class and professional African Americans, but generally, black soldiers should be directed away from alcohol and dancing and toward educational activities and religious study. The same group of black professionals demanded also that black women, whom the middle class considered the moral centers of the home and family, hold the positions of recreational assistants.

Yet, fears of newly empowered African Americans, particularly of African American women, also gripped the army in the early days of American involvement in the war. In establishing a black officers' training camp at Camp Dodge in Des Moines, Iowa, in October 1917, the Department of War had addressed African American demands for higher ranks and greater opportunities for black men in the military. But the army had no plan for resolving the numbers of southern black wives, girlfriends, and families who had also relocated to Iowa to be closer to the officers-in-training. So apprehensive was Iowa Governor (and future U.S. president) Warren Harding of the southern women migrants that he wrote the governor of the country's most segregated state, Charles Henderson of Alabama, "to do everything possible to discourage negro women from moving to Iowa at this time." Since many of the black officers-in-training and their families resided in Alabama, Harding believed that Henderson's control extended over the state's black emigrants. Harding insisted that the weather was inhospitable to black women, and he added that there was no available housing for black women in Des Moines. Additionally, "the labor situation here is such that they will not be able to find employment." Harding did not specify in his correspondence the methods he hoped Governor Henderson would use to inhibit the migration, but he hoped Henderson would use his office "to disseminate information as to the conditions here, and thus assist in persuading these people from leaving their homes and coming here." Governor Henderson replied that he would publicize as much as possible the conditions in Des Moines among the blacks of Alabama.[32]

In addition to allaying fears of the presence of black women around military campsites, the Hostess Houses also came to represent black women's patriotism, though the Houses were based on middle-class expressions of status and propriety. Professional African Americans shared white fears of the proximity of soldiers and working women. The casual relationships between soldiers and young women might lead to disastrous violations of social morality. Alice Dunbar-Nelson described the attraction as "the lure of the khaki," though she explained it as an "expression on the part of the girl of her admiration for the spirit of the men who are willing to give their lives, if need be, in the defense of their country."[33] Other war workers claimed that it was the fault of the soldiers, who, in taking a sexual interest in innocent and unaccompanied young women, "found out the section where they lived and that they were easy prey, with results that were disastrous to both soldiers and girls."[34] In both cases, the Hostess Houses and their secretaries interceded in these situations and worked to provide a wholesome, chaste atmosphere for both men and women to congregate. With the opening of the Hostess Houses on camp property, the Hostesses provided entertainment and chaperones for dances, silent movies, and Bible study so that men and women could meet each other in structured and supervised environments.

It was in this complex atmosphere that Camp Upton, located in Yaphank, New York, on Long Island, opened the first YWCA Hostess House for African American soldiers in November 1917. The opening took place at the same time and place that the all-black 367th Infantry was undergoing combat training at Camp Upton.[35] Hannah Smith took charge as Executive Hostess, and her first duty was to renovate the property designated for the Hostess House. The barracks, she found, were barn-like, an "open house in more senses than one, for wind rain and snow came in uninvited," Smith remembered.[36] Smith immediately set to work to renovate the space, with the help of black troops stationed at Camp Upton. They cleared the area around the house, removing fallen branches and leaves from the oak trees close to the foundation. Two months later and in the dead of winter, two other Hostess volunteers joined Smith to run the Hostess House, despite the rustic conditions where they waded "through a snow drift when going from bedroom to kitchen" on the bitterly cold winter mornings. Still, Smith kept a cheerful and positive attitude for her work, and maintained that though establishing the house was a difficult challenge, it could not compare "to the joy of being a pioneer in the work of our boys who needed us, and we came very close together in that barren, old room which we all loved."[37]

From its sparse beginnings at the outset of winter 1917, the Camp Upton Hostess House grew rapidly into a mainstay of the Camp Upton African American community by spring 1918. One volunteer noted that Smith's achievement in administering the House "made it possible for other Houses to be erected and perhaps did more than anything else to break down the prejudice of officials against colored women as leaders." Under Smith's direction, the original House opened as a one-room enterprise with writing tables, a piano, and a few chairs, and quickly progressed to a three-room greeting center with its own cafeteria. When the building proved too small for the 5,000 visitors a month, another Hostess House was added in April 1918 at Camp Upton. Soon after, the families, friends, and troops overran that House too, with 4,000 visitors in the first two weeks alone. At its peak, the Camp Upton Hostess Houses greeted nearly 5,000 people per week, and came to represent the success of the nationwide Hostess House network, which included eighteen camps from Ohio to Texas. Other base camps followed suit, and established Hostess Houses in Georgia, Iowa, Illinois, Kansas, Kentucky, Massachusetts, North Carolina, Texas, and Virginia.[38]

Lugenia Burns Hope, the executive Hostess of the second House at Camp Upton, considered the Hostesses the last vestiges of feminine influence on the troops before they were thrown into the tumult of war. "We think about men rushing off fiendishly into combat," she wrote for the *New York Age*. "So much devolves upon women to maintain and promote real civilization in the midst of this present orgy of death and destruction."[39] The women redecorated the house with comfortable furniture, magazines, colorful curtains for the windows, and a piano.[40] The Hostess Houses also provided academic and social activities for the troops. The Hostesses taught literacy courses and Bible workshops, led group hymns, and in many cases volunteered their time after hours with soldiers who needed individual instruction. One soldier declared that the sight of usually raucous troops sitting quietly with the Hostesses in community sings surprised him so much, he requested that the Hostesses "write his mother [telling her] that soldiers actually sing hymns as well as swear and gamble."[41] "You mean you miss your mother," recognized Smith, "and you like to be near a woman of your own kind."[42]

The success of the Houses symbolized an important accomplishment for African American war workers across the nation, proving African American women as effective organizers of their own war work. Eventually the number of Hostesses in one camp expanded from a single individual to four women at each House, and the duties evolved equally among the volunteers. Each House had a variety of Hostesses: the Executive Hostess, responsible for the entire House, who reported to the camp director, usually the executive of the white Hostess House; the Information Hostess, who answered questions at the information desk and helped families find individual men stationed at the camp; the Cafeteria Hostess, who oversaw not only the cafeteria but also home economics courses; and, finally, the Business Secretary, who handled the financial matters.[43] This arrangement laid the foundation for a training program of new Hostesses at Camp Upton, where Hostesses-in-Training gained four weeks of experience in all four sectors of House management. They also received instruction in leading programs for troops and families within the camp community. The Hostesses often taught classes in a variety of subjects, including French study, war cookery, knitting, and sending comfort kits for enlisted men.[44] The Houses served many functions at the camps and in the lives of the visitors. They filled the gaps in war work and volunteer service that the white agencies could not fill entirely, as in the case of the YWCA, or declined to address at all, as in the case of the Red Cross. Nationwide, there were about one hundred fifteen African American women actively engaging in war work for the

YWCA, including twelve national workers, three field supervisors, thirty-four Hostess House workers, and sixty-three other paid workers.[45]

Despite the popularity of the Hostess Houses, the number of women assigned or accepted into this work fell far behind the number of troops enlisted in the war. Eva Bowles issued another call for volunteers to oversee the Hostess Houses and recreation centers, but she added that by "this time, Hostess Houses were already granted at twelve camps. The difficulty was recruiting proper leadership."[46] Relative to the demands of the enlisted men abroad and at home, few African American women were chosen to address the needs of hundreds of thousands of African American men. Though the Hostess House network grew in popularity and success by spring 1918, the Colored Work Committee realized by summer 1918 that 150 workers and approximately twenty houses were not going to be enough. One volunteer on the Committee on the Welfare of Colored Soldiers admitted that "the YWCA did not adequately meet the needs of the colored girls in the South; that there were not enough Hostess Houses for colored troops."[47] Partly to blame were the narrow criteria for the type of woman the YWCA approached for Hostess House work. Just as the NACW drew its membership from a relatively small pool of middle-class, college-educated African American women, so did the YWCA also attract the same type of woman, if not the same woman. Most of the women graduated from college or normal school and prepared to become homemakers, nurses, educators, or social workers. Their backgrounds involved a certain level of religiosity, given the underpinnings of Christian rhetoric in the YWCA and NACW. The women expressed and maintained a sharp awareness of social hierarchy, that is, separate, gendered spheres in social interaction, minimal contact between unmarried men and women, an acute awareness of class and status, and reserved interaction between whites and African Americans.

In the meantime Bowles proposed a "branch relationship" between the African American and white YWCAs, where the African American branches followed their own agendas but reported to the white supervisors of the central headquarters of each community. The Hostess Houses replicated the branch relationship in that the executive of the African American Hostess House reported to the camp directors, often the Executive Hostess of the white Houses. "The director handled all matters pertaining to camp policies and conducted negotiations with camp authorities, in this way centralizing the work and maintaining the same standard for all Y.W.C.A. work in the camp," explained a YWCA publication on how the two races interacted.[48] African American women led their local branches with as much autonomy as the National Board and local headquarters allowed them, but

African American women's war work still occupied a lower rung on the ladder of administrative hierarchy.[49]

As the war progressed, African American women in the YWCA assured the organization that they had put off an aggressive petition for equally distributed resources within an interracial organization, allowing the organization to pursue its biracial programs. In 1918 the YWCA established several African American branches, including one in Germantown, Pennsylvania, another in Dayton, Ohio, and a social club for young women in Detroit.[50] In areas with high populations of working African American women and girls, the Colored Work Committee employed the resources of the YWCA to provide a recreational area for women only. In several southern cities, such as Columbia, Little Rock, Richmond, Atlanta, and Charlotte, the Colored Work Committee also operated individual assistance centers. Fashioned as comfortable homes and living spaces, the centers served primarily working black women. African American women dined and listened to addresses on a variety of issues, from food conservation to financial planning during the war. In Louisville, Kentucky, for example, the YWCA refurbished a house for 2,000 African American women working at the local factories. For the African American women of Washington, D.C., the Colored Work Committee erected a new building, which "is to be conducted as a model of community recreation, a cafeteria system, and an executive center."[51] In the cities with a high African American population, Eva Bowles lobbied continuously for the allocation of funds to programs affecting African American women, urging that African American women be given the same resources as programs for white women. Alice Dunbar-Nelson, in Emmett J. Scott's *The Official History of the American Negro in the World War*, wrote that African American women working at the YWCA and YMCA envisioned their work as a part of a larger paradigm for racial progress. "[Negro women] offered their services and faced them freely, in whatsoever form was most pleasing to the local organizations of white women. They accepted without a murmur the place assigned them in the ranks. They placed the national need before local prejudice; they put great-heartedness and pure patriotism above the ancient creed of racial antagonism."[52]

While the YWCA's programs appeared to be the model of biracial cooperation, only the Colored Work Committee actually conducted the work done for African American women. The World War provided opportunities for national women's organizations to expand their service to include more African American women; yet, much of the onus of these programs fell on the racialized subdivisions responsible for overseeing all areas of African American communities. African American women championed their own causes. Otherwise, programs for African American women would not have been initiated, especially within white women's organizations. The success and the incongruity of African American women's war work illustrated the vagaries of institutionalized repression. Though the YWCA was a well-meaning charitable organization, black social workers and community organizers used their experience in circumventing Jim Crow to combat racial prejudice in the YWCA in order to advance programs for African American women. The World War had not changed this paradigm, but the work of African Americans mounted a challenge to the structures supporting segregation in the YWCA. The World War interwove the fates of working black women and white women, concluded Eva Bowles. "Unless the white girl sees her responsibility to the colored girl, and makes her understand the standards of work and wages, much that has already been accomplished will be undone and the white girl herself be injured."[53]

The Hostess Houses officially closed in August 1919, but their success had two important effects on a postwar civil rights agenda. For one, the success of the Houses demonstrated the limited reach of a charitable organization divided by racial segregation. The white agencies and workers praised the Hostesses for a job well done, but when the war ended, so did the program. In the postwar period, the YWCA attempted to shift backward, to its prewar formula of limited resources, individual and institutional prejudice, and restrained acknowledgment of black YWCAs' labors and accomplishment. The reaction strained the relationship between the YWCA and the NACW. At its first postwar biennial conference in 1920, the NACW Executive Committee petitioned the National Board of the YWCA for prompt and equal representation of African American women. The NACW said that "all organizations, bodies, and groups having to do with anything affecting Negro Womanhood, shall have on its representative body, a Negro Woman, thus insuring direct representation and more effective work." At its 1920 convention, the NACW also refused to endorse the YWCA's national program until the YWCA appointed an African American woman to the National Board.[54] The YWCA acknowledged, at Eva Bowles's insistence, that the "Federation of Colored Women's Clubs is a very powerful organization and it is necessary to have the cooperation of such sister organizations of the Y.W.C.A. is to be successful in its purpose."[55] In response, the National Board of the YWCA invited Charlotte Hawkins Brown, noted African American teacher and founder of the Palmer Memorial Institute in Sedalia, North Carolina, to sit on its governing board.[56]

A few months after the Hostess Houses officially closed for good in summer 1919, Eva Bowles praised the Hostesses for their services, adding that the country now owed them a debt of gratitude. Her objective for the future of African American women's politics was simple. In the summer of 1920, Bowles's vision for an autonomous black women's division of the YWCA came to fruition, when the YWCA established the Bureau of Colored Work, the second significant consequence of the Hostess Houses' wartime success. With Eva Bowles as the director, the Bureau of Colored Work oversaw black YWCAs in twenty-one states across the country and Washington, D.C., all of which had an industrial and recreational center for black women and girls.[57] Bowles signaled the shift in black women's activism when she concluded, "Our present status of the Colored race and the real leaders of the country is due to the fact that as Colored Women we have shared in the plans and promotions with equal justice and opportunity. We can never afford to lose this fundamental principle through compromise."[58]

# 4

## Supporting Black Doughboys in France

When Addie Hunton and Kathryn Johnson arrived in Paris on 21 June 1918, neither could have predicted the enormity of the tasks that awaited them as YMCA secretaries. They spent much of the summer of 1918 attending conferences, enjoying various social activities, and sorting out their work instructions. Kathryn Johnson recounted many of the experiences in a letter to her friend, Fred R. Moore, editor of the *New York Age*. She told of the World Conference of Allied War Workers in August 1918, "a wonderfully inspiring conference and [after] we had the opportunity of visiting the home of Mrs. Theodore Roosevelt, Jr., attending a banquet at the Hotel Palais d'Orsay and a reception at the home of President and Mrs. Poincare. Of course, both of us appreciated these privileges very much." The women knew that they had entered a war zone and that they were certain to encounter death and destruction during their yearlong assignment. Johnson told Moore about the bombing of Paris in seven separate air raids she had witnessed. One of the raids killed several people, and "the next morning the buildings on the block where the bomb was dropped looked as if they never had a window in them." Johnson already had some inkling of the tasks before her, because she spent one week at a camp in northwestern France, which had about 20,000 black soldiers but only one black chaplain who interacted with them on a daily basis. But she hadn't yet grasped that the number of black soldiers they were sent to assist would swell to ten times the number that she saw in the first weeks after their landing.[1]

In their capacity as YMCA secretaries, Addie Hunton and Kathryn Johnson, who were later joined by Helen Curtis, maintained mess huts, taught literacy classes, wrote letters home for illiterate soldiers, helped soldiers count and save money, ran kitchens, and led Bible study classes for nearly 200,000 African American soldiers stationed at or near the Western Front. They were among a handful of black volunteers sent to assist black soldiers in France, and they were the only black women in August 1918 through April 1919. Soon after their return, Hunton and Johnson published their remarkable story in 1920, entitled *Two Colored Women with the American Expeditionary Forces.* Their narrative also revealed an important discussion on the intersection of race, class, and gender, as the authors recorded the uniqueness of their circumstances and their identities as black people, as race women, and as Americans.

While Hunton and Johnson described their war work as a watershed moment in the advancement of the race, they also created a separate intellectual and cultural space, which Darlene Clark Hine has called the "culture of dissemblance." A key subject missing from the commentary on race relations in *Two Colored Women* is a public discussion of gender—in roles, relations, communications, or tensions. As a paradigm to describe a consciousness crafted by black women facing sexual oppression, Hine writes that the culture of dissemblance expresses "the behavior and attitudes of Black women that created the appearance of openness and disclosure but actually shielded the truth of their inner lives and selves from their oppressors." Yet, the culture of dissemblance also allowed Hunton and Johnson to shift their extraordinary narrative away from the private sphere and their inner lives. For instance, Hunton never mentioned that she had two children whom she had to leave behind in America, nor did she explain who took care of her children while she was in France for twelve months. As Hine cogently argues, college-educated, middle-class black women were largely concerned with representing elite black womanhood, and *Two Colored Women* was no exception.

Hunton and Johnson focused the retelling of their experience on race, and specifically on African American soldiers. In this respect, they never intended to reveal whether their experiences in France influenced their postwar dreams. Early in *Two Colored Women,* Hunton and Johnson explained their motives for offering their memoir: "The authors have written because to them it was given to represent in France the womanhood of our race in America—those fine mothers, wives, and sisters and friends who so courageously gave the very flower of their young manhood to face the ravages of war. That we then should make an effort to interpret with womanly comprehension the loyalty and bravery of their men seems not only a slight recompense for all they have given, but an imperative duty." In their status as "super-moral women," as Hine notes, these women engaged in a discourse that necessitated black soldiers' affirmation of the women's respectability as race women.[2]

Instead, exposing Jim Crow was the primary undertaking of *Two Colored Women*. Hunton and Johnson's overseas vantage point politicized the mistreatment of black soldiers abroad. So shocked were Hunton and Johnson at the level of inequality within the armed forces that the race women returned to the United States advocating a militant black response to Jim Crow. "We believe that undervaluation is a more subtle and unkind foe than overvaluation," explained Hunton at the beginning of the memoir, "so that we have not refrained in our story from a large measure of praise for a large measure of loyal and patriotic service, performed oftimes under the most trying conditions."[3] In this case, "the most trying conditions" were inadequate housing for black soldiers generally, harassment of African American soldiers, and propaganda about African American cowardice. The tone of the narrative reiterated constant African American support of the Allied cause and also expressed that the women considered themselves and the soldiers "crusaders on a quest for Democracy."[4]

Moreover, Hunton, Johnson, and Curtis critiqued Jim Crow in an international context as race women and cultural ambassadors. Few African Americans utilized an international forum to debate American race relations.[5] But Johnson, Hunton, Curtis, and *Two Colored Women* became both commentators and critiquers of white supremacy and racial discrimination in the United States. Hoping for widespread embarrassment with an international condemnation of Jim Crow, they essentially asked, How can America treat her loyal blacks this way? And that central question, formed by Hunton, Johnson, and Curtis as eyewitnesses, helped create black women's political agenda and consciousness after the war.

African American women turned to the Young Men's Christian Association (YMCA) for the organization's resources in uplift work. The YMCA had a long history of working to uplift middle-class African American men, but also of institutionalizing white ambivalence toward black success. In 1853, Anthony Bowen, a former slave, established a YMCA for free blacks in Washington, D.C., but it was William Alphaeus Hunton, a Canadian-born descendent of former slaves, who directed the newly incorporated Colored Men's Department of the YMCA during the most troubling and dangerous period in African American history, the nadir between 1890 and 1914. As historian Nina Mjagkij explores, William Hunton was both a staunch ally and vocal critic of the YMCA. He raised several objections to the institutionalization of Jim Crow early in his tenure, arguing that the Christian organization occupied unchristian terrain by cooperating with institutions that humiliated and oppressed black people. At the strongest point of the nadir, William Hunton modified his critique of the YMCA, calling for less direct confrontation and more focus on employing African American men to carry the YMCA's message to impoverished and disenfranchised African Americans. Joined later by his assistant Jesse Moorland, who later headed the Colored Work Department during the World War, William Hunton favored gradual change over political pressure until his death in 1916. By 1914, the first year of the World War, the YMCA's Colored Work Department had become a formidable black uplift institution, navigating Jim Crow by advocating segregated black advancement. During the war, the YMCA called on its black war workers to undertake the same objectives.[6]

Ironically, the Young Women's Christian Association (YWCA) made no provision to include African American women as overseas volunteers. In fact, early in the war no opportunities to travel outside American borders were afforded to African American women. But since white American women were also virtually excluded from international travel, few African American women pressed the issue. Then came the reports of low morale among African American troops indicating that black soldiers needed relief. The YMCA was the only international organization to accept African American women in its programs of international service. No other predominantly white organization approached African American women for war work, either in nursing or in assistance in hospitality services, including the Red Cross, the Salvation Army, and the Knights of Columbus. In this respect, the YMCA progressed far beyond its counterparts. Altogether, the YMCA ("Y") sent over 7,850 Y relief workers, 1,350 of them women. Of this large group, eighty-four were African American, including twenty-three African American women.[7] But in comparing the number of women attending black soldiers, the disproportional ratio of African American volunteers to African American recruits was staggering. Of the twenty-three African American women the organization eventually employed, only *three* were in France during the actual fighting. No more than seventy-five Y workers served in France at any one time.[8] With 367,000 African American soldiers in an American military force 2.3 million strong, just over 1 percent of the 7,850 total number of Y workers traveled to France to care for nearly 16 percent of the military force.

Responding to the petitions of African American troops and Y secretaries alike, the YMCA hired three African American women for canteen service. Though the YMCA employed African American women intending to be fair, the lack of African American women in these vital roles, a byproduct of segregation in the armed forces, had a subtle, morale-evaporating impact on the entire fighting force. The problem of Jim Crow not only divided the YMCA's resources but also divided the loyalties of its black members and volunteers, and the shortage of black women volunteers was felt on a level deeper than the practical and material. Shortly after returning to the United States, Johnson and Hunton wrote of their experience as volunteers in their memoir. Hunton and Johnson considered this work as a necessary element of their service to African American soldiers, who would otherwise not receive any aid at all. *Two Colored Women* aimed not only to commemorate African American participation in the war but also to convince white Americans of the moral debt they owed to African Americans. Moreover, since there is no other extant narrative of African American women overseas during World War I, Hunton and Johnson's memoir links gender, race, and citizenship to form a prescription for the improvement of American race relations at a critical juncture in African American history. In *Two Colored Women*'s opening chapter, Hunton wrote, "This volume is written at a time when, after the shock of terrific war, the war has not yet found its balance— when in the midst of confusion, justice and truth call loudly for the democracy for which we have paid."[9]

## Recruiting African American Women to the YMCA

The cultural and biographical backgrounds of the YMCA's female secretaries provides insight into their public narrative of their service in France. All three women, Addie Hunton, Kathryn Johnson, and Helen Curtis, had long and detailed careers in social work, club work, and civil rights activity. They shared similar backgrounds, they had the same religious affiliation as members of the African Methodist Episcopal Church, and, with only five years separating them, they were in the same age group. The women drew from their experience as constituents of diverse national organizations. They were college-educated, and they were members of the National Association of Colored Women (NACW). They were active in the college-educated black middle class, and their values, particularly their educational and social values, left a deep imprint on their labors as Y workers in France.

Helen Curtis graduated from Southern University in New Orleans in 1900. In conjunction with her education at Southern, she studied dressmaking for over a year in Paris. Her history in the black uplift movement of African American women began with her tenure as vice-president of the YWCA's Harlem Branch, and she was head of the Camp Fire Girls from 1907 to 1915. Drawn to the YWCA Hostess House program at Camp Upton in Yaphank, Long Island, Curtis joined Hannah Smith and Lugenia Burns Hope as a director of the program for a brief period. Curtis's career in wartime volunteer service often intertwined with that of her husband, James L. Curtis, in his position as minister resident and consul general to Liberia. In 1915 the couple moved to Liberia. James Curtis's artful diplomacy persuaded Liberia to support the Allied cause in the war. Though her husband died in 1917, Helen Curtis's dedication to Liberia remained fully intact. After the war, Curtis returned to Liberia for nearly a decade to conduct missionary work and teach in the capital of Monrovia.[10]

Addie D. Waites Hunton also maintained an active professional life alongside her husband, William Hunton. Married in 1893, William Hunton's career with the YMCA elevated him into national prominence in the 1890s, while Addie Hunton's civic work in African American women's organizations began in 1896, when she served as a founding member of the NACW. Addie Hunton was a staunch supporter of the NACW and its commitment to social welfare work among middle-class African America women. She wrote several articles promoting the NACW in the leading black magazines and journals of the period, including the politically conservative *Colored American* magazine and the progressive *Voice of the Negro* and *The Crisis* magazines. Of middle-class black women's duties to uplift the race, she wrote, "Women, the most cultured of the race; women, students only of the great school of humanity, but with keen desire and courageous hearts; women from every section came flocking, that through the National Association of Colored Women they might be united into a working force."[11] Hunton's association with the YWCA developed into a distinguished career by 1907, when she was appointed secretary of work among colored students. Like many African American social activists, Hunton also pursued an opportunity to view the United States from an international perspective in 1909, when she and her two children toured Western Europe. While in Germany, Hunton took classes at Kaiser Wilhelm University. After her family returned to the United States in 1910, Hunton continued her work for women in the YWCA. In 1916, Hunton wrote a biography of her husband after his death, detailing his successful career with the YMCA. She continued her work with the YWCA until she left for France in April 1918.[12]

Prior to her career in France, Kathryn Magnolia Johnson directed her energies toward education and social work in charitable organizations. Graduating from Wilberforce University in 1902, Johnson taught for ten years at various schools around the country, and for a brief period she was dean of women at Shorter College in Little Rock, Arkansas. When the NAACP was founded in 1909, Johnson became the organization's first field worker, organizing branches around the country, primarily in the South and West. From 1911 to 1916 she excelled in this work, and developed great skill as a lecturer and public speaker. But after she was passed over for promotion as national secretary in 1916, Johnson left the organization for a yearlong job as associate editor of the African American women's magazine, the *Half-Century*.[13] The position honed her skills as a writer and literary critic, and provided for her the best training for chronicling her experiences as a war volunteer in France. Johnson wrote several essays for the *Half-Century* magazine on the World War and the recruitment of black soldiers. During the early years of the war, her articles focused on the economic benefits to African Americans, and she anticipated that "the entrance of the United States into the conflict will open the door of opportunity" to African Americans.[14] In a similarly optimistic outlook, Johnson also viewed the establishment of a black officers' training camp in Iowa as an opportunity to report that "war is a great leveler, and the bringing of the World to its knees in a baptism of blood and tears, will no doubt, result in an obliteration of all color lines."[15] By the time the United States entered the war in April 1917, Johnson was anxious to reignite her career as a civic leader and activist. She joined the YMCA in 1917 as a service volunteer, and was selected to travel to France with the African American soldiers in April 1918.[16]

Embarking in early April 1918, Helen Curtis was the first of the three to sail to France for volunteer service with the YMCA. The women expected to be assigned immediately to the front. Kathryn Johnson, writing of her eagerness to serve with the fighting forces, illustrated how the war was easily romanticized, especially the perilous conditions. "We desired in all earnestness of heart to serve whatever other colored regiments were marshaled in battle array against the foe; those who were facing the shot and shell; the poison gas and liquid flame; . . . and who offered themselves as a supreme sacrifice to help make the world safe for Democracy."[17] In June 1918, Hunton and Johnson sailed together on the *Espana,* and after about ten days on the sea, the women arrived at Bordeaux, a key port city in southwestern France, famous for its red wine. A few weeks later they entered

Figure 3. Addie Hunton sits with a black unit in an unnamed French town. Hunton and Kathryn Johnson ultimately praised the YMCA for its immense programs for black soldiers. However, the need for more black YMCA social workers greatly outweighed the numbers sent. Black troops and social workers also were confined to the small towns, for fear of racial intermingling with the French townspeople. For recreation, the YMCA social workers organized a number of activities, from boxing and basketball to reading and church services. *Courtesy of the Kautz Family Archives/University of Minnesota Libraries.*

Paris, beginning their war service as Y secretaries under the direction of Dr. John Hope, then president of Morehouse College. Hope's colleague, Matthew Bullock, told the secretaries once they got to France which areas most needed their assistance. John Hope was also the husband of Lugenia Burns Hope, famed social welfare activist and founder of Atlanta's Neighborhood Union, and he possibly knew the women since they and Lugenia occupied the same social and activist circles.

Contrary to their expectations, the women were stationed not on the war fronts with the fighting units, but with the Service of Supplies Unit (SOS) and other noncombatant troops. Comprised of stevedores and labor battalions, the SOS forces were the primary division where black troops were sent during the war. The SOS units were located all over France, but were concentrated near the Belgian and Swiss borders, rarely facing combat on the Western Front. But these forces were indispensable in providing the Allies with materiel and other resources in fall 1917 through summer 1919. They unloaded ships, dug trenches and latrines, constructed docks and warehouses, delivered mail, transported supplies, and exhumed and reburied the war dead. They often worked twelve- to sixteen-hour days. Overcoming their initial disappointment, the Y secretaries gained an appreciation for the labor and service that these labor battalions provided.

The three women were assigned separately to three different camps for the duration of the war. In September 1918 Addie Hunton began work at YMCA Hut 5, Camp One in St. Nazaire, a harbor city on the mouth of the Loire River in northwestern France.[18] Kathryn Johnson was also stationed in St. Nazaire at the same time, but at Camp Lusitania. Soon after her arrival, Helen Curtis served in a YMCA hut in the small town of Montoir, about six miles away from St. Nazaire.[19] African American soldiers, for the most part, gathered in one particular area for relaxation, a segregated rest area at Camp Lusitania. White and African American soldiers often had leave time in the same areas, but the YMCA offered separate huts for the two races of soldiers. Though other camps for African American soldiers were established in western French cities such as Bordeaux, Brest, and Le Mans, or in eastern French spa towns such as Challes-Les-Eaux and Chambery, Camp Lusitania operated for the longest period and served the largest number of African American soldiers during the war.[20]

## Jim Crow in France

The YMCA played a large organizational part in the treatment of black troops. Attempting to address the high poverty and illiteracy rates among African American recruits, the YMCA organized a number of educational activities. Since many of the black recruits were from the rural South, the YMCA conducted classes in reading and writing, as well as basic arithmetic for handling payroll checks and other financial matters. Troops with a high-school education or an advanced degree benefited from French classes and lectures on music, art, and literature. All black troops were ordered to attended lectures on social hygiene and social morality, a serious concern for the YMCA for both white and black troops.[21] But the most fulfilling work was providing literacy classes and libraries, and for many black soldiers the classes and books were the first organized educational lessons and resources they had ever been given. "This offered a special opportunity for colored welfare workers to give another kind of training to soldiers that thousands were unable to get in their home cities. In very few cities in the South are any library facilities provided for the colored people. They are not permitted to go into the public libraries, and only a few cities have colored Branch Carnegie Libraries," Kathryn Johnson wrote, describing the value of the lessons and the books.[22]

Despite the outward attempts at black uplift, however, anti-black prejudice and routine denial of basic goods and services undermined the YMCA's role as a charitable agency. Trouble with the African American secretaries started soon after Hunton and Johnson landed in France in the summer of 1918. In August, a group of five YMCA African American secretaries was asked to leave a soldiers' camp in Bordeaux, because Helen Curtis, one of the secretaries, had talked about the race problem in the United States. Curtis ran the canteen in Bordeaux, and she worked in close proximity with white officers and YMCA secretaries. One of her white colleagues turned her in. Mr. Kidder, who worked with Curtis at the base camp, testified in a confidential memorandum that he "invited her confidence regarding some unpleasant conditions and then reported her remarks to the general in charge. She and her colleagues were suddenly ordered away from Bordeaux without opportunity of explanation."[23] Matthew Bullock, a YMCA secretary who had also served with the all-black 369th Infantry, wrote about his sudden removal to Jesse Moorland, the general supervisor for the African American YMCA secretaries. After detailing the activities the black Y secretaries led for black soldiers, including literacy classes, religious services, athletic events, and a canteen service, Bullock told Moorland "there we found that it had been requested that we be removed and—by innuendo at least—that white secretaries be used in our place."[24] Hunton and Johnson met the party of black YMCA secretaries in Paris in late August 1918, a few days before the outgoing secretaries would sail back to the United States. The group described its experiences to Hunton and Johnson, who then recorded the episode in *Two Colored Women*. Hunton and Johnson speculated that "sectional prejudice" caused the removal of the black secretaries, since it had "resulted in the detention of many secretaries, both men and women, sailing for quite a period, and no more women came for nearly ten months, thus leaving three colored women to spread their influence as best they could among 150,000 men."[25] Helen Curtis was transferred to Lyon instead of being sent home after she pleaded her case to the YMCA.[26]

Jesse Moorland, in addition, faced an attack on his reputation in France. The effort to recruit more African American secretaries nearly ended after the incident. As William Hunton's successor, Moorland oversaw the Colored Work Department of the YMCA, and was chiefly responsible for preparing the YMCA secretaries for their service in France. For a year after the incident in Bordeaux, the War Department and the YMCA closely scrutinized Moorland about his racial objectivity. His professional superior at the YMCA, General Secretary William Knowles Cooper, complained to Lucien T. Warner, member of a subcommittee appointed to investigate Moorland, that Moorland's race and his background in racial politics had compromised his judgment in selecting war work volunteers. In particular, Cooper suggested that Moorland had selected disloyal YMCA volunteers who had openly criticized Jim Crow. Though he was certain that Moorland would never consciously betray his country, Cooper added in the correspondence, "[Moorland] is a negro with the deepest sympathy for his race and he feels, as you and I would feel, the injustice that is often visited upon his people and he is occasionally given to utterances of ideas which may be capable of misconstruction." But Moorland's colleagues and former assistants rushed to his defense. One former YMCA secretary, A. L. James, the secretary of the Florida Colored YMCA, wrote in a letter of support that at times Moorland was too patriotic, often urging the YMCA's workers in France "to be faithful and to be patient and joyful in the service which we were rendering to our country."[27] Moorland was eventually cleared by the YMCA, as the subcommittee convened to investigate him found that the charges of disloyalty were baseless. After the investigation ended, Frank Nichols, representing the American Expeditionary Forces, praised Moorland and the African American secretaries for "keeping up the morale of the colored troops and impressing upon them the necessity of concentrating all their efforts toward winning the war."[28]

But the damage had already been done in France in 1918 and 1919. While many African Americans hoped that patriotic service might transform the language of racial politics, their earliest encounters in France curtailed their racial utterances. In effect, criticizing or talking openly about racial segregation, the unequal treatment of African American soldiers, or white secretaries' unwillingness to interact with African American troops were seditious and potentially harmful views that the YMCA would not tolerate. After Bullock and his colleagues were sent back to the United States, Kathryn Johnson wrote Moorland in veiled language, "I, too, feel that we can afford to let our most vexing questions wait for a solution; and I'm sure that the war will do much towards bringing about the condition for which we all do earnestly pray."[29] The reference to the "most vexing questions" that demand prayer implicates the host of indignities characterizing racial practices in the American military. But Johnson and Moorland were bound by an open secret that separated and segregated even the language they used to describe race relations in wartime. Johnson's letter continued, "I appreciate fully our words of caution about delicate situations. . . . But we are simply trying to help the men see a brighter day in the future."[30] In *Two Colored Women,* Johnson wrote of a bar fight between a white American officer and a French resident after the resident's sister was called an "insinuating remark" for having lunch with a black recruit. The fistfight moved into the street and threatened to escalate into a race riot, "until the French people mounted a machine gun in the middle of the public square, to restore order."[31] Bullock's letter to Moorland mentioned "innuendo" about his dismissal, and in the memorandum clearing Moorland of unpatriotic speech and activities, the investigative committee reasoned, "No fair-minded men could expect the type of people desired as Association representatives and leaders to be opinionless or absolutely unemotional under the circumstances so common in their case."[32] As World War I had unleashed waves of repression of political speech, one of the far-reaching consequences was to change the way African Americans spoke about Jim Crow in France. Nichols's letter of support to Moorland admitted, "The attitude of the Colored Personnel was, that a problem that could not be solved in America in fifty years, certainly could not be solved in France in a few years."[33]

As Hunton and Johnson assisted black troops in tolerating Jim Crow in France, they turned to the troops for their firsthand accounts of individual prejudices and institutional discrimination in the army. For instance, in her duties as a canteen worker, Johnson worked at making the huts as hospitable and relaxing as possible. Early on, however, she recognized in Camp Lusitania that a tense atmosphere had developed between white officers and black recruits. She found "signs prohibiting the entrance of colored soldiers [that] were frequently seen during the beginning of the work in that section." Johnson also noticed, "There is no doubt that the attitude of many of the white secretaries in the field was to be deplored. They came from all parts of the United States, North, South, East, and West, and brought their native prejudices with them."[34] Before the arrival of the YMCA secretaries, the soldiers had no one to assist them. This situation spread across the Western Front. In Camp Pontanezen, located in the northwestern port city of Brest, Johnson saw that "in the absence of colored women, white women, sometimes as many as five in a hut, gave a service that was necessarily perfunctory, because their prejudices would not permit them to spend a social hour with a homesick colored boy, or even to sew on a service stripe, were they asked to do so."[35]

Restricted movement also vexed black troops in France, as the army curtailed the areas to which African American troops could go outside the camp for relaxation or tourism. Addie Hunton remembered an incident where white American officers recommended the French citizens turn away the African American soldiers from hotels and restaurants, fearing close interactions between black men and white women. In another incident that Hunton described, "[The black soldiers] were going to a neighborhood summer resort—a miniature Coney Island. It had been arranged for them to tent on the beach. . . . They went but came back dumb in the despair of outraged truth and justice. A runner had preceded them, and the French restaurants and places of amusement had been warned not to receive them since they were but servants of the white soldiers."[36] In contrast, the YMCA printed several pamphlets for white soldiers interested in local excursions in the French countryside and the main cities. In the northwest corner of France, white soldiers were encouraged to visit Tours, using as a guide the YMCA pamphlet, *Tours and Surroundings,* or to drive to Cannes, a resort town on the Mediterranean, using the tour books the *YMCA Automobile Guide* and *Spend Your Leave in Cannes.*[37] The same pamphlets simply did not acknowledge the existence of black soldiers. There were no images of black soldiers or suggestions of camps for black soldiers to visit. Getting passes to go off the base were "as hard to secure as American gold," while white American soldiers were given leave to travel freely.

Similarly, when venturing outside of the camp, the white officers in the army gave strict instructions to hoteliers and restaurateurs in neighboring towns to provide the minimum of services and goods to black soldiers. After speaking with her French hosts, Johnson described in *Two Colored Women* how the French residents in Brest had been forewarned about black men's lewdness, particularly that "the story of the roughness of the colored men was being told to the civilians in order that all possible association between them might be avoided."[38] *The Crisis,* the official journal of the NAACP, collected some of the propaganda literature disseminated in France illustrating the same order, citing from a secret document, "Americans are afraid that contact with the French will inspire in black Americans aspirations which to them [the whites] appear intolerable. It is of the utmost importance that every effort be made to avoid profoundly estranging American opinion."[39] In the end, however, African American troops were able to change the minds of their French hosts, particularly by the war's end, when American eyewitnesses frequently overheard the French expression *"soldate noir, tres gentile, tres poli* [black soldier, very genteel, very polite]."[40]

Jim Crow had also caught the attention of German enemies. On the Western Front in August 1918, the German army attempted to convince African American combat troops that they were fighting a losing battle for a dubious cause by dropping propaganda leaflets over the heads of the 367th Infantry in the 92nd Division, an African American unit nicknamed the "Buffaloes." Urging the men to "come over to the German lines," the leaflet continued, "Do you enjoy the same rights as the white people do in America, the land of Freedom and Democracy, or are you rather not treated over there as second class citizens? Can you go into a restaurant where white people dine? Can you get a seat in a theater where white people sit? Can you get a seat or a berth in a railroad car, or can you even ride, in the South, in the same street car with white people? And how about the law? Is lynching and the most horrible crimes connected therewith a lawful proceeding in a democratic country?"[41] To their credit, the 367th and the rest of the 92nd Division gave little thought to the propaganda attempt, except in retrospect, that "the invitation had no effect other than to present an intimate view of German methods and to confirm in our men a loftier conception of duty," as Emmett J. Scott explained in *The Official History of the American Negro in the World War.*[42] Kathryn Johnson, however, included the German circular amid a lengthy description of the army's mistreatment of African American troops. She let the German circular make her point that the black soldier's most troubling problem was *not* fighting against the Germans, but rather soldiering as "colored regiments [who] were marshaled in battle array against the foe" and against what Johnson called "the biting and stinging thing which is forever shadowing us in our own country." At the time, the best Johnson and Hunton could do was to record the incidents for a future audience. Still, the battle lines were slowly being drawn of a long-simmering postwar race riot.[43]

The reprinting of provocative propaganda and other primary accounts in *Two Colored Women* also revealed Johnson and Hunton's intention to use their memoir as a means of expression of black troops' frustration during the war. Back in the United States, a typical wartime confrontation involved an African American soldier, from a state where segregation was not institutionalized, and a white business owner, determined to uphold local laws and social customs mandating the separation of the races in public facilities. Similar to the reprinting of the German propaganda circular, *Two*

*Colored Women* also published a damning bulletin from Camp Funston, Kansas, which demonstrated the hostility that black soldiers encountered when stationed in rural or southern cities. The incident recorded at Camp Funston in March 1918 fit the pattern. An African American sergeant in the medical department entered a theater in the town near Camp Funston, located in northeastern Kansas, despite the division commander's orders "that all colored members of his command . . . should refrain from going where their presence will be resented." The bulletin acknowledged that the black sergeant had a legal right to enter the theater, as well as a legal right to complain when he was given an unsatisfactory seat at the theater. But Major General C. C. Ballou, the division commander, charged that the sergeant should have been cited for instigating the hostility by going into a theater where his presence was not wanted and "by making it possible to allege race discrimination."[44]

Hunton and Johnson were sensitive also to the fact that by openly demonstrating their discontentment, the soldiers' fates might end like that of African American soldiers in Houston during the war. In Houston in 1917, a crisis between white townspeople and black soldiers ended with a race riot that left nineteen dead, two blacks and seventeen whites. Seventy-four black soldiers from nearby Fort Logan were arrested and court-martialed for participating in the riot. Thirteen were put to death by hanging, without the right to appeal their sentences, while the other sixty-one soldiers were given lengthy prison terms. None of the white troops or townspeople who contributed to the riot were prosecuted.[45] The Houston riot took place one year before Johnson, Hunton, and Curtis set sail for France, and the news story made headlines in African American newspapers for months after the riot. To the charge that they lacked journalistic distance in retelling black troops' stories of segregation and discrimination, Hunton and Johnson responded, "it was to these troops that we felt we owed all that could be given of service and devotion . . . ; and consequently our chapter . . . must be a record of facts which we have gathered from officers and men of the different programs who have so kindly and willingly come to our assistance."

Soon, a reversal in gender roles took place, one in which Hunton and Johnson became the narrators of *the* African American experience in France. One intriguing shift in gender relations hinged on Hunton and Johnson's obligation to protect black men's virtue and honor. The environment in which the women worked also allowed for intense interactions and shared experiences between black men and women, which were hidden from white

Figure 4. Addie Hunton and two unnamed women (probably Kathryn Johnson and Helen Curtis) seated during their lunch break in France. The photo is undated. *Courtesy of the Kautz Family Archives/University of Minnesota Libraries.*

view. For instance, the women took on the roles of wives and sweethearts, which they were comfortable in assuming, as long as the roles maintained the boundaries of propriety. Hunton and Johnson bought gifts for relatives, or they helped black soldiers with "letter writing and the wrapping and sending home of little presents that had been approved by the company commanders."[46] The holidays presented extra challenges, particularly the Christmas of 1918, the only Christmas they spent in Europe. The women celebrated the holiday with thousands of troops, a few hundred at a time, or with as many as could squeeze into the YMCA huts. At one YMCA hut, Hunton remembered, "There were men crowded in every space even to the rafters—more men then we had ever seen in any one room."[47] The numbers were overwhelming. But the women saw themselves as surrogate relatives, which mitigated much of the intense admiration that was focused on them.

Gradually the women's roles as canteen workers evolved from asexual surrogate mothers and siblings to symbols of the female sexual presence.

Hunton remembered how the soldiers with families eagerly shared pictures of their mothers, wives, and children back home. Given the lack of attention from the white secretaries and her own recently widowed status, Hunton readily acted as a surrogate mother, at times the "trusted guardian of that home back in America." Describing the maternal relationship with many troops, Hunton wrote, "[The canteen worker] must be ever ready to laugh with him, but she also be ready to go down into a heart-breaking alley with her soldier-boy when he would get a bit of bad news . . . ; or, worse still, once in a great while the tragedy of faithlessness was made known to him."[48] Hunton remembered how some troops "shed tears at their first sight of a colored woman in France."[49] One soldier, upon meeting Hunton at the YMCA hut, exclaimed, "There must be a recess in heaven." One secretary had witnessed one soldier who had heard about an African American secretary at the leave area, "and walked [seven miles] in double time, that his eyes might behold the sight."[50] On more than one occasion, the men offered to pay the women for the privilege to look at them. "One man came to us saying, 'Lady, do you want to get rich over in France?'" Hunton wrote, remembering one proposition. "We gave an affirmative reply and questioned how. He said, 'Just get a tent and go in there and charge five cents a peep. These fellows would just be glad for even a peep at you.'"[51] Though the comment unnerved Hunton, the man was right. Soon after this remark, another enlisted man approached the women. "'Lady I just want to look at you,' he said. 'If you charge anything for it I'll pay you—it takes me back home.'"[52] Though the intense staring and constant attention surely alarmed the women at first, the women regarded their posts as YMCA secretaries as the living embodiment of women who kept the home-fires burning, "that home which every kept for him a beckoning candle in the window, and a fire that was ever aglow."[53] Before he sailed back to the United States, Bullock told Moorland that the black troops at the rest area in Bordeaux "sent her flowers, made pieces of furniture for her, and just before we left one Company presented her with a diamond ring."[54]

It was a rare glimpse into the personal lives of women dedicated to maintaining a proper, public face in their work. "Over the canteen in France we learned to know our men as we had not known them before, and this knowledge makes large our faith in them." Hunton remarked that her service in France deepened her respect for the troops, and she "learned to know that colored men love their own women as they could love no other woman in the all the world."[55] Of the immediate boost, one observer among the YMCA secretaries said that the presence and work of the African American female secretaries "built up morale instantly. . . . Had many times their number gone to France, probably many of the complaints made by the Negro soldiers would not have been heard."[56] As for the women, they were not shy about appreciating the attention. While Hunton admitted that the work placed "a tremendous strain on their Christian ideals," she also said "that she had come to France to be truly proud of the fact that she was a Negro woman."[57]

In a matter of weeks, Johnson's work in Camp Lusitania expanded from providing basic services to making up for the lack of attention given to the soldiers before she arrived. Once all three women arrived, they realized they first had to sort through a substantial backlog. Johnson's service at Lusitania included simple tasks: assisting in religious work; setting up the library with books, chairs, tables, and decorations; writing letters for illiterate soldiers; establishing a system of dispatching money orders, which sent out as much as $2,000 a day; talking with lonely soldiers; showing American movies; teaching illiterate soldiers to read and write; and, in some cases, shopping for soldiers who had little time for it themselves.[58] Much of their time was spent on sitting down with soldiers and talking about their lives back in America and their ambitions once they returned. "A glass of lemonade with a sympathetic touch" usually initiated many of the relationships between the women and the soldiers.[59] With so many responsibilities to complete, the women worked almost continuously between the summer of 1918 and the spring of 1919. "Of course, this is the real work for which I came," remembered Johnson. "The canteen work is only a means of contact by which the soul of the soldier can be reached."[60]

At the height of their work in France, the authors of *Two Colored Women* became regular witnesses to the toll that racial segregation exacted from the black soldiers. When Hunton began her work at Camp One in St. Nazaire, she found that the appearance of African American women transformed the area. "The St. Nazaire Area, more than any other in all France at that time, warmly welcomed and gave opportunity to the colored Y secretaries to demonstrate their spirit and ability to serve their own soldiers," Hunton explained.[61] However, the condition of the canteen and Y huts for black troops at St. Nazaire contrasted with the YMCA's description of the area in one of its guidebooks. In St. Nazaire, the army and the YMCA promised, "Here you will find a piano, victrola, small games, free paper and envelopes, and a canteen where soft drinks, sandwiches, cakes, chocolates, ice cream, etc. can be purchased at the lowest possible prices. If the prices sometimes seem high, compare them with the cost of similar goods elsewhere and remember that we're in a war and a long way from home."[62] In actuality, the price of using the canteen was prohibitively high, since black soldiers were physically intimidated or threatened with military action if they entered the white-only canteens, or "sometimes other signs would designate the hours when colored men could be served," reported Kathryn Johnson.[63] "It was pathetic," Hunton wrote, "to see long lines of men patiently waiting for a cup of chocolate and a cookie—to find many coming from distant camps not alone for the refreshments, but for the good cheer they found with us."[64]

Between January and April 1919, Hunton and Johnson observed the early moments of a postwar political movement, based on the frustrations they experienced and witnessed in France. The seeds of grassroots politics were planted in the black response to difficult assignments or to rumors of black malfeasance. For example, in the winter and spring months, the American Expeditionary Forces (AEF) assigned African American soldiers to exhume and rebury the war dead on the Western Front, a task nearly universally hated by the troops. African American soldiers performed this duty exclusively, while the former combatant countries worked toward a peace treaty. Hunton and Johnson, as well as the African American troops, were aware of the gravity of the responsibility. "Strange that the value of such a task did not gather full significance in the minds of American soldiers. Strange that when other hands refused it, swarthy hands received it!" Alone, grumblings about reburying the war dead did not amount to much of an attack on Jim Crow. But toward the end of their assignment, Hunton suggested in *Two Colored Women* that the troops had begun to challenge "the very heart of the United States for the rights of the twelve million of its citizens whose loyalty had thus endured the test."[65]

The black troops were further antagonized by rumors that African American fighting regiments suffered widespread desertions, or that the combatant troops did not adequately prepare themselves for battle. As Barry Stentiford explains, when black troops were trained well and given adequate supplies, they performed admirably. Robert Edgerton pointed to the 92nd Division and 93rd Division, both all black, as studies in contrast. Poor combat training, few supplies, and a stridently racist social order hamstrung the 92nd Division, which was stationed at base camps in the Deep South. The failure of the 92nd Division on the battlefields of the Western Front was cited as "'proof' that blacks were naturally unfit for battle." Yet, the 93rd Division, which was loaned to the French in 1917, drilled with proper equipment and leadership. Edgerton writes that members of one black regiment of the 93rd Division, the 369th, were known as the "hell fighters" and the "men of bronze" who "received 550 decorations by the French and Americans, including 180 awards of the Croix de Guerre."[66] The accusations of cowardice fed long-standing resentment among black troops.

Beyond the claims of cowardice, African American troops also faced rumors of rape, assault, and even murder. Robert Moton overheard the conversation of two white women on their way to France, both of whom had been told that for their own safety, a high-ranking white officer should escort them through a camp of African American soldiers. Another rumor claimed that the soldiers of the 92nd Division, one of the two African American fighting units, committed thirty individual acts of rape on white French women.[67] The false claims added to a general atmosphere of bitterness, suspicion, and tension among the African American soldiers. Though African American soldiers maintained special relationships with French civilians, these insinuations, many of them initiated after the war's end, devastated African American morale. "Another rumor, equally malignant and damaging was to the effect that the fighting units commanded by Negro officers had been a complete failure," found Moton, who was Booker T. Washington's successor as principal of the Tuskegee Institute and a special observer sent by the president and the secretary of war.[68]

Moton traveled to France after the war to investigate the charges and the rumors. Arriving just as the Paris Peace Conference had begun, Moton's inspection of the morale and condition of the troops uncovered circumstances nearly opposite to the rumored ones. Although five African American soldiers were convicted of rape and one African American officer crumbled under the pressure of combat, African American soldiers performed their duties effectively and patriotically.[69] Moton argued successfully for a reduction in the number of working hours for all African American troops and for greater access to the educational programs developed by the YMCA. In an attempt to boost the troops' morale, Moton commended them in a public address, "You have been tremendously tested. You have suffered hardship and privations. . . . Black mothers and wives, sweethearts, fathers, and friends have joined with you and with our country in your record."[70] Moton also cautioned the soldiers to avoid even the appearance of disloyalty upon their return home. He advised them to take satisfaction in their hard work, not to take the rumors at all seriously, to accept the slow pace of change in the United States, and to take care of their families once they returned home. "If I were you," recommended Moton, "I would find a job as soon as possible and get to work. To those who have not already done so, I would suggest that you get hold of a piece of land at home as soon as possible, and marry and settle down."[71] African American soldiers and secretaries, for the most part, regarded Moton's message as a subtle warning not to rock the boat. Moton warned that the rather cosmopolitan perception of American race relations from an international perspective would only antagonize an American public not ready to accept racial equality. In April 1919, the YMCA secretaries and African American soldiers alike were dissatisfied with Moton's public admonitions. W. E. B. Du Bois, who sailed to France with Moton en route to the First Pan-African Congress of 1919, commented that Moton "rushed around as fast as possible," without taking time to consult directly with the troops or the secretaries. Other observers noted that Moton had also told the soldiers "not to be arrogant" when they returned home.[72]

Yet, the charges of cowardice and desertion in the face of battle already had changed the tenor of the discourse on race. For their part, Hunton and Johnson did not refer directly to Moton's speech to African American troops in *Two Colored Women*. Rather, the women emphasized how hard the troops worked around the time of Moton's visit, as well as how disappointed they were at the continuing dismal state of race relations. Johnson commended all the troops heartily, writing, "In the midst of oppression, circumspection, intrigue, and false and wicked propaganda spread against them by their own countrymen, these colored soldiers fought as bravely as any Americans overseas, and worked with a greater will."[73] Johnson, in fact, was amazed that African American soldiers worked as hard as they did. The experience of working with Europeans, Johnson found, had reinvigorated her faith in the coming transformation in the United States. "They [African American soldiers] caught the vision of a freedom that gave them new hope and a new inspiration. . . . While they traveled they learned that there is a fair-skinned people in the world who believe in the equality of the races, and who practice what they believe," concluded Johnson.[74]

The three secretaries continued their work for another four months, and they eventually got relief in April 1919. Several notable African American women, many with experience in club and charity work, signed up as secretaries, including Mary B. Talbert, then-president of the NACW. The addition of sixteen more African American female volunteers, all traveling on appointment with the YMCA, lightened the load tremendously. All of the new secretaries joined Hunton, Johnson, and Curtis on the former front, at times helping to run the leave areas at Chambery or setting up new YMCA tents at Marseilles and Le Mans.[75] The YMCA secretaries, including Hunton, Johnson, and Curtis, remained with the African American troops until they were sent home in August 1919. Johnson directed the closing of the last YMCA hut on 3 August 1919, and soon after she joined Hunton and the other YMCA secretaries on the voyage back to America.

After their lengthy and arduous service, Hunton and Johnson agreed with the growing number of African American intellectuals, including W. E. B. Du Bois, James Weldon Johnson, A. Philip Randolph, and Mary Church Terrell, who placed the onus of civic equality on white society. Kathryn Johnson remembered, in retrospect, "Some were not too anxious for the colored soldier to take a part in the great World War. They felt that it would be a needless sacrifice for something that would bring no tangible results by way of alleviating his present condition; others felt that if he offered his life upon the altar for the principles of a new freedom, the remaining shackles that have so long bound him would be wholly broken. Neither were correct; for while the shackles have not been wholly removed from his body there have been some wonderful results accomplished that have in some measure removed the fetters from his soul."[76]

By the spring of 1919, clearly the political winds had shifted, as increasingly violent race riots crowded out the hopes and expectations of real democracy for African Americans. Fred Moore, the editor of the *New York Age* who lobbied for more black nurses in the American Red Cross, represented black opinion accurately when he wrote, "Our people have done their part in war loans, in Red Cross contributions, and by the hundreds of dollars, if you measure service by dollars. They richly deserve the square deal that they are asking for."[77] In the summer of 1919, African Americans, particularly newly discharged black soldiers, were not inclined to wait for what they asked. American politics took a reactionary posture in the postwar period, and African American politics met backward motion and greeted it with equal intensity. J. E. Blanton, a YMCA worker serving along with Hunton, Johnson, and Curtis, predicted that in the next war, "it goes without contradicting that we should pull and howl for colored workers all along the line and also for the 'Colored men with shoulder straps.' In no other way will we get anything like the same treatment for whites as well as blacks."[78]

Addie Hunton and Kathryn Johnson's return trip to the United States in August 1919 serves as a fitting conclusion and poignant metaphor for African Americans returning to the structures of racial segregation after the World War. Along with the group of sixteen black nurses who had arrived in France four months earlier, Hunton, Johnson, and Curtis sailed back to the United States, assigned to second-class cabins on a deck below the white nurses and secretaries who were making the same passage. At sea for nearly two weeks during the most humid days of August, the party of African American women were also "placed in an obscure, poorly ventilated section of the dining room, entirely separated from the other workers by a long table of Dutch civilians." When Johnson complained to the ship's captain about the accommodations and the service, "the reply was made that southern white workers on board the ship would be insulted if the colored workers ate in the same section of the dining room with them; and, at any rate, the colored people need not expect any such treatment as had been given them by the French."[79] In essence, Hunton, Johnson, and Curtis had returned to the same America that they had left. Their voyage back to America, perhaps, served as a period of re-acculturation, when they would become accustomed to the social, economic, and, in this case, physical subservience to whites. The women quietly endured the insult for the remainder of the passage. But when they got home, Hunton and Johnson carefully arranged their experiences into a book-length narrative, which described their attempts to assist black soldiers to navigate similar humiliations and racial practices. Their narrative, of course, is *Two Colored Women with the American Expeditionary Forces.*

The richness of *Two Colored Women* rests not only in its narrative of life in France during the World War but also in its illustration of black frustration confronting a reinvigorated Jim Crow in the postwar period. The women's experiences and the experiences of the African American soldiers in France formed the foundation of a collective transformation in African American perceptions of American race relations. Many whites in 1919 and 1920 had argued that the war had made black soldiers at home and abroad arrogant. Many African Americans had chosen to participate in the World War, hoping that their full involvement would lead to recognition of blacks' full citizenship. *Two Colored Women* serves as a postwar call for civil rights long overdue to African Americans. But the memoir also illustrated the extent to which black identity had been transformed. Describing the shift, Johnson concluded, "We learned to know there was being developed in France a racial consciousness and racial strength that could not have been gained in a half century of normal living in America."[80]

One could make the case that the Red Summer of 1919 started not in June or July, but in March and April, on the second-class ships and trains with the substandard accommodations that epitomized the country and the white supremacy to which the black soldiers would return. Too often a race riot had been narrowly avoided on the base camps where black secretaries witnessed the marginalization and oppression of black troops. In 1919, race riots became nearly inevitable. It was a violent clash of failed expectations—whites expecting African Americans to return to subservience, and African Americans expecting whites to repudiate Jim Crow and grant all African Americans full citizenship. But a grassroots political movement among black women had already formed in those key months in the postwar period. And it was a grassroots movement that, along with the catastrophe of the race riots, signaled that a new Negro would appear in the 1920s.

# 5

# Gender Relations and the New Negro

By December, the year 1919 had entered history as the bloodiest on record for American race relations since the turn of the century. It could have been called "the Year of the Red Rope." In the course of twelve months, seventy-seven black men and one black woman were lynched by hanging, shooting, burning, and other means. Eleven of the men were war veterans, some of whom were lynched in their uniforms. Most troubling, in 1919 one lynching took place every week between March and December. According to the NAACP and records of *The Crisis* magazine, this was the most since 1910, when eighty blacks were lynched.[1] But the year 1919 also had been coined "the Year of the Red Scare," when a post–World War I labor movement came under fire on most sides, and the newly formed Bureau of Investigation rounded up 2,500 suspected Communist agitators. And, when nearly two hundred blacks perished in race riots in a period between May and October 1919, James Weldon Johnson called this period of intense racial violence "the Red Summer."[2]

Race riots seemed to have erupted in almost every area where blacks and whites lived next to each other. Several cities, at least ten and probably twenty, were devastated by the riots, all fueled by roving bands of gangs, drive-by shootings, retaliatory shootings, snipers on rooftops, acts of self-defense, and police actions. The first riot of the Red Summer took place on 10 and 11 May 1919, in Charleston, South Carolina. The riot broke out when a rumor circulated that a black man had shot a white sailor. The white sailors, stationed at Fort Sumter in the port of the naval city, sought revenge and hundreds of them chased down and killed two black men.[3] The deadliest riot of the Red Summer took place in Chicago, between 27 July and 2 August, after an altercation between white and black beachgoers led to the drowning of a black youth, Eugene Williams. Thirty-eight men were killed in Chicago, fifteen whites and twenty-three blacks, and over five hundred were wounded and thousands left homeless. Ten women—seven white, two black, and one of unknown race—were wounded, including Roxy Pratt, a black woman who was chased down "Wells street from Forty-seventh by gangsters and was seriously wounded by a bullet." In 1922, the Chicago Commission on Race Relations, after a lengthy investigation, found that several, interdependent reasons led to the conflagration and loss of life: black migration to urban areas, simmering racial tensions, inadequate and expensive housing, loss of employment, rumors and exaggerated stories of assaults on women, and white anxieties about the increased political power and social standing of black migrants.[4]

The Chicago riot and the Red Summer of 1919 marked a moment of transition in black consciousness, with regards to politics, resistance, and gender roles. First, the Red Summer stood out for acts of black resistance. While the human toll numbered in the hundreds, African Americans resisted the destruction of lives and of property for prolonged periods, before being finally overcome. Secondly, the Red Summer revealed a postwar black male consciousness, which rejected white supremacist beliefs about black male criminality and stressed black men's rights to protect their communities. In the course of the Chicago riot one African American man stated, "These things [riots] will keep on until we peaceable, law-abiding fellows will have nothing left but to prepare to defend our lives and our families."[5] Thirdly, the Red Summer indicated a change in the politics of black gender roles, where the wartime prominence of middle-class black women and their politics, which focused on uplift and reform, was gradually replaced by the postwar dominance of middle-class black male institutions, which stressed political identity and a cultural renaissance. Black women's political activism remained vital parts of the community, but, after 1919, black women's grassroots politics were recast in tightly prescribed roles in the era of the New Negro.

## Race Riots and Gender Roles

Though black migration and short-term economic dislocation formed the foundation of the Red Summer, one of the primary triggers of the lynchings and riots were assaults, actual or perceived, on white women. An insult of a southern white woman especially stirred up the deep hatred of black sexual manhood and of interracial marriage. Thus, the prohibition of "social equality," or of black men marrying white women, was enforced with the ghastliest forms of retaliatory violence during the Red Summer.

Figure 5. Northern industrial centers presented increased employment opportunities to rural black farmers. Higher wages in bustling cities encouraged southern African Americans to migrate northward, as described in this political cartoon, entitled "I Hear Yo' Callin' Me." The 1923 cartoon depicts the migrating black family as humble in origin, but eager to join the economic boom times in unspecified cities. *Courtesy of the Tuskegee Institute News Clipping Files, reel 18, "Labor Migration Movement."*

And yet, in each of the riots the sexual relationship was never proven, since the lynch mob seized the charged man shortly after his arrest and the testimony of the white woman was never questioned.

Three race riots—in Washington, D.C., Omaha, and Longview—began after accusations spread of black men having or trying to have sexual contact with a white woman. For instance, the Omaha riot of 28 September began with the arrest and gruesome murder of Will Brown, who was seized by a lynch mob after Agnes Loebeck accused him of rape. According to a report for the *Crisis* magazine, the local vice gang further incited "the mob's anger by saying that black men sleeping with white women had become a rampant problem in Omaha." Omaha's black residents repelled the rioters and there were no further deaths, but a blanket of fear fell over the city's black population, driving many to abandon the city and move back east.[6] In Longview it was rumored that a prominent white woman of the city had confessed her love for Lemuel Walters, a black laborer in the city. She hoped to elope with Walters, and move away from the city. When Walters's nude and bullet-riddled body was found on a roadside in Longview, a riot erupted on 10 July. In the wake of the riot, several black families were left homeless, many blacks were wounded, and the city of 19,000, evenly divided between whites and blacks, was overtaken by vigilantes and lynch mobs.[7] The causes of the Washington, D.C., riot, breaking out just nine days after the Longview riot and continuing until 23 July, also stemmed from rumors of interracial sexual contact. One rumor was that a black fiend had assaulted several white women in the city, while another rumor held that a black rapist had attacked the wife of a sailor stationed in the city. Fanned by racist propaganda and provocative editorials in the daily newspapers, the riot claimed the lives of between fifteen and forty people, primarily on the "Colored Boulevard," the nickname for the section between U Street and New Jersey Avenue. Like previous riots in the Red Summer, the military quelled the violence after the mayor established martial law.[8]

But the conflagration in the nation's capital was also heralded as a critical juncture in black consciousness. The editorial column of the *Washington Bee,* a weekly black newspaper, concluded, "When the colored men in the Southwest [district] were attacked, they defended themselves. When they exercised their constitutional rights, they were called 'crapshooters' and 'bootleggers' . . . . The black man is loyal to his country and his flag, and when his country fails to protect him, he means to protect himself."[9] Several months later, an NAACP investigation, led by James Weldon Johnson, concentrated on the responses of the black residents and their defense of their homes and communities: "If the white mob had gone unchecked—and it was only the determined effort of black men that checked it—Washington would have been another East. St. Louis." Furthermore, as black armed resistance kept the violence from overtaking the entire city, Johnson described it as "the turning point in the psychology of the white nation regarding the Negro problem."[10] Afterward, black organizations of the 1920s advanced their agendas for political rights by proclaiming that they wanted no part of social equality. As M. E. Lawton, president of the New York Federation of Colored Women's Clubs, expressed, "The white people think we want social equality. We don't. We're content with our own society. We don't want white people to invite us into their homes, because we're not going to invite them into ours."[11]

In other riots of the Red Summer, black challenges to Jim Crow and economic racism affirmed Johnson's assertion of a turning point underway. As scholar Mia Bay has suggested, the disappointed and angry response to anti-black violence in the shadow of the World War fueled the fury and destruction as much as the desire to participate fully in American society.[12] And yet, the riots and their representation in the African American press also reinforced the masculinizing effect of this new consciousness. Contemporary accounts of the race riots in Chicago were quick to point out that the riots were outgrowths of racist reactions to black men's resistance to white economic supremacy. Walter White, in an investigation for the NAACP, cited eight reasons for the riot: "racial prejudice, economic competition, political corruption and exploitation of Negro voters, police inefficiency, newspaper lies about Negro crime, unpunished crimes against Negroes, housing, and reaction of Whites and Negroes from War"—all gender-neutral reasons, initially. In the weeklong Chicago riot, not one woman, white or black, was killed, revealed the 1922 Chicago Commission on Race Relations and its report, *The Negro in Chicago*. Rather, women had been drawn into the frenzy of the riot, via rumor and innuendo. One rumor, published in the white *Chicago Tribune* and *Chicago Herald-Examiner*, spread the story that two white women, one holding an infant, "were attacked and wounded by Negro mobs firing on street cars."[13] An almost identical rumor, printed in the widely read black *Chicago Defender*, held that "an unidentified young [Negro] woman and three-months-old baby were found dead on the street at the intersection of Forty-seventh and Wentworth."[14] *The Negro in Chicago*, however, found that there were no police reports, hospital records, church minutes, or coroners' reports of any killing of "a woman or child, white or Negro." Walter White concluded that the violence in Chicago had been repelled by black men who "saw their own kind being killed, heard of many more and believed that their lives and liberty were at stake. In such a spirit most of the fighting was done."[15]

But White's investigation did not examine the riot's effect on black settlement houses, club programs, and community organizations, all run by black women activists in the city. Most notably, Ida B. Wells-Barnett, a longtime resident of Chicago, led two delegations to the mayor's office in June 1919, warning of simmering racial tensions, but was turned away twice for her efforts.[16] After the riot, Wells-Barnett wrote in an open letter that the riot had been instigated by the South, "smarting under the loss of her black population, which she has driven from her by lynching, by burning human beings alive, by disfranchisement, and by segregation," and by the black men of Chicago, who felt "that it [was] glorious to fight and die for the protection of the liberty of foreign nations it ought to be equally glorious to die for his own liberty in this free land of liberty." Finally, Wells-Barnett suggested that a joint committee of "the best men and women of both races" discuss the underlying causes of the riot and deliberate on ways to prevent further violence.[17] Though Wells-Barnett's idea came to pass three years later in the form of the Chicago Commission, the landscape of racial politics had changed since the Red Summer. But the NAACP investigations of the riots in Washington, D.C., Chicago, Omaha, and Longview in the waning months of 1919 helped affirm the NAACP as the primary race organization of the 1920s.

## Race Man, Race Woman, and the New Negro Movement

As a prologue to the New Negro movement and its gendered politics, the Red Summer both redefined and reprioritized black women's political activism. The race riots of 1919 can be divided into two types of outbreaks—lynch mobs sparked by interracial sexual contact, and riots motivated by black political challenges to racial segregation and white economic hegemony. Both types were underpinned by responses to or expressions of white supremacy. But the gender dimension emerged differently, such that the lynching of alleged black male rapists propelled black women's politics in the postwar period, but the drive toward black political equality after the war narrowly defined black women's political space and power. In the wake of black male defiance of racist violence, the status of black women's political consciousness fell or shifted downward at the same time that black men's political consciousness rose or shifted upward. In short, the Red Summer relegated black women's political voices to a secondary position as black men's political voices rose to prominence. Historian Margaret Higgonet explains the process of forward-then-backward motion in the wake of war as the "double helix," when "the lines of gender can therefore be redrawn to conform to the prewar map of relations between men's and women's roles. Even when material conditions for women differ after the war, the fundamental devaluation of the tasks assigned to them remains."[18]

Moreover, when the Red Summer ushered in a new phase of gender relations within the black middle class, it reaffirmed black men's political agency, and reinforced the linkage of black women's politics to the advancement of the race, not the equality of sexes. Gone was the period when African American women connected wartime volunteerism to women's political empowerment. Instead, bloodshed and violence joined the idea of black masculine power to the militancy of the new political movement. The Reverend Florence Randolph, president of the Jersey City Federation of Colored Women, expressed the transformation in the following way: "If every time a colored man is lynched several other colored men would learn to die with him, and carry as many white men as possible with him—above or below, whichever place they might go—the white people of the South would stop their lynchings. . . . It's going to happen. There'll be bloodshed. The country must be prepared for it. And out of it all we're going to get our civil and political rights."[19]

As African American political identity evolved in a new era, decidedly masculine organizations, such as the Universal Negro Improvement Association (UNIA) and the NAACP, set the course of racial politics. The gendered dimensions of the Red Summer illustrated that sexual exploitation of white women was provocative propaganda for vengeful animosity. At the same time, black armed resistance to the Red Summer was characterized in the male normative language; that is, the term "Negro" represented both black men and women, or simply black men alone, but never black women alone. If Claude McCay's "If We Must Die" remains most often associated with the spirit of the Red Summer generation, then historians must also admit that the poem articulated a postwar identity meant only for black men. The poem, in part, reads: "O kinsmen we must meet the common foe! Though far outnumbered let us show us brave/ And for their thousand blows deal one deathblow! What though before us lies the open grave? Like men we'll face the murderous, cowardly pack/ Pressed to the wall, dying, but fighting back!"[20] Though the movement invoked black women as sym-

bols of race uplift and virtue, the shift toward black masculine consciousness amounted to the most formidable challenge to the future of black
women's organizations.

Mary Church Terrell and Mary Talbert stood at the forefront of the New
Negro Movement almost before the movement had been officially recognized as a political and cultural watershed. And, at first, the foremost figures in the National Association of Colored Women focused their political
speeches on condemning American racial practices after eight months of
racial violence in 1919. With less emphasis on transforming white attitudes,
Talbert and Terrell suggested that the New Negro, who is "thinking and
thinking straight—no longer bound by ancient superstitions," was the
strong, black response to Jim Crow and white supremacy in a period of new
black identity.[21] Angered by the violence of the Red Summer in 1919 in her
home of Washington, D.C., Mary Church Terrell, for instance, wrote in
1920, "Since the war one hears practically nothing about Democracy. Not
only has no real, concerted effort been made to establish it in the United
States, leaving the 'World' entirely out of consideration, but it is almost
never referred to and is rarely if ever discussed. Therefore colored people
have lost faith in the white man."[22] Similarly, when invited to the 1920 International Council of Women Conference representing the NACW, Mary
Talbert told her audience, "The black race of humanity is asking that the
races of the world recognize it as a part of God's great humanity—possessed
with the same endowments of reason, virtue and ambition that others have.
Because of the superior opportunity you women of the other races have,
you are duty bound to lift your voices against the ills that affect your sisters
of color both in America and elsewhere."[23]

However, amid the emergence of the New Negro Movement in the
1920s, Talbert's and Terrell's style of politics, which drew its direction and
resources from women's organizational activism, was in jeopardy of falling
from national prominence by the end of the decade. The wide array of black
politics in the New Negro Movement focused on a few unifying objectives
—ending segregation, securing voting rights, abolishing lynching and mob
violence, reaffirming the legitimacy of black culture. What the NACW
sought by mid-decade was a national platform, one that spoke to the key
unifying issues facing African Americans in the 1920s, fostered interracial cooperation, and reaffirmed their standing as race women. As scholar
Wanda Hendricks has argued, black clubwomen after the war defied gendered and racial conventions openly, "willing to change the social order"
with a broad agenda of work for the postwar period.[24]

Though fully committed to the voting rights, officeholding, and the political visibility of African American women, middle-class black women empowered themselves and their political agency primarily by choosing to follow the paradigm of racial politics over gender politics. In fact, black clubwomen's politics did not uniformly pursue gender equity per se, since black clubwomen consistently articulated that they felt more challenged due to their race than due to their gender. However, due to the success of the suffrage movement and the emergence of black identity movements among the working and middle classes, the politics of black middle-class women stood at a crossroads. Indeed, the pressures of race and gender in black women's politics came not just from within, as in battling two forms of oppression, but also from without, as in having to choose one form of politics over the other. Not that gender equity was less compelling than racial advancement and equality; rather, the racial discourse of the New Negro Movement offered a more dynamic political platform. The challenge facing middle-class black clubwomen, in the evolution of the New Negro Movement, was to determine the course of their politics that satisfied traditional gender roles and promoted the objectives of modern race womanhood.

In due course, however, the forceful rhetoric that had characterized the NACW during the World War would be put on the back burner during the 1920s. Thus, the state of male-female partnerships in racial uplift called for the prevalence of male-dominated institutions in national politics, like the NAACP, UNIA, and the Urban League. And, over the long haul, the future relationship of black women in national civil rights movements was defined by the gender roles in black politics of the 1920s, as the NACW sought to make the political voices of black clubwomen matter amid the rise of the NAACP in the 1920s.

Longstanding clubwomen, such as Ida B. Wells-Barnett, believed that the NACW might lose its voice in support of the NAACP, writing that black clubwomen's support in the 1920s "seemed bent on making the National Association of Colored Women's Clubs a tail to the kite of the National Association for the Advancement of Colored People."[25] The conflict in black women's politics in the 1920s had much to do with the incongruence of mainstream, integrationist ideology to the race woman and gender equity. The postwar black consciousness widened the arena in which black politics and intellectual thought found expression, and it stimulated new ways of thinking about black heritage and culture. And yet, the New Negro Movement, with the NAACP as its standard-bearer, drew on restrictive notions

of gender and women's work, reinforcing gender stereotypes of men's politics, like anti-lynching and mob violence investigation as men's issues and
community service and social work as women's issues. As Wells-Barnett had
feared, the New Negro Movement had sought to redefine black women's
politics, shifting them from the public sphere during the World War to the
private sphere in the 1920s.

The gradual shift in black politics had begun by 1922, and the NAACP
became the organization that entered the public mind first as the organization of the New Negro. Through focusing on key unifying issues, and with
the help of persuasive self-promotion among the African American intelli-
gentsia, the NAACP became the male normative institution, or rather, the
organization that came to best represent the interests of the Negro, but
without committing many resources to women's activism and politics. It
heralded the work of Mary B. Talbert in rescuing the Douglass home, but
it had not formed a black women's department or committee, and it did
not regularly pursue the input of the NACW or other black women's organizations in advocating its core issues. The NAACP's steady advancement
in the 1920s seemed linked to the slow decline of the NACW and the
falling visibility of black women's clubs by the end of the decade. As black
politics fell largely within the range of the NAACP and the New Negro
Movement, black clubwomen turned in the 1920s to their political base in
social welfare and community service, seeking local support for the issues
that were once central to black grassroots politics, including education,
prison reform, community development, anti-lynching, and interracial cooperation. If black clubwomen's politics were to remain relevant in the
1920s, then the NACW would have to craft a new relationship, or at least
a modern arrangement, of the paradigm of the Talented Tenth, the Race
Man, and the New Woman. Hallie Q. Brown, president of the NACW
from 1920 to 1924, remarked in her open letter to clubwomen in 1921
that the NACW needed a progressive, active political agenda to sustain its
race work: "Now as never before must Negro Women stand solidly together
for the elevation of her own to the very highest and best in spiritual, intellectual and industrial achievement. The National Association of Colored
Women shall more thoroughly and sincerely direct its attention toward assisting its women to attain the heights of true culture and refinement."[26]

However, the philosophy of the Talented Tenth and the traditional language of gender had the combined effect of masculinizing the New Negro
Movement soon after the decade begun. Ushering in a period of the Race
Man with renewed vigor, the New Negro Movement fell under "a masculine influence," as Deborah Gray White suggests, rejecting racial concilia-

tion in favor of an affirmation of black men's independence, leadership, and primacy.[27] The ensuing renaissance in black arts and letters discouraged black women from embracing the movement with equal vitality. For instance, the *New York Age* asked, "The New Negro—What Is He?" in its January 1920 issue, leading to a series of editorials on the future of black consciousness. The Old Negro, readers wrote, "suffered disfranchisement, jim crowing, and discrimination" but never entirely yielded and "achieved things, even to the governorship of states." The New Negro, in contrast, "not despising his inheritance of forbears," looked ahead "to the day when his accomplishment of success will shine the brighter because he had no name of fame to help him on to eminence." Though the language of the *New York Age* at times used the term "the Negro" to mean both African American men and women, the foregone conclusion of the editorials was that the New Negro was a male Negro. One respondent wrote, "Although the Negro has endured many hardships, it has been the means of bringing them closer together. And this is going to be one of the greatest factors in aiding the black man to obtain his rights."[28] In a similar statement, the *Atlanta Independent* declared that the new racial awakening was due to the New Negro's revelation that "he has powers of mind and soul like other men and that he has a great destiny to work out for himself and his posterity."[29]

The most important essay explaining the vision of the New Negro Movement also did not mention black women at all. Alain Locke's "The New Negro," which represented the core philosophy of the New Negro, wrote that the movement, borne out of migration from the south, crafted a modern black consciousness "as the advance-guard of the African peoples in their contact with Twentieth Century civilization; the other, the sense of a mission of rehabilitating the race in world esteem from that loss of prestige for which the date and conditions of slavery have so largely been responsible." With the urban heart of the movement in Harlem, Locke assigned to the "thinking Negro" the task of the rehabilitation of the image of African Americans, to aid and direct "the rise from social disillusionment to race pride, from the sense of social debt to the responsibilities of social contribution, and offsetting the necessary working and commonsense acceptance of restricted conditions, the belief in ultimate esteem and recognition." Indeed as David Levering Lewis has suggested, though Locke largely ignored the primary economic and social causes of the southern black migration, he described the New Negro movement as led by male migrants who were "radical on race matters, conservative on others," and who were primed to remake America and the African American in their own image of authenticity.[30]

Elise Johnson McDougald in a separate essay, "The Task of Negro Womanhood," examined the contribution of black women to the New Negro movement. By the mid-1920s, a new generation of black women leaders, trained to critique primarily racism and white supremacy, had come to characterize black women's empowerment. Though McDougald's professional career overshadows much of her personal life, she worked as a journalist and teacher during the New Negro Movement. Most notably, she contributed to Alain Locke's *Survey Graphic,* the literary journal of the Harlem Renaissance.[31] In the course of articulating black women's agency within the movement, McDougald argued, "On the whole the Negro woman's feminist efforts are directed chiefly toward the realization of the equality of the races, the sex struggle assuming the subordinate place." McDougald focused on the classes of black woman—elite, middle class, or working class—and the question of whether one class should represent all of black womanhood or all of blackness in America. She argued, "The Negro woman does not maintain any moral standard which may be assigned chiefly to qualities of the race, any more than a white woman does." In the same manner, McDougald wrote that the images of the black mammy and Aunt Jemima had been widely misunderstood and misused among white people: "She is most often used to provoke the mirthless laugh of ridicule; or to portray feminine viciousness or vulgarity not peculiar to Negroes." Instead, McDougald suggested that there were four types of women who exemplified race womanhood in the New Negro ideology— women of the leisure class, women of business and industry, women of the middle class, and women in domestic work.[32]

The divisions by class and gender revealed the few problematic blind spots of the essay. McDougald shared Locke's opinion that the New Negro Movement was best exemplified by middle-class, college-educated black people. Women of the leisure group, "the wives and daughters of men who are in business," were most likely involved in influential reform movements like anti-lynching and settlement houses, but they also shared "acutely in the prevailing difficulty of finding competent household help." Though she praised the important labor that domestic workers provided, she described their sacrifice primarily as a benefit for other types of women, explaining, "Through her [the domestic's] drudgery, the women of other groups find leisure time for progress. This is one of her contributions to America." McDougald argued for comradeship between men and women, as black women gained educational and cultural capital, and as black men, trained in new schools of thought, began "to show a wholesome attitude of fellowship and freedom for their women." The men of the younger generation were more freethinking and open-minded than their working-class counterparts, whose "suppressed desires to determine their economic life are manifested in overbearing domination." McDougald argued that the task of black womanhood in the movement was to use her moral strength to change white prejudices, "to rise above and conquer negative attitudes," particularly to counter prevailing attitudes of black women as lazy, immoral, vulgar, or "without grace or loveliness." Representing the progress of the race still fell to black women, and as McDougald concluded, "The wind of the race's destiny stirs more briskly because of her striving."[33]

Thus, as Mia Bay has argued, the impact of the New Negro Movement on black politics was that it reduced the number of powerful black organizations—such as the NACW, the Universal Negro Improvement Association, and the National Equal Rights League, who argued for political diversity in racial uplift at the beginning of the 1920s—to one black organization, the NAACP, which championed integrationist and mainstream ideology by the end of the decade.[34] Furthermore, voting rights and political equality, popular political themes among all the national black organizations, were taken up with heightened visibility by the NAACP after mid-decade. The NACW supported the Republican Colored Women of America, and the NACW's president, Hallie Q. Brown, also headed the political lobbying group. The organization promoted increased voter registration drives among African American women in the South, joining with the Negro Women's National League to campaign for the "Republican party, liberty, equality, justice, and to lift the race to a higher plane of American citizenship."[35] Yet, the Republican Party, out of expediency and political pressure, worked most closely with the NAACP on gaining the support of black communities. By 1925, the NAACP's national network established twenty-seven state or local branches, and was especially active in states where African Americans had been disenfranchised or where the number of lynchings were on the rise.[36] Also, the NAACP proposed that a closer partnership between black women voters and the nonpartisan League of Women Voters would be beneficial and preferable. The Executive Committee argued that black women and their best chances at national political leadership were with the League of Women Voters, "which is really an organization intended to influence women's votes as the situations represent; that colored women as delegates are vitally important and perfectly possible from non-prejudiced states."[37]

In combating lynching and mob violence, the NAACP also emerged as the organization that best rallied black public opinion. The organization reportedly had spent over $35,000 in exposing lynching and funding investigations of race riots. Nearly $12,000 went to the NAACP's legal defense of twelve men convicted in the Elaine, Arkansas, riot of 1919. The riot broke out in the summer of 1919 between black farmers and white landowners after the landowners tried to break up a union meeting. The NAACP and Ida B. Wells-Barnett both investigated the cause of the riot, and both contested the shaky criminal case against the convicted men. Wells-Barnett visited the convicted men in jail to gather evidence of the terrible prison conditions, and she authored one of her provocative pamphlets, the *Arkansas Race Riot,* to drum up support.[38] But, when the case became a cause célèbre among black leaders, the NAACP claimed that "the personal investigations of lynchings by the Association's staff were the ONLY ONES to be made in this country, and were often DANGEROUS TO THE LIVES of the investigators," which was just partly true.[39] The legal case eventually reached the Supreme Court in 1925, and the court ruled that due to prosecutional misconduct, the men's convictions must be overturned. As Linda McMurry has observed, the NAACP took the credit for the release of the twelve, plus demanding that Wells-Barnett reimburse the association for money she used in her part of the legal defense campaign.[40]

However, in the Tulsa race riot of 1921, the NAACP and UNIA were the sole black organizations to send assistance and investigators. Walter White, the executive secretary of the NAACP, interviewed the residents of Greenwood, Oklahoma, and his report was published in the progressive magazine, *The New Republic.* The NAACP also raised $3,500 for the victims, and UNIA sent at least thirty Black Cross nurses to the scene, who provided medical aid and support for relocation.[41] The complete destruction of the black suburb of Greenwood, the fierce white opposition to black autonomy, and, most importantly, the false rumor of the rape of a white woman, sent shock waves through African American communities, as legal scholar Alfred Brophy explains.[42] But unlike the aftermath of the East St. Louis riot of 1917, when the NACW sent petitions and telegrams directly to President Wilson demanding that he condemn the riot, or in the wake of the Chicago riot in 1919, when the organization pressured local and congressional politicians to investigate the cause of the violence, after Tulsa the NACW had not formulated an immediate response to the riot. While the NACW pressed for the passage of the Dyer Anti-Lynching Bill that had come before the House of Representatives at the same time as the riot, it was the NAACP that most loudly publicized the impact of the riot across the country.

## Mary B. Talbert and the
## Anti-Lynching Crusaders

As the NAACP made gains on issues such as migration, discrimination, and Jim Crow, one black women's group galvanized public opinion against lynching at a time when the NACW had begun its deceleration. The Anti-Lynching Crusaders, prompted by the success of fundraising efforts during the World War, undertook the cause of anti-lynching amid a period of heightened nativism and racism in the 1920s. Isolationism and white supremacy exerted pressure on Congress to initiate and pass the Quota Act of 1921, which limited the number of immigrants from southeastern Europe to just 3 percent of their 1910 immigrant numbers. The National Origins Act of 1924, and its secondary proviso of 1929, further restricted immigration by reducing the number of foreign-born migrants to just 2 percent of the numbers recorded in the 1890 census. In similar nativist activity, the Ku Klux Klan grew in popularity and members in the 1920s, primarily in Midwestern states such as Ohio, Illinois, and Indiana. In its efforts to combat the resurgence of white supremacist groups, the Anti-Lynching Crusaders drew upon the breadth and depth of black political networks, especially the multitude of organizations connected to the NACW. African American women gathered support from the associations of clubwomen, working women, and churchgoing women, all of whom had already forged working relationships during the World War.

"The most admirable feature of the whole movement is the fact that it is the Negro women themselves who have seized upon this opportunity, not only to enforce justice for their race, but to remove one of the ugliest stains that has been put upon the United States by its own people," argued an early press release from the Anti-Lynching Crusaders. "For this service," the item concluded," all the citizens of the democracy should be grateful to its Negro women."[43] The Anti-Lynching Crusaders (ALC) embraced a form of confident activism, signifying a step beyond the low-profile approach of the NACW. A national organization tied to the NACW and the NAACP, the ALC emerged in the postwar years as an example of African American women working for and by themselves to achieve clear and discernible goals in the near future. In this way, the ALC would be one of the very few national groups originated and headed by African American women for the next fifty years.

The idea for a group of anti-lynching activists sprung from a speech given in Newark, New Jersey, in June 1922 by Republican Congressman Leonidas C. Dyer of Missouri. Dyer had made several attempts to introduce an anti-lynching law to the U.S. Congress. But the proposed legislation never made it past congressional debate. Dyer then issued a challenge to the delegates at the annual NAACP conference in Newark: "If 1,000,000 people were united and demanded from the Senate that the Dyer Bill be passed, there would be no question of its passage."[44] The ALC constructed a straightforward plan of action for African American women. "The Anti-Lynching Crusaders are a band of women organized to stop lynching," the group's publicity pamphlet read. "[Our] slogan is: 'A Million Women United to Stop Lynching.' [We] are trying to raise at least one dollar from every woman united with them and to finish this work on or before January 1, 1923."[45] The ALC aimed to gather as much financial support as possible in support of the Dyer Bill between 1 October and 31 December, then disband thereafter. A small committee of women met immediately after the conference to organize as many African Americans as possible within the three-month period at the end of 1922.[46]

Since the ALC offered a morally unassailable position with a clear line of attack, the popularity of the ALC spread across class lines, political affiliations, and traditional gender roles. The goal of 1,000,000 African American women armed with $1,000,000 attracted a large cross-section of African American constituents, including members of the black intelligentsia, the professional class, recent emigrants from the South, and, of course, black clubwomen. The group's organizers borrowed the patriotic language of the World War to publicize their effort. "In the typical fashion made familiar during the war through 'drives' for Liberty loans and Red Cross membership, a 'drive' has been started for 'a million members and a million dollars' to fight and conquer lynching."[47] Less than a month after the NAACP Newark convention, twenty-eight women immediately signed onto the project and became directors of the state branches for the ALC.[48] Historian Dorothy Salem has explained that the ALC had a broader national base than the NAACP, although its staff received no pay in order to give all the funds raised to the anti-lynching effort.[49]

The appeal of the Dyer Bill rested on its pledge to combat several crimes at once. Consisting of six separate sections, it called for: the prosecution of a group of three persons or more who put to death any citizen of the United States; a charge of murder for the entire group involved; a fine of $5,000 to $10,000 levied against the county in which the murder occurred, to be used for the family of the victim; a guilty charge for peace officers and presiding judges who "neglect or omit all reasonable efforts to prevent the putting to death"; a fine of $5,000 and up to ten years in prison for the peace officers and judges who have custody of a citizen taken from them by a group of three or more persons; and finally, the disqualification of police officers and judges from "the impartial and unprejudiced trial of the case, and [who shall] also be disqualified to serve as a juror."[50] The wording and intent of the bill antagonized senators from southern states, who claimed a federal bill compromised states' rights and state sovereignty. The ALC acknowledged the fierce opposition to the bill, and the organization publicized the need for widespread public support to ensure the Dyer Bill's passage. Every African American woman and her dollar counted. While civic equality and social justice occupied an ideological plank in the ALC platform, the ALC's uncomplicated tactics and direct approach worked to bring as many women into the fold as possible. While it was closely associated with the NAACP and NACW, the ALC worked with independent plans and objectives. It aimed to be national in character to draw its volunteers from all economic backgrounds, levels of education, and types of employment.

The ALC employed simple weapons in their political and ideological battle: extensive publicity of atrocities to the American and international public, loud and continuous support for federal anti-lynching legislation, increased pressure on the clergy across the nation to denounce lynching, and nationwide prayer meetings held simultaneous to these efforts. In a statement drawn with the aid of the NAACP, the ALC explained its plan of attack: "The Anti-Lynching Crusaders are . . . determined to raise $1,000,000 or as much as is possible by January 1 [1923], and to turn this sum over to the Anti-Lynching Fund of the N.A.A.C.P. in trust to be used to pass and enforce the Dyer Anti-Lynching Bill and to put down mob violence."[51] The group never once doubted that the Senate would approve the bill at its next go-around, despite the long odds. Previous efforts backed by Congressman Dyer and others had been filibustered, but they passed in the House on subsequent attempts.[52] In May 1922 the Dyer Bill managed to pass the House again, but was blocked when a group of southern senators questioned the constitutional basis of a federal anti-lynching bill.[53] Ever stalwart, Talbert assured the members of the ALC, as well as supporters of the anti-lynching cause, that at the next congressional vote in December 1922, the Senate would approve the bill and send it on to the President. Confident in the bill's chances, the ALC promised to disband with or without passage of the bill on 31 December 1922. "I have no fear of our campaign. We are bound to startle America," gloried Talbert in the opening weeks of the campaign.[54]

The ALC's members approached their objective with the combined zeal of deeply pious Christianity and longtime experience in club work. In fact, prayer meetings became an essential component for raising awareness and gathering support, especially from the clergy. The *Woman's Forum,* a magazine edited by Ida B. Wells-Barnett, published an open request to its readers from the ALC, which declared:

**First:** Gather about you as a large a group of women as possible.
**Object:** To unite one million women to suppress lynching.
**Membership:** Every woman and girl in your locality.
**Sunrise Prayer Meeting:** October 1st.
**Noonday Prayer:** "Pray daily without ceasing."
**Special Sermons:** October 1st–November 5th—Against lynching by every pastor in your city.
**Sacrifice Weeks:** First weeks of October, November, December.
Help in this crusade to make Dyer Anti-Lynching Bill a law.
Read enclosed pamphlet and talk about the 83 women known to have been lynched.[55]

The group distributed index cards that were printed with individual entreaties urging every woman to pray for the abolition of lynching every time she attended church. "Let Every Women in This Church Join the One Million Women United Throughout the Country," one handout stated, "in Prayer to Almighty God at This Hour That the Crime of Lynching be Stopped."[56] In New York state, the ALC gave specific instructions to its members at every available instance, including prayer of some sort for the entire three-month period. "First—Attend sunrise prayer meeting October 1st—7 a.m. Michigan Avenue Baptist Church—To your knees and don't stop praying until God answers. . . . Fourth—Pray every day at noon. Fifth—Sacrifice every non-essential during the first week of October, November, or December. Give this sacrifice to stop lynching."[57] General publicity about the group, news reports in the American and foreign press, prayer meetings across the United States, and direct lobbying of the Congress all contributed to the fervor of the ALC's anti-lynching lobbying campaign.

Particularly, Talbert's vision carried the ALC through to the end. Her efforts, along with those of Mary Jackson and Grace Nail Johnson, energized the movement. The group focused on publicizing the number of African American women lynched and shoring up its membership and financial bases. Throughout their campaign the Crusaders enjoyed broad support from a number of organizations, national and international in outlook. The Crusaders' success relied on several favorable conditions, including an open accounting of the funds raised by the ALC, the prompt and eager donation of these funds to the NAACP and popular support of the Dyer Anti-Lynching Bill.

Talbert also had previous experience in directing African American women for coordinated anti-lynching and NAACP efforts. She expressed interest in anti-lynching projects while president of the NACW. She also conferred with NAACP Secretary John Shillady about an anti-lynching department. "I want to send out 3000 letters to our club women," she wrote to Shillady, "urging them to *form* or join local branches, and also urging them to help on this lynching fund and the fund we are to raise for legislative purposes. *This will be part of a general letter which I want to send out at once.*"[58] Talbert also served on the board or included her membership in several African American organizations of the period. "One million staggers, *but I can do it,*" she wrote James Weldon Johnson in the early stages of the campaign. "I will enlist every secret or gaming action in every state. And every church, including Colored Catholics. I believe it can be done."[59] She knew the right people to contact and the money needed in order to make this group a success. Her enthusiasm for the cause converted many skeptics of the ALC's effectiveness into her corner. As historian Rosalyn Terborg-Penn has found, Talbert also led the NACW during her presidency to a full endorsement of the Dyer Bill, while individual state federations, such as the New Jersey and Northeastern Federation, supported the bill throughout the early 1920s.[60]

Talbert's leadership of the ALC also underscored how African American women privately formed their politics of race and gender. The World War and the ensuing war work efforts revealed that gendered interracial cooperation came about begrudgingly and only under infrequent circumstances. For instance, after the right to vote had been confirmed for all American women in 1920, the National Woman's Party (NWP), headed by legendary suffragist Alice Paul, denied Talbert the opportunity to speak at the organization's convention in 1921. Paul complained that Talbert's representation of the NAACP, a race organization, was the primary reason. Emma Wold, headquarters secretary of the NWP, explained, "If there were an organization of colored women having a purpose similar to those of the organizations which have been named, that is, a feminist rather than a racial program, there would be a place for a representative from that organization in the session at which the work of woman's organizations is presented."[61] Evidently, Talbert's two-time presidency of the NACW made no difference. For many white women's organizations, African American women's groups

were governed by race first and gender second. Although Mary White Ovington, president of the NAACP, urged Paul to reconsider, Talbert declined
to go. Writing to Ovington she added, "I thank you for your trial to put me
on the program of the Woman's Party but I do not believe I am eligible as
they see it, although I have no doubt that Mrs. [Mary Church] Terrell will
try and get on the program. I do not believe Alice Paul is at all sincere. I
doubt her very much on the color line."[62] The incident left an immense rift
between the NACW and the National Women's Party, but Talbert's familiarity with white women's organizations reinforced the necessity of autonomy for the ALC.

But the reluctance of the NWP to support black women's issues was not
the case for all organizations with a predominant white female membership.
Anti-lynching, in fact, unified white women's activism in the 1920s. As
Jacquelyn Dowd Hall has argued, "the dramatic force of a group of white
southern women" emphasized both the barbarity of the act of lynching and
the illegitimacy of lynching's purpose with a force that southern black
women had not been granted.[63] For instance, nearly a year before the formation of the ALC, the Committee for Interracial Cooperation (CIC), an
interracial southern organization, led a letter-writing campaign in 1921 that
explicitly condemned lynching. The Georgia CIC urged the police to uphold the law against the formation of mobs, and the group sought to ban-
ish the Ku Klux Klan as well. In an open letter, the Georgia CIC added "no
false appeal can be made to southern manhood than that mob violence is
necessary for the protection of womanhood, or that the brutal practice of
lynching and burning of human beings is an expression of chivalry."[64] Later,
the Alabama CIC pursued the issue at its annual meeting. Two hundred
delegates pledged to uphold the group's resolution condemning "all mob
violence by any race for any crime" and the claim "that lynching is necessary for the protection of white womanhood." Though the Alabama CIC
qualified their statement insisting that it did not support social equality (or
interracial sex) or the repeal of Jim Crow laws, it confirmed in the minds of
African Americans that anti-lynching attracted biracial, crossover support.[65]
However, as historian Cynthia Neverdon-Morton has found of the CIC, its
organizational style preferred compromise and gradual change, and it preferred to enlist in their efforts "thoughtful, educated Negro leaders, as
earnest in their desire for equality but willing to be patient and work with
whites" over radical blacks who demanded progress at once.[66]

While Mary Talbert and several other ALC members recognized the
vital importance of anti-lynching to some white women's groups, the ALC

asked that white women's advocacy be limited to publicity and pressure on clergy and congressmen. Talbert contacted southern white women's groups directly, and asked for their fellowship in this cause. "We are anxious that southern white women as well as northern white women shall join us," Talbert wrote. Invoking the fresh memory of the World War, she stated, "White women know that no better group of women could be found than the colored women during the perils of the Great War and they also know that no better group of women could be found for loyalty and support at any time. Our country, our state and our cities of our families are in danger. . . . This is the first time in the history of colored women that they have turned to their sister white organizations and asked for moral and financial support and as we have never failed you in any cause that came to US, we do not believe that YOU will fail us now."[67] Like the NACW, the ALC brought race and gender to the fore. "This crusade promises to be the biggest and swiftest movement ever undertaken by colored women," pledged the ALC to a group of key women from Buffalo in September 1922.[68]

The ALC counted on the participation of one million women, never once imagining that any woman, African American or white, would choose not to involve herself in the cause. Just a few weeks into October 1922, Talbert wrote her sister crusaders of the group's warm reception from other organizations. "The executive Board of the National Council of Women has endorsed our Crusade, and letters are coming to me from the white women Presidents of National Organizations."[69] Talbert often confided in Grace Nail Johnson, wife of James Weldon Johnson, about the group's success. In mid-October, Talbert wrote Johnson reporting the good notice the ALC attracted. "The campaign is flourishing. I believe we are going to put it over," Talbert stated.[70] A few days later, Talbert wrote, "My dear Mrs. Johnson, it is nothing short of marvelous how the women are falling into this crusade."[71] After depositing a check for $2,500, adding to its account of $1,040, Talbert wrote Johnson to say, "We made our first strike and how. I am hoping to have a check for another $2500 within a week."[72]

At the beginning of the campaign and throughout its duration, the American and international public responded favorably. Paul Kennaday from the Foreign Press Service corresponded with the ALC on several occasions between October and December 1922. Members of the European press, he reported, were alternately aghast at the crime of lynching in the United States and amazed by the tenacity of African American women for their broad support of the Anti-Lynching Bill. Kennaday wrote to Johnson in December 1922, "You may be interested to see from the enclosed that

. . . two of the Belgian newspapers here have run your story about your anti-lynching crusade."[73] The two papers, *La Gazette* and *La Nahon Beige,* joined the Foreign Press Service in the denunciation of lynching. In a report entitled "The Shame of America," the Foreign Press Service related:

> It is a fact that in the United States human beings are still being burned alive at the stake, that as many as twenty-eight people were publicly burned by American mobs in the four years from 1918 to 1922, that more than 3,000 people have been lynched in the United States in a period of thirty years, and that eighty-three of these victims of mob frenzy were women.
>
> The [ALC] bringing the facts of lynching before the attention of the American public . . . consists of women, of both races, who have banded together to put an end to conditions which, more than any other evil of American life perhaps, have aroused horrified condemnation abroad.[74]

"The Shame of America" report gave further credence to the women's crusade, and the group sought particularly this form of public notice. When the foreign press reported on the ALC's cause and the impending vote on the Dyer Anti-Lynching Bill, the group also collected more political currency. With the foreign press covering the issue, the prospects for the bill's passage gained momentum.

Not every anti-lynching activist felt the same optimism. Ida B. Wells-Barnett considered the effort a waste of time and energy.[75] Making her case as editor of the *Woman's Forum,* Wells-Barnett neither embraced the group nor sanctioned its efforts to enact the Dyer Bill. She wrote, "The whole scheme is utterly unworthy of you Mrs. Talbert and a direct insult to the intelligence of the Negro womanhood of the land."[76] Skeptical that the ALC could help the passage of the bill through prayer meetings, buttons, and sacrifice weeks, Wells-Barnett excoriated the ALC for all the efforts the group did not make. "If you had started a crusade to get every voting woman out to the polls this month and next to work and vote against those congressmen and senators up for election who are known to be against making lynchings a federal crime—then indeed you would have done something."[77] Her magazine published the ALC advertisement as a favor, but Wells-Barnett refused to defend the group's activities.

Wells-Barnett's criticism continued. She called for more direct action. She questioned where the money was going, why one million dollars was needed, and demanded a direct accounting of how the money would help the passage of the bill. "The only thing needed to put an end to lynching is the enactment of the Dyer Bill, and votes, not money, is what is needed to achieve that."[78] Wells-Barnett wrote of her disappointment particularly in the NACW for not heading up the drive. "They already have the large group of women nearer to getting a million women united to suppress lynching than a new organization." Ultimately, Wells-Barnett thought the women could do better. She saved a few words of praise for Mary Talbert, "a very capable and energetic woman," but she saw the entire effort as misguided, poorly organized, and ineffectual.[79] The help of the NACW would have increased the group's coffers at least two- to threefold, but the ALC refused to ask for monetary aid from the NACW. The ALC explained, "The Committee does not believe in duplicating organizations. We have enough and more organizations already for the work there is to do. What we need is concentrated effort for specific objects."[80] At the core of Wells-Barnett's criticism was her disappointment that the NACW had not initiated its own anti-lynching organization, given its resources and extensive network.

By the mid-1920s the NAACP took full leadership of the anti-lynching movement, though the NACW could have shared the responsibility. For Wells-Barnett, the sustained interaction between the two organizations only allowed the NACW to become the middle-class wife of the NAACP. To Wells-Barnett's accusation, however, the NACW executive body did not offer a response. The 1920s had just begun, and African American women engaged much of their club work on using their newly won vote effectively. Other urgent matters of the decade overshadowed working with the NAACP as a pressing matter.[81] Wells-Barnett feared that with the loss of a central focus, the NACW would lose its autonomy in advocating African American women's issues. "The National Association of Colored Women's Clubs is the only organization in this country—outside of the secret orders and the church—which is truly National in character," maintained Wells-Barnett. "When the president speaks she can reach all over this country and be heard. When the delegates come to her call and do her bidding, they and their interests should come before all else."[82] While Wells-Barnett offered grudgingly high praise for the NACW, she focused her criticism on the absence of a discernible objective for the organization in comparison to the NAACP.

Yet, Wells-Barnett foresaw accurately for the ALC the difficulty in the bill's passage through Congress. She had worked in the anti-lynching movement for almost thirty years, and she knew all too well the obstacles facing the enactment of any federal anti-lynching bill. On the issue of gathering one million women, Wells-Barnett's commentary proved true. The ALC only gathered several thousand women to its cause by the end of December 1922, and if its savings account at the Guaranty Trust Company was any indication of its solvency, the group also raised about $12,000.[83] Though it fell short of its goal of one million women and one million dollars the ALC persevered, confident that their efforts had boosted the bill's chances of passage.

On 30 November 1922, nearly two full months into the ALC campaign, the Dyer Bill finally reached the Senate floor. As they had during the war, African American women, led by the ALC, held particularly high hopes for the vote on the Dyer Bill in 1922. And similarly, these expectations were dashed. Though the Republican Party worked to amass the necessary votes, a filibuster mounted by senators of the Democratic Party blocked any chances of even the consideration of the bill by the Senate. In addition to the filibuster on 30 November, the Democrats forced the issue off the Republican platform altogether just a few days later when they threatened to hold extra sessions of the Senate and continue their filibuster if the Republican party tried to vote on it again. By early December 1922, the Dyer Bill was dead. President Harding, a supporter of the Dyer Bill, refused to comment on its defeat, while leaders of the Republican Party officially abandoned the bill. The Dyer Anti-Lynching Bill and similar legislation sponsored by like-minded senators would be presented to Congress again, and these bills too stalled before the Senate. The defeat of December 1922 spelled the end of federal anti-lynching legislation for the rest of the twentieth century.[84]

After the bill's defeat, Talbert wrote her sister Crusaders, "No Negro's life is safe anywhere in America, now."[85] The failure of the bill to pass the Senate deeply saddened the Crusaders, and Talbert was especially hard-hit. At the same time, Talbert pledged not only to continue her efforts but also to redouble them and increase the pressure on Congress to pass the bill the next time it was introduced. "To do effective work in 1923, we must immediately place in the hands of the Anti-Lynching Committee of the N.A.A.C.P. one hundred thousand dollars," Talbert wrote the state directors of the ALC. By this time, the NAACP became the primary anti-lynching organization in the country. She further urged, "Do not stop or hesitate in your work because somebody asks where the money is going. Every cent of it will be sent to the Guaranty Trust Company to be placed in the hands of the Anti-Lynching Committee to protect and insure your life."[86] True to its word, the group disbanded a few weeks later, on 31 December 1922. Talbert continued her support of ALC members who carried on their activity for anti-lynching through other means. She also maintained a firm connection with the NAACP, corresponding with various members of the executive committee.

In September 1923 Talbert fell ill with a serious cough and frayed nerves. The strain of the campaign, added to the successful filibuster of the Dyer Bill, took its toll on Talbert's health. She never fully recovered from the stress, and she died on 15 October 1923.[87] Nannie H. Burroughs eulogized Talbert as "a matchless and magnificent woman."[88] Mary White Ovington, chairman of the Board of the NAACP, personally thanked Talbert just days before Talbert's death, affectionately stating, "I want you to know that the work that you did for the Anti-Lynching Fund was of incalculable worth . . . I might say you are largely responsible for it was you who made our publicity work and so much else we did possible."[89]

The Anti-Lynching Crusaders and the extent of their efforts showcased both the strength and fragility of the African American women's networks in the 1920s. The Crusaders' energy unified African American women toward a distinct goal with an enthusiasm that had not been seen since the World War. Though the Dyer Bill had been filibustered, the Crusaders' success in reaching African American women nationwide signified the continuing need for an organization for and by African American women. Yet, the anti-lynching work also showed that the NACW had lost much of its energetic drive in the 1920s, as the organization had been quietly eclipsed in prominence by the NAACP. At the same time, the NAACP made anti-lynching its first priority in its national program.[90] Thus, anti-lynching work no longer occupied much space in the activity of the NACW, despite its impact on African American women across the nation. The ALC turned out to be one of the last national efforts led by African American women prior to the Depression to change federal policy and advocate social justice.

Politically speaking, without anti-lynching as a primary objective for the NACW, the network of black clubwomen's activism gradually withered in the 1920s. Additionally, the masculine political ethos of the New Negro Movement slowed the pace of female-driven civil rights activism, as the NACW withdrew into the background in the 1920s and the NAACP filled the space. One critic of the NACW in the 1920s commented that the organization had become indifferent and inactive in the wake of the failure of the Dyer Bill. Mrs. Charles E. Hall, a clubwoman in Washington, D.C., urged clubwomen to better organize themselves or risk becoming irrelevant: "Our organized efforts will be of no avail unless our programs consist of practical methods, and are pushed with the same vigor and consistency, and are outlined with the same thought, purpose and determination of other groups. This is the only course that will solve human problems. Do we realize this fact?"[91] Hall's call had not fallen on deaf ears. Other clubwomen posed similar questions, intending to evoke a response from the leadership about the NACW's progress. An anonymous writer asked in the *National Notes,* "Is the National Association of Colored Women becoming a political machine that anybody finds it necessary to flood the membership with letters campaigning for a desired office?"[92] Despite the calls for more active political campaigns and longer partnerships with other organizations, by 1924 the organization had decentralized, giving authority to its regional federations, where local and state clubs first reported to the Northeastern, Southeastern, Northwestern, and Southwestern federations, remaking the NACW into a looser national body with little power for the president to embark on a wide political agenda.[93]

As Deborah Gray White explains, the organization's gradual unraveling had much to do with its own inability to adapt. The decade of the 1920s, with the Jazz Age, New Negro, and New Woman, offered a period ripe for transformation. But by shunning the overt sexuality of the New Woman and the working-class appeal of jazz, the NACW became an old-fashioned organization.[94] Gertrude Rush, a clubwoman and attorney from Des Moines, complained that the "flapper mother," "wolves in social guise," and "exalted immorality" caused much social delinquency among black girls, continuing, "Because a woman has reached the age of second childhood, it is not necessary to advertise the fact by bobbing her hair and donning baby doll clothes, and assuming school girl frivolity. Grow old gracefully and with dignity. There is no one more pleasing to the eye than a dignified old lady."[95] As for organizational politics, the NACW played an important role in the founding of the International Council of Women of the Darker Races, which former club presidents Mary Church Terrell, Mary Talbert, Margaret Murray Washington, and others formed in 1920 as a global advocacy group for women of color. However, as Ula Taylor argues, the International Council adopted a middle-class, institutional approach to the study of race history. Its noble objectives for global uplift left working-class and poor women on the outside, leaving the women of UNIA, especially Amy Jacques Garvey, to speak more directly to the politics and economics of working women.[96] The International Council disbanded after five years in operation.

The active presidential terms of Hallie Q. Brown and Mary McLeod Bethune interrupted the gradual decentralization of the NACW in the 1920s. At the 1924 Chicago convention, Brown initiated a fundraising drive to collect $50,000 for the higher education of African American women. While the project lacked the attention of previous NACW objectives, it raised $12,000 at the 1924 convention and provided a platform on which the clubwomen could base future programs.[97] Furthermore, the NACW issued a national call for support on two other political issues, blocking the passage of an anti-intermarriage bill and condemning the proposed construction of a mammy statue in Washington, D.C. Senator Arthur Capper and Congressman Louis Fairfield, both of Indiana, proposed a bill that prohibited "the marriage of epileptics, insanes, [the] feebleminded, those afflicted with communicative diseases, and of blacks and whites." The bill's defeat was assisted by the vigorous protests of the NACW, whose president, Hallie Q. Brown, said the legislation insulted black men and women. It particularly hurt women, she said, "upon the ground that such a law would sweep away the legal resources a Colored woman still has in nineteen states against the white man who seduces her"; that is, the legislation undermined protections in nineteen states that could force a white man to marry a black woman whom he seduced or sexually abused.[98] In a similar protest, the Daughters of the Confederacy's proposal for a statue honoring the black mammy met the same fate after a successful publicity campaign, led by Hallie Q. Brown. Brown's rallying cry to black clubwomen read, in part, "If the Daughters of the Confederacy wish to make restitution let them visit the courts and note the injustice meted out by the dispensers of law when the black man is arraigned. Let them witness the lynching of the mammy's children, the burning of their homes and the fear that broods over the land, away from the protection of the town and city."[99]

Despite its loss of visibility after 1924, the NACW remained indispensable in the evolution of black women's politics in the twentieth century. As the New Negro Movement held the promise and the future of black politics in the Jazz Age, black clubwomen returned to the private sphere. Though the women of the NACW would be loath to call themselves "feminists" according to the late-twentieth-century understanding of feminism, they embraced consciousness-raising as a form of community development. Black women's political voices preferred consciousness-raising over militant politics, though their community programs, such as child health, day care, school reform, and housing reform, operated within the narrowly prescribed women's arena of family care, social welfare, and education. These were roles that the traditionalists in the NACW comfortably undertook by the end of the 1930s, and as Stephanie Shaw has argued, development work provided crucial services to black communities, especially in poor, rural black areas.[100]

And the modern spirit of the organization would inspire a second generation of social activists, coming of age during World War II and the emergent civil rights movement. The direct line connecting the New Negro

Movement to the post–World War II civil rights movement ran straight through gender. Traditional notions of gender established a paradigm of black women working on the less visible, logistical tasks of keeping the movement running in a forward direction. Despite the sexism that divided the civil rights agenda into women's work—community development and social welfare—and men's work—leadership and national visibility—black women's politics maintained a special vision of a racially equal society. Much of this special vision was dependent on class, as Elise Johnson Mc-Dougald described, and much of it was based in the prevailing belief that one civil rights agency could symbolize all of the different facets of African American life and culture. Still, it is important to recognize that the NAACP's middle-class, masculine approach to civil rights did not represent all viewpoints, and that black women's politics informed the debate on authentic blackness and the future of the race.

Take, for example, Christia Adair, an active clubwoman from Texas who was instrumental in the reform work of the Art, Literary, and Charity Club of Houston. Eighty-three at the time of the interview, Adair told an interviewer in 1977 that she was directly inspired by the pioneering race work of the NACW: "Our motto is 'Lifting as We Climb.' This means that we have not tried to major on the woman who has already reached her zenith, but the woman who needs us, the woman who hasn't had the advantages, the woman who is down and needs to be lifted." For Adair and countless other clubwomen, the NACW afforded a guidepost not only for black women's political activism in the 1910s and 1920s. The organization's political influence, reform objectives, and public politics set the standard for the development of middle-class black women's politics within male and white institutions. Adair explained the NACW's social and cultural objectives for black women throughout the twentieth century, concluding her interview, "WE need to climb. WE also know that in order to climb, we have to have strength and we have to have enough influence if we want her to follow us. So we major our interest on the woman that perhaps is sometimes not recognized by her church. But if we feel like it takes recognition to give her a push and a start in life, we give it."[101]

# 6

# National Party Politics through
# the Depression

The NACW embarked on its reformist and social welfare agenda in 1920, with much of its political influence undiminished by the World War and the Red Summer. At its July 1920 biennial convention at Tuskegee, Alabama, the NACW and its 700 delegates spent the weeklong conference debating the organization's future. The lukewarm relations with white women's organizations during the war and the growth of black consciousness groups, such as Marcus Garvey's Universal Negro Improvement Association, had forced a change in consciousness in the NACW after the riot-filled summer of 1919. As for the NACW's impact on black women's politics, the organization had gained political capital since the end of the war. The migration of a half-million blacks from the South to the North and the effects of the Red Summer increased political pressure on urban reform. Black women's politics maintained a separate ethos and outlook from white women's politics, but the linkages between black women's organizations and white women's organizations, were still undetermined.

The organization had found an opportunity to declare its political plan of action vis-à-vis white politics. In 1920, Warren G. Harding was the Republican candidate for president, and the GOP assembled a platform on lynching and mob violence. Yet, instead of endorsing the Republican candidate, as the NACW had in every presidential election since 1896, the NACW, by an overwhelming majority of its voting delegates, rejected both Harding and the Republican Party. The organization criticized the party for half-heartedly defending the Dyer Anti-Lynching Bill, calling the GOP's position "not a plank, but a splinter, against lynching."[1]

The NACW's decision went against mainstream opinions. Harding had won the Republican Party's nomination handily in June 1920, and the Warren Harding–Calvin Coolidge ticket was welcomed by Republicans. James Weldon Johnson, national secretary of the National Association for the Advancement of Colored People (NAACP)—who sat on a black advisory committee to the GOP—met with Harding on several occasions, and in these meetings, Harding promised that the Republican Party would address black grievances.[2] From most outward appearances, Harding and the GOP took the civil rights agenda of black people more seriously than Woodrow Wilson, the two-term Democratic president who had re-segregated the nation's capital and strongly resisted women's suffrage.[3]

For his part, Harding contacted the NACW executive council at Tuskegee personally, writing via telegram, "Let me express the hope that the Association will be guided by that broad and uplifting spirit which characterized the founder of the Tuskegee Institute."[4] Harding also added his personal chef, Inez McWhirter, to his front-porch campaign, as he chose to make political speeches from his home in Ohio rather than travel across the country. McWhirter, an African American migrant from Atlanta who moved to Ohio during the World War, worked as the principal cook for then-senator Harding. Harding hoped that featuring McWhirter would persuade black women voters that he supported industrial education and job opportunities for African Americans in the North, and he eventually appointed her as the head of cooking in the White House.[5] But Harding's efforts in the summer of 1920 were to little avail. Harding won the nomination and presidency in 1920, but without the support of the Republican Party's most steadfast followers.

The women of the NACW not only rejected Harding at Tuskegee but also challenged him again a year later. Harding initially supported a petition, signed by 500 government clerical workers, opposing the appointment of an African American Register of the Treasury. Though few African Americans worked in the federal government prior to 1950, the Register of the Treasury historically had been filled by an African American with political ties to the Republican Party. Hallie Q. Brown, president of the NACW, told Harding in an open letter, "Mr. President, if these clerks would find it so 'intolerable' for a Negro to be chief in the department . . . , there are several hundred American Negro ex-servicemen who have fought for democracy and won high praise on foreign fields, ready to relieve their white brothers of the onerous task and save them from chagrin and shame. Furthermore, we have in the organization, [which] I have the honor to represent, 1,000 educated, competent, reliable women ready to fill with honor and integrity the places of those 508 petitioners."[6] The NACW's appeal, combined with sharp criticisms from the NAACP and black organizations, led Harding to rescind his support for the petition. Harding later appointed 140 blacks to civil service positions, including Solomon P. Hood as minister to Liberia.[7]

As historian Evelyn Brooks Higginbotham has written, black women's active role in 1920s electoral politics has been largely and mistakenly overlooked, "as if it was an unimportant, even impotent factor in the profound political changes underway."[8] In fact, far from becoming ineffectual or invisible, in the 1920s black women's political organizations carried a good deal of clout in their networks and alliances. Both political parties attempted to sway black women's opinions, either by openly courting them or attempting to suppress them. Moreover, black women's politics drew from the disappointment of their exclusion from the suffrage movement, the shrewd diplomacy learned during the World War, and the worldview gained during the New Negro Movement. By the presidential election of 1924, the NACW had become an integral part of the Republican Party machine, championing the GOP and its candidate, Calvin Coolidge, as well as Herbert Hoover in 1928. Middle-class black women's politics became even more visible through their efforts to enlist women's clubs in registration drives, to form voting leagues to educate black women about their rights, and to link themselves to the Republican Party, the dominant national party of the 1920s. In essence, middle-class black women's organizations had politicized black women's experience by shaping national, white-party politics to suit their communities.

Though the ratification of the women's suffrage amendment ushered in the 1920s, an insidious debate accompanied the enfranchisement of white women and focused on the ways and means of disenfranchising black women. And yet, at the end of the decade, middle-class black women became central figures in national politics and crafted national Republican strategy. Alain Locke, the principal philosopher of the New Negro Movement, wrote that it was voting rights and political equality that made the New Negro "new." It was a sentiment that black women utilized to gain entrance to new corridors of power. Of the NACW's position in the development of New Negro women's politics, the *Birmingham Reporter* commented, "The Negro woman of America is truly getting ready for the big things that are to come in this Twentieth Century. What the Negro people must do is to get ready."[9]

### African American Women's Suffrage Activism

On the eve of the ratification of the Nineteenth Amendment, establishing black women's electoral legitimacy, that is, establishing in the minds of dubious whites that black women were deserving of the vote, proved an exceedingly difficult enterprise. The disenfranchisement tactics that were devised long before the passage of the women's suffrage amendment found new life after the amendment passed. At issue were two anti-suffrage beliefs—that women's suffrage would unleash a black menace, and that black women were intellectually or socially unworthy of the vote. The notion of a growing black menace was particularly persuasive. W. E. Cardwell, a white resident of Norfolk, Virginia, claimed that black women's votes threatened the white community. "And if the [white] women don't hurry up and decide whether they prefer white or black supremacy, the Republicans will have the battle won before the women get through being advised as to what they are politically."[10] A letter to a Montgomery, Alabama, newspaper, *The Advertiser,* captured the white public's misgivings for African American suffrage. The "Daughter of the South" regretted that the ratification of women's suffrage had become the burden of the white women of the Democratic party. But white women had been chosen "to defend, as they believe, the sanctity of their homes, and to resist the progress of the social equality underlying the movement; to impose upon them the obligations and responsibilities of meeting at the polls the ignorant and irresponsible negro woman and negro man."[11] Moreover, conservative notions of gender roles were based on the position that politics was still a masculine business, that women should follow their husbands and fathers in making political decisions, and that without male guidance, women were certain to grow disinterested with the voting process. Black men's keen advocacy of women's suffrage also reinforced fears that black men would use the vote to legalize interracial marriage.

However, black suffragists could not turn to white suffragists for support in the twelve months before the ratification vote of the Nineteenth Amendment. Despite the instances of rather close cooperation in the nineteenth century, by 1919 white suffragists and national party politics actually knew very little about black voters, particularly black women voters. In her study of the women's suffrage movement of the nineteenth and twentieth centuries, historian Rosalyn Terborg-Penn has detailed the racial exclusion of black women from the movement, due to presumptions of white intellectual supremacy and black inferiority. In the twentieth century, this rhetoric turned to political expediency, as white suffragists "realized that African American women were feared because whites, especially in the South, believed Black women were not worthy of the right to vote."[12]

White suffragists, conversely, did not consider racial segregation and disenfranchisement of African Americans as problems in need of urgent reform. The disenfranchisement of black men in the southern states, which some white suffragists advocated, led them to disregard the multiple layers of oppression facing black women suffragists. Alice Paul, president of the National Woman's Party, called black women's suffrage "nonsense," since black men were not permitted to vote in South Carolina, nor should black women be granted the right once women's suffrage was ratified.[13] John Shillady, secretary of the NAACP, publicly rebuked Paul, insisting that she retract her comments. The National Woman's Party should answer for Paul, if "it is in reality the democratic organization we have been led to believe it is, it will repudiate instantly the statements ascribed to you."[14] Paul stood by her assertions that supporting black women's suffrage and black political equality would have cost southern votes in the ratification process. Similarly, the National American Woman Suffrage Association (NAWSA) had long since abandoned black women's contributions to the movement, and catered to the same anxieties of social disorder.[15] Anna Howard Shaw, president of NAWSA, told a white audience in Waco, Texas, that NAWSA did not promote the political superiority of black men over white women, as was the case as long as black men were enfranchised but white women were not. Instead, white women should have the right to vote in order to correct the social imbalance. Shaw continued, "There is not a color from white to black, from red to yellow; there is not a nation from pole to pole, that does not send its contingent to govern American women. If American men are willing to leave their women in a position as degrading as this, they need not be supervised when American women resolve to lift themselves out of it."[16]

Black organizations like the NAACP, and individual black male voters in their states and cities, supported and defended black women's suffragists throughout the movement. Having played integral roles in the women's suffrage movement and racial uplift since the nineteenth century, middle-class African American women knew that the suffrage rights of black men and women were indispensable to African American advancement. The franchise separated the New Negro from the Old Negro, and political autonomy was destiny. The resources provided by black men were vital to the success of black women's political activism, because they offered institutional support and widespread influence in national party politics. Furthermore, without the votes of black men, the women's suffrage amendment would not have had enough votes and the Republican Party would have lost its control in Congress. In states where women's suffrage had not yet been ratified, black men joined black women in the argument that gaining the vote would give black people greater power to reform social ills, such as illiteracy, poverty, drunkenness, and mob violence. Black women in

Atlanta urged black men, as respectable fathers and husbands, to pay their poll taxes and to vote on the critical issues affecting the welfare of the community:

> Into our churches, shops, homes, and on the streets we shall ceaselessly go, and with this question ever on our lips, "HAVE YOU REGISTERED? IF NOT, WHY NOT?" And by this answer, we measure your manhood in this critical period.
>
> Your vote is necessary to secure for our children the privilege to study and to play in modern sanitary places.
>
> Your vote is necessary to secure for our teachers equal pay.
>
> Your vote is necessary to secure complete civil and political protection and absolute justice before the law.
>
> Register now and spread the gospel of good citizenship.[17]

The NAACP also contributed to voter registration initiatives. In its June 1920 national conference, the organization endorsed defending the franchise for all African Americans. W. E. B. Du Bois added in 1920, "They may beat and bribe our men but the political hope of the Negro rests on its intelligent and incorruptible womanhood."[18] Indeed, throughout the 1920s, the executive committee of the NAACP joined with *The Crisis,* its official news organ, and routinely encouraged black men to support women's suffrage and to rally African American women to register.

However, across the states controlled by the Democratic Party, legislatures wasted little time instituting methods to disenfranchise African Americans after the ratification of the women's suffrage amendment in August 1920. Efforts to delegitimize black women's right to vote took two forms— legal disenfranchisement, through tests, taxes, and grandmother clauses, and illegal coercion, through violence and intimidation. The displacement of the white voting population and the ouster of the Democratic Party were fears that gripped much of the South, further invigorating the disenfranchisement schemes. For example, W. P. Pollock, a former senator from South Carolina, in 1919 suggested instituting a grandmother clause if women's suffrage was approved. Since the 835,000 blacks outnumbered the 680,000 whites in South Carolina, a disenfranchised black population guaranteed the political supremacy of the white population.[19] Pollock's plan was to require birth certificates of all voting applicants extending back three generations in order to prove the applicants' legitimacy. "If such an amendment was adopted in various states, there would never be any danger from the vote of Negro women," Pollock asserted, as the law would have banned granting voting rights to people with proper papers and it would "place a ban on illegitimacy and it would encourage marriage and the keeping of the family relation sacred."[20] Pollock's grandmother clause never passed into state or federal law, and Pollock voted for the women's suffrage amendment.[21] But the idea of educational and property qualifications for voters, which excluded black men and women alike from registration polls, was instituted throughout South Carolina after the Nineteenth Amendment was ratified.

In North Carolina, the debate on grandmother clauses resumed in 1921, although the Supreme Court had found the clauses unconstitutional in 1915. Since the Supreme Court's decision had not been enforced, Senator Dewar proposed that the grandmother clause be extended to 1925 for "many white illiterates [who] have hitherto been registered."[22] In the same way, nearly one thousand blacks were arrested for registering illegally in Carter County, Oklahoma, in 1924. Election officials charged that the black registrants had "failed to announce a change in party affiliation ninety days before Election Day." The black residents won a permanent injunction against the election law, but the Oklahoma State Supreme Court overturned the injunction on appeal.[23] Cora Trotter, of Birmingham, Alabama, also sued her local county registrar after she was denied the right to vote for not knowing enough about the Constitution. In her lawsuit, she charged that she was "a property owner, has paid her poll tax, [was] a citizen of age, and therefore, [was] entitled to vote."[24]

When legal disenfranchisement failed to reduce the numbers of black registrants, paramilitary groups threatened or used violence to achieve this objective. As historian Tera Hunter has written, groups like the Ku Klux Klan experienced a resurgence of membership when D. W. Griffith's "The Birth of a Nation" portrayed African Americans taking gross advantage of the electoral system, leaving whites were powerless to oppose them.[25] Such prejudice had a practical effect on black women's voting rights, particularly in Florida, where election fraud and intimidation, tinged with the fears of a black menace, became widespread problems. For instance, mobs and paramilitary groups harassed and physically beat several white male representatives of the Republican Party. Some representatives were threatened with lynching for helping black women to register to vote, as was the case of B. J. Jones, who, according to the *Cleveland Advocate,* was taken from his bed one night in 1920, "a noose placed about his neck, and taken out of town in his night clothes, and then allowed to escape on threat of death if he returned, and all because he had been active in encouraging Colored women to register."[26]

In addition, white newspapers loyal to the Democratic Party promoted the use of violence in order to keep blacks from the polls. The *Miami Post* encouraged its white readers to take up arms "to keep colored men out of politics" when the Republican Party, who had few members in the state, encouraged blacks to gain access to the ballot by registering as Democrats, then voting the Democrats out. The *Post* continued, "The majority of the people in Dade County are opposed to the re-entry of the Negro into politics, for they do not consider the Negro their social equal. There is no reason why the Negro should not be give a square deal, so long as they know their place and stay in it."[27] Similarly, a report authored by Walter White of the NAACP found that when the number of black women registrants dramatically increased in the city of Jacksonville in 1921, a headline in the highly partisan *Jacksonville Metropolis* blared, "DEMOCRACY IN DUVAL COUNTY ENDANGERED BY VERY LARGE REGISTRATION OF COLORED WOMEN." The headline was accompanied by descriptions of questionable election practices, such as allowing white women to enter voting booths unhindered, but placing physical obstructions in front of black women. The fraud in Jacksonville was reinforced by racist violence, also described by the NAACP investigation. White supremacist retaliation led to the killing of six African American men after the Ku Klux Klan "sent word to the colored people of Orange County, that no Negroes would be allowed to vote and that if any Negro tried to do so, trouble could be expected."[28]

At first, the waves of disenfranchisement efforts evoked vigorous debates on appropriate local, state, and federal responses. Just seven months after the ratification of the women's suffrage amendment, black clubwomen called for a probe of the disenfranchisement activities. Political activists sympathetic to black women's voting rights even presented their concerns to the National Women's Party, which remained one of the most outspoken organizations for women's rights. At the February 1921 conference of the National Women's Party held in Washington, D.C., black clubwomen made their appeals for the National Women's Party to join them in demanding a federal investigation of disenfranchisement laws. Mary Church Terrell, the former president of the NACW, addressed the resolutions committee with a proposal that the National Women's Party undertake the electoral needs of black southern women "who need the ballot as a weapon of defense and protection more than any other group of women in the United States." Florence Kelley, the president of the white progressive National Consumer's League, made the case for reframing disenfranchisement as a feminist issue. Kelley told the resolutions committee, "If burning men at the stake when they try to show women how to vote is not a feminist question, I don't know what IS a feminist question."[29] However, the resolutions committee, in effect the National Woman's Party, declined to officially support a federal investigation of racist electoral practices.

Thereafter, and over the rest of the 1920s, the gendered political domain linking black and white women disintegrated as the radical former suffragettes continued to distance themselves from African American voters. In truth, the cleavage between black and white suffrage advocates had emerged long before the passage of the amendment. And yet, race, or rather American racial practices, had become the most decisive and divisive element in American women's politics of the twentieth century. White voting rights activists misunderstood the interwoven layers of racial oppression embedded within black women's lives, and black clubwomen misjudged the readiness of white feminists to challenge the racist political discourse perpetuating black women's disenfranchisement.

### Exercising the Right to Vote

White fears of black inability to use the vote properly were reinforced by deeply held assumptions about black gender roles, particularly regarding the private space of the home and the control of the household. Neither the conservative NAWSA, on one hand, nor the radically feminist National Woman's Party, on the other, knew what to expect of black women and their exercise of the franchise. One of the primary racist beliefs about black women and their roles within the private sphere of the home was that black women had usurped black men's authority and had become the heads of the family. As George Frederickson has written, negative depictions of African American character had been fully formed during slavery, contributing to a system of white supremacy in which blacks were inferior to whites in almost every measurable aspect.[30] In the 1920s, post-suffrage racism fixated on the notion that black women had emasculated black men, by taking away from men the power to lead the family. The complex paradigm of racist gender roles portrayed all black men as lazy, shiftless, submissive, ignorant, and dangerous. In contrast, professional and middle-class black women were described as shrewd, ambitious, calculating, and undermining. In other words, black women were too smart for the vote, and black men, when they weren't threatening white women, were too dumb, according to the racist rhetoric advocating the disenfranchisement of African Americans.

For instance, Mrs. Smith, a white southerner, suggested to the *Louisville News* that black men's votes could be easily controlled, but a black woman was "more independent and would be more apt to vote as she wanted."[31] Similarly, the *St. Louis Argus* printed the sentiments of George Lockwood, a prominent attorney, who was concerned that "[s]uffrage for white women is alright, but for Colored women this will never do. . . . Colored women are so much smarter than Colored men, that once they get the ballot, they will use it."[32] The Writers' Club of the South Georgia State Teacher's College conceded the same point, especially that "the Negro woman is more business-like in every way than the man. She is also always on the alert to everything out of which she may gain."[33] However, the Writers' Club argued that the vote might give black women too much influence, and it would grant black husbands political authority by proxy. Partisan politics played a crucial role in the general reluctance to extend the franchise to African Americans, particularly the Democratic Party's worries that that blacks and reform-minded white women would vote the Democrats out of power. And yet, though many states argued that extending the franchise to blacks was an issue of states' rights presiding over federal mandates, the negative stereotypes about black women specifically illustrated two prevailing anxieties: first, there was considerable fear that the wrong people had won the right to vote and were certain to misuse it; and second, there was considerable uncertainty that regardless of how black women voted, their choices would be unpredictable and uncontrollable.

Even Kelly Miller, a vocal opponent of Woodrow Wilson during the World War and the dean of Howard University's Junior College, considered black women's political leanings as difficult to manage, though he was certain that black women would never stray too far from the party of Lincoln. Writing in support of the NAACP, which had backed the Progressive Party's candidate, Robert La Follete, Miller continued, "Doubtless many thousands of negro men will vote for the Democratic and Progressive tickets, but comparatively few negro women will do so. The mind of the negro man has grown somewhat indifferent to recital of the wrongs that the race has suffered at the hands of the Southern Democrats. But the woman is stirred with each recital. The acute politician knows how to capitalize on the negro woman's emotions."[34] In fact, Miller was correct that in 1924 black women remained some of the most loyal supporters of the Republican Party and its candidate, Calvin Coolidge. However, Miller did not acknowledge that Alice Dunbar-Nelson, a veteran of state and local politics in Delaware, supported the Progressive Party in 1924 and was chosen as the party's eastern organizer of black women voters in the months leading up to the presidential election.[35]

In order to challenge the various stereotypes about black women and their political motivations, middle-class black women reframed the debate on black women's political equality, explaining voting rights as a civil right and an act of personal responsibility. For instance, in 1922, Louise Dodson, the director of the Republican Women's National Executive Committee, told the Virginia Federation of Colored Women at its annual convention that an organized effort of women could bring voting education to the homes of black and white women throughout the state. Despite the partisanship of her position, Dodson urged black women to remember their duty as citizens, continuing, "Most of us resent the political conditions in Europe where, by inheritance, certain citizens are the governing class, yet we by our own wills in this country, which is the freest country in the world, in our failure to vote confess our ability to be governed by others than ourselves."[36]

In Georgia, the Savannah Federation of Colored Women printed a full-page advertisement in the *Savannah Journal,* explaining that new registrants must satisfy three of the five provisions used to judge registration applications. But the Savannah Federation was certain that black registrants could satisfy all of them, including the good character, educational, and property clauses. Though the Savannah Federation was forbidden to help registrants with the educational tests, the organization challenged the miseducation of black women by reminding them that no one was too old to vote, that the poll tax cost one dollar, and that the all-white Democratic Party primary was not the same as the general election. The Savannah Federation concluded, "Rally, Negro women, you have never lacked courage even when the days were darker. . . . Do not rest until you, your family, your neighbor, your community, your whole state have met the requirements of this your state, your country, whose laws are made of the people, by the people, for the people."[37]

Other themes within black voting rights activism described voting as a patriotic duty and as a form of protection of the private sphere. In November 1920, shortly after the ratification of the Nineteenth Amendment, the editors of the *Houston Informer* applauded the "loyalty, patriotism, and fealty" of the African American women of Texas, who, in demonstrating their patriotism, "saved the day for genuine republicanism and undefiled Americanism and voted in such large numbers and with such intelligence that it drew consternation in the ranks of even the democrats." Though it made no attempt to hide its partiality to the Republican Party, what mattered most to the *Houston Informer* was that black women had confronted the attempts to disenfranchise them by redoubling "their efforts and urging every qualified voter to go to the polls."[38] Dr. R. H. Butler of Atlanta explained that a Christian, African American woman had several obligations: to be a church worker, to take proper care of her home, to honor her husband and her children, and to be "a registered voter in her city, county, and state to make her a full-fledged citizen of her country."[39]

The rapid growth of black voting clubs and registration drives, often led by middle-class black women, changed the tenor of the debate from a character-driven discussion on black women's intellect to a multifaceted argument of education, women's duty to protect the home, and black identity. Across the country, a grassroots movement of voting clubs in black communities emerged, but the clubs were the most popular in the South, as were the efforts to get black women to register. In Birmingham in 1921 the black women of the city formed the nonpartisan Colored Women's Voters' League, for the purpose of educating black citizens about the vote and to encourage the members to pay their poll taxes. The league selected a regular meeting space and composed a network of ministers, churchgoers, and social workers. The league was particularly important since, just eight months earlier in September 1920, black women had been compelled to recite the Constitution before registering or had been turned away from the polls altogether in Birmingham.[40]

Similar groups had formed in other southern states. In order to dissuade black women from registering to vote in Columbia, for instance, white registrars issued a series of loosely defined literacy and education requirements —reciting the Constitution, defining legal terms such as "mandamus," explaining the appeal process, and accurately guessing the revenue payments made by the Baptist Church to the state of South Carolina.[41] And in Lowndes County, Georgia, only two African American women were allowed to register to vote. Yet, in Chatham County, Georgia, the Woman's Suffrage Club made an appeal to every woman in the county to educate themselves on Georgia's complex suffrage clauses. The club organized adult night school classes five times a week, for the 175 people who signed up.[42] In Richmond, nearly two thousand women registered to vote in September 1920, just one month after the ratification of the women's suffrage amendment. The registration activity in Richmond was particularly important for black women, as the chairman of the all-white Democratic Committee, John Purcell, tried to impose a literacy test on the black registrants and was confronted "with nearly fifty women, a majority of them colored, all of whom were busily engaged in writing out their applications."[43]

Voting clubs also had the effect of consciousness-raising about the process of voting and maintaining a high interest in registration. Suffrage clubs educated black women to maneuver around a common form of disenfranchisement at the time, the poll tax, by encouraging black citizens to pay it. By not paying the tax, newly enfranchised black women gave white registrars reasons to reject their applications and to declare that black women had no interest in politics. Indeed, supporters of black voting rights claimed that whites had deliberately misrepresented black women's commitment to voting, by using the flawed data of poll tax receipts to show that black people had not paid them and, thus, were not interested. Alice Paul, of the National Woman's Party, said, "We are organizing the white women in South Carolina but have heard of no activity or anxiety among the negresses," a statement that was largely untrue, since South Carolina had tried on several occasions to disenfranchise black women.[44] But the *Southwestern Christian Advocate* advised black women to ignore the degrading treatment at the registration booths, particularly the "harsh and disrespectful manner of address by the registrars" and the "proferred familiarity toward the applicant," and to carry forward with their voting duties.[45] The Colored Woman's Suffrage Club of Baltimore joined with the YWCA and held citizenship and information meetings for black women.[46]

Voting clubs argued that every registered voter, black and white, was required to pay a poll tax. In Texas, an editorial piece in the *Houston Observer* blared, "YOU ARE NO MAN!! If You Don't Pay Your Poll Tax," insisting that the road to political equality for black men was impassable without paying the poll tax.[47] Also in Texas, Mrs. E. P. Jackson-Hurd, the secretary of Houston's Republican Women Voter's League and the first black female notary public in Texas, contended that poll taxes validated the political legitimacy of male and female voters. She argued that the one dollar tax would help fund overcrowded schools, underpaid teachers, insufficient facilities, "and many other phases of our public school system the lack of which impedes the greatest progress and educational development of the voting citizens of tomorrow."[48] The Houston Voter's League played an instrumental role in registering black women to vote, after Judge J. D. Harvey, of the 80th District Court, in 1920 ruled that it was unconstitutional to demand that black women and men of voting age present a receipt proving that they had paid their poll tax.[49]

Naturally, the success of black women's voting clubs galvanized the African American base of support for the Republican Party. Though some of

"LONG 'BOUT CAMPAIGN TIME"

Figure 6. African American voters contemplated abandoning the Republican Party in the 1920s, after the Republicans failed to enact an anti-lynching bill. In this 1924 political cartoon, "Long 'Bout Campaign Time," an unnamed politician, presumably from the GOP, attempts to lure black voters. Ultimately, southern disenfranchisement laws after 1920 had the effect of driving black women toward the Republican Party, popular in the northern states and among progressive southern blacks. *Courtesy of the Tuskegee Institute News Clipping Files, reel 19, "Political Party Affiliation."*

the clubs pledged nonpartisanship, most were directly affiliated with the Republican Party and the clubs' leading members were outspoken members of the GOP. Critics of black voting clubs charged that the clubs were thinly veiled attempts by the Republican Party to lure in new voters. The critics urged black women to consider third-party candidates, such as the Black-Tan Party of Houston, the Lincoln Independent Party of Louisville, the Socialist Party of Hartford, and the national Progressive Party. But the Republican Party courted black women voters as a separate voting bloc, particularly among middle-class black clubwomen, who long advocated for the Republican Party in their social activism. Black women were far from disinterested in electoral politics after the passage of the women's suffrage amendment, and their relationship with the GOP, growing ever tighter with the growing popularity and necessity of black voting clubs, was elevated to national visibility just a few years later.

The watershed in black women's politics did not arrive in one moment or in a series of moments, but rather in a wave of significant advances in officeholding and Republican Party politics. Black women's achievements within the Republican Party, beginning with political appointments and moving into electoral politics and registration, formed the summit of middle-class black women's political expression in the 1920s. Their politics adhered to the ethos of political and cultural advancement critical to the New Negro Movement. Though the New Negro Movement was often blinded by its own sexist assumptions about gender roles and politics, its philosophy of a new black consciousness, new political tactics, and new strategies for confronting white supremacy also shaped black women's political expression. Middle-class black women engaged in artful political exchange with the GOP in the 1920s. In the interests of their own politics, middle-class black women chose not to endorse the Republican candidate for president in 1920, and yet rose to high ranks within the same party by 1924.

Political appointments were particularly important for the advancement of black women's politics in the 1920s, since an appointment provided the crucial entry point into public politics for black female professionals. The appointees were often the first black person and first woman to be granted commissions and representation in their districts. In Ohio, Blanche Van Cook received a permanent appointment as clerk for the Superintendent of Markets in Columbus's Municipal Civil Service Commission, a notable achievement, given white male professionals had always served in the position previous to Van Cook's employment.[50] In another important political appointment, Fannie Barrier Williams, one of founding members of the

NACW who addressed the 1893 Chicago Exposition on "The Intellectual Progress of the Colored Woman," was granted a seat on the Chicago Library Board, a powerful office since the Library Board held governance over all of Chicago's public libraries and worked directly with the Chicago City Council. Williams was also the first woman and African American to be seated on the Library Board.[51] In Arkansas in 1922, Mrs. J. T. Warren was the first black woman to hold office in the history of the state, when she was appointed a justice of the peace and a notary republic for Hot Springs.[52] In most southern states, political appointments were the only doors open to black women in local and state politics.

Rosalyn Terborg-Penn writes that the significant numbers of black women running for office also signaled their increased political presence. By 1924, black women ran for, and sometimes won, local and state political posts across the northern states, and in the southern states they rose to prominent levels of leadership within black Republican politics. Candidate W. L. Presto linked the progressive politics of feminism and civic equality for black women in her run for the Washington State Senate in 1920.[53] Similarly, Laura Brown ran for a seat in the Pennsylvania State Assembly in 1922 on a platform of working-class rights, law enforcement, "racial development, and world wide consciousness."[54] In a hotly contested race in the Connecticut State Assembly, Mary Seymour, a Hartford-born labor organizer of tobacco workers, ran under the Farm-Labor Ticket, the third party in the state. Though the Farm-Labor Ticket won few votes, Seymour received more votes than any other candidate in the third party. Seymour said that she did not expect to win the election for secretary of state for Connecticut, yet she told the *Bridgeport Herald* that "the organization of the union of women [tobacco workers] was a great step—the naming of a colored woman on the ticket of the Farm-Labor Party is a still greater one."[55]

Equally important, in the critical half-decade after the passage of the Nineteenth Amendment, black women formed or joined advisory groups for the purpose of directly lobbying the Republican Party. Black women's groups were organized within the Republican National Committee, such as the unofficial Republican colored women's organization, led by NACW clubwomen Mary Church Terrell, Victoria Clay Haley, and Lethia Fleming. Though the group operated with a substantial budget of $15,000 a year, it worked with the men's committee to evaluate national and state legislation affecting African Americans.[56] The GOP in Georgia also authorized the organization of the Women's Republican Advisory Committee, which set aside twenty-five seats for white women and twenty-five seats for black women. While the two groups worked and reported to the Republican

State Committee of Georgia separately, both groups followed the same purpose—increasing the number of women voters in Georgia, or, as the *Atlanta Independent* reported, "to bring out the women voters . . . of the state to the end that the honor conferred upon the women shall be a means for good to the party and nation."[57] After pressure from groups like the NACW on issues such as anti-lynching and voting rights, the Republican Party political machine continued to fill its visible positions with African American clubwomen. The GOP recognized that African American loyalty to the party had remained steadfast, despite the rancorous debate on the intellectual worthiness and political readiness of African Americans in the use of the ballot.

Thus, when Henry Lincoln Johnson, the sole African American member of the Republican National Committee, nominated Mary Miller Williams in 1923 to a seat on the Women's Auxiliary to the National Republican Committee, the decision, at first, was welcomed for its boldness. However, when Williams, the former president of the Georgia State Federation of Colored Women, was also granted a position at the Republican National Convention for the 1924 presidential election, white members of the Republican Party from Georgia strenuously objected. They argued that Williams, a black woman, would have the same rank and privileges as white women from other states, and that she "would sit as a representative of the white women of Georgia," a position they considered unsuitable for a black woman.[58] The issue of political visibility, particularly regarding race relations and electoral representation, struck at the heart of the division between black and white women's political activity, and remained a sore point largely due to the reluctance of white women activists to cross racial boundaries and work with black women.

In response to the nomination of Williams, high-ranking members of the GOP advised Johnson to rescind his selection, and when Johnson refused, they suggested that Johnson resign from his position within the Republican National Committee. Owing to the "recalcitrance of the Republican National committeeman," the GOP put Williams's appointment on indefinite hold.[59] But Williams's nomination was revived in April 1924 when the Republican National Committee relented just a few months before the party's presidential convention. When her nomination was approved, Williams was granted the position as associate member of the National Committee of the Republican Party, working as the ad hoc representative of black women's interests within the party. In recognition of Johnson's steadfast support, Williams remarked in 1924, "This is the first time Georgia has had a Republican woman appointed, and the first time in the history of the country that a colored committeewoman has been authorized to take a seat in the National Convention."[60] Williams was soon joined by Mary Booze of Mississippi, the reported daughter of a slave owned by Jefferson Davis, who was the also the first black women to represent the Republican Party from the heavily Democratic state.[61]

The highpoint of black women's success within the Republican Party came with the 1924 nomination of Calvin Coolidge for president. Before then, the GOP had recognized black Republican women by supporting their lobbying efforts or by selecting black women for positions within the party machine. But in September 1924, the Republican Party, at its national convention in Cleveland, responded to pressure from its black constituents for a national Republican organization committed to black women voters. In fact, input from the NACW assisted the GOP in selecting Wilberforce University professor and former NACW president, Hallie Q. Brown, as president of the National League of Republican Colored Women. The National League of Republican Colored Women aspired to galvanize the voting power of black women to influence party and national politics.[62] The league was constructed along the framework of the NACW as well, as Brown was the national director who supervised state chairmen from twenty-one states and nine national organizers.

A methodical and deliberate undertaking, the league employed the state chairmen to organize Republican women within their states, while the national organizers collected reports within their regions and met with the national director. When Brown wrote to the NACW clubwomen that "[Negro women] have shown integrity of purpose, indomitable courage, unswerving fidelity to the Republican party in the face of enemies who would destroy the fundamentals of our government and the onslaught of our constitutional rights," she not only celebrated the success of black women's politics within the GOP but also refuted the suffrage movement's argument that the Republican Party would not risk its resources on the unpredictable political whims of black women.[63] In the interest of educating women "all over the country in the exercise of their citizenship rights, and to urge that they use the ballot in an honorable, intelligent manner," black women's party politics had become quite sophisticated by mid-decade in challenging the GOP to engage more black voters. By working with the GOP, middle-class black women increased the profile of the black constituency in national politics.[64]

The ultimate goal of the black women's Republican groups was to increase the number of southern women on the registration rolls regardless of political opinion, though these efforts were also driven by the desire to dismantle the Democratic Party in the South. For instance, the Colored Women's National Political Study Club, a committee of black political activists in Washington, D.C., endorsed Coolidge in a long letter, detailing African American support of the Republican Party since the Civil War. The Study Club pledged "to do all in our power to lead back to the path of Republicanism those of our group that have blindly strayed" to the Democratic party, as the "Southern oligarchy . . . has manifested no interest whatever in the conditions affecting our people in the South."[65] Similarly, the National League of Republican Colored Women determined that it should "urge the advisability of voting for the Republican party" and to "raise funds for the support of the Republican party" as a part of its general campaign to increase voter registration among the black electorate.[66] As Evelyn Brooks Higginbotham writes, the political lines between the NACW and the league were blurred due to the large number of black clubwomen active in the Republican Party in the 1920s. Yet, the National League found considerable recognition with the Woman's Division of the GOP, and by 1926, the league enjoyed a direct affiliation with the GOP, leaving black clubwomen to reestablish ties with the League of Women Voters.[67]

Apart from the critical issues of visibility and leadership, black women's political advances within the Republican Party provided a temporary halt or deceleration of Jim Crow in 1920s black politics. By allying themselves with the GOP, black leaders, particularly middle-class black clubwomen, found that their national platform for civil rights gained a measure of credibility among sympathetic white politicians, to the extent that the Democratic Party of the South appeared ineffectual by comparison. In addition, black women's networks within Republican politics laid the groundwork of the modern civil rights movement. By establishing and furthering a paradigm of black participation in party politics, black women's networks actively worked toward the unseating of the Democratic Party in the South. In turn, they focused on the Republican Party's promises to eradicate lynching and discrimination in housing and employment and its promotion of educational reform and other areas of social welfare. However, black women's political achievements may have come at a cost to black plans for civic equality in the long run. In the effort to institutionalize black women's politics, the number of black women's positions within the Republican Party remained relatively small, with even fewer elite posts. At the end of the 1920s, black women would come to expect to play a pivotal part in sustaining the black electorate, but it was the Democratic Party that would capitalize on black women's networks and expertise.

## Political Visibility and the Republican Party

After the NACW's organizational success in the World War and its political rebirth in the New Negro Movement, the future of black women's politics in the 1920s was left to Mary McLeod Bethune. Bethune's political career reframes the discussion of black women's politics in the 1920s, as she
moved across the private sphere of the education of the black family to the
public sphere of the government-backed civil rights policy in the New Deal;
in short, Bethune reformed middle-class black women's politics by shifting
them from the private, less visible realm to the public, governmental arena.
Bethune is arguably one of the most recognizable black female historical
figures, along with Ida B. Wells-Barnett, Harriet Tubman, and Sojourner
Truth. Bethune is certainly the most famous clubwoman, whose work within the NACW, the National Council of Negro Women, and the New Deal
launched black women's politics into greater visibility. As historical intersection and as narrative explication, the professional development of Mary
McLeod Bethune was also the story of the ascension and institutionalization of black women's politics at the end of the 1920s.

Like the NACW, Bethune's considerable accomplishments in social work
and community welfare had emerged at the turn of the century. One of seventeen children of former slaves, Bethune's youth was spent in rural poverty
in Mayeville, in Sumter County, South Carolina during the Reconstruction
period. But an early exposure to Booker T. Washington's philosophy of economic empowerment deeply influenced her education ambitions, as historian Joyce Hanson explains. Bethune's education began at Scotia Seminary
in Concord, North Carolina, and was followed by studies in Chicago at the
Moody Bible Institute in 1894. Her marriage to Albertus Bethune in 1897
led to the birth of her son, Albert, and the relocation of the family to Georgia, then Florida where the family settled. While in residence, Bethune en-
acted her vision of girls' education, and she gathered funds to establish the
Daytona Educational and Industrial School for Negro Girls in 1904. The
school merged with the Cookman Institute of Jacksonville in 1923 to become the Bethune-Cookman College. Bethune was president of Bethune-
Cookman College for thirty-eight years.[68]

But it was apparently the World War and the suffrage movement that
launched Bethune into national prominence. While serving as principal of
the Daytona Educational and Industrial School, Bethune was also the president of the Florida Federation of Colored Women. During the war, Bethune led the Florida Federation into closer cooperation with the Red Cross,

the Circle For Negro War Relief, and the Liberty Loan campaigns, enterprises that strengthened her association within the NACW. After the passage of the women's suffrage amendment, Bethune, the president of the Southeastern Federation of Colored Women's Clubs, joined other influential NACW members in authoring an open letter to southern white women, appealing for "the sympathy and cooperation . . . in the interest of better understanding and better conditions, as these affect the relations between white and colored people."[69] The Southeastern Federation, much like the NACW national platform, urged southern white women to condemn lynching and mob violence, to support black women's voting rights, and to encourage reform in working conditions of domestic workers. And the women with whom Bethune served, including Lugenia Burns Hope, Charlotte Hawkins Brown, and Margaret Murray Washington, all at one point or another, enjoyed lively and successful careers in social work in their private spheres and helped form the NACW's national anti-discrimination, anti–Jim Crow platform. They also put the onus of racial reconciliation on white women's shoulders, ending, "we are stating frankly and soberly what in our judgment, you as white women may do to correct the ills from which our race has so long suffered and of which we as a race are perhaps more conscious now than ever."[70]

In 1924, Bethune was elected president of the NACW and began a bold initiative of reshaping the organization and institutionalizing its objectives in electoral politics. As historian Elaine Smith has written, Bethune lent to this position a talent "to facilitate greater cohesion within an organization. She strove to bring organization affiliates closer in structure, methods, and goals, and members of differing affiliates closer in their relationship to each other." Though the organization faced gradual irrelevance, Bethune encouraged the NACW membership to guard against "stagnation, decomposition, death."[71] Bethune moved the NACW toward the goals of economic development, individualism, and political activism, or rather, she urged NACW members to follow a platform of "self-support as a primary essential of self-government and service as the 'acid test.'" As the NACW allied itself with the Republican Party, via interorganizational cooperation with the National League of Republican Colored Women, Bethune advised the NACW to "assume an attitude toward all big questions involving the welfare of the nation, public right and especially the present and future of our race." Even in international policy and politics, Bethune envisioned the NACW serving as a beacon of black women's humanitarianism, "carrying the torch of freedom, equal rights, human love, [and] holding it high and brightening the world with rays of justice, tolerance, and faithful service in God's name."[72]

In 1927, the NACW financed a delegation of black academics and politicians on a goodwill tour of Europe, which included Bethune and other high-ranking NACW officials. Bethune's journey included a private meeting with Pope Pius XI and extended research of the poverty-stricken peasants of southern Europe. "One gets many different ideas—we are not the only sufferers and burden bearers of the world," recalled Bethune of her trip. "I stiffened my back and got new courage to come back to American with greater appreciation for the blessings we did have."[73] Returning from the trip invigorated with new ideas for cooperative efforts within black women's politics, Bethune tried to instill NACW members with the same enthusiasm. She proposed an NACW biennial in Europe or Africa, adding, "How woefully ignorant of true conditions! So few of us have seen and actually know. The time has come when, instead of [going] as individuals, we must go as an organized unit. The more informed people we have, the easier our work. . . . We shall have experts, who have been abroad, to plan our trip . . . THIS IS NO DREAM WOMEN."[74]

Bethune's goals had the effect of infusing the NACW with much-needed direction and energy. Her tenure of the NACW concluded with the founding of the NACW's national headquarters in Washington, D.C., the dispersal of initial funds for the National Scholarship Fund for young women, the monthly publication of the *National Notes* journal, and the establishment of a caretaker's home for the Frederick Douglass home in Anacostia, the property that the NACW bought and restored in 1916. She wrote her colleagues in 1926 of her vision to bring more visibility and prominence to the NACW during her tenure, so that the NACW might progress into "a national body of colored women not merely [of] national influence, but also a significant link between the peoples of color throughout the world."[75]

Yet, Bethune's vision also put the NACW on a narrower path within racial politics. By the last year of her presidency in 1928, the NACW struggled to promote education and citizenship, while anti-lynching, anti-discrimination, and anti–Jim Crow efforts were hardly mentioned after Bethune's departure. Not that the NACW could no longer afford to concentrate on the core, unifying themes within black public consciousness. Rather, they were taken up fully by the NAACP, which, by the Depression, had fully eclipsed the NACW to become the predominant organization promoting the economic empowerment and political equality of African Americans. Sallie Stewart, a longtime and dedicated clubwoman from Indiana, was elected president of the NACW and took over the helm of the organization in 1928. Tempered by a gradual decline in financial resources, growing tension among members of the executive committee, and a general shift in the African American political outlook, Bethune founded in 1935 a new black women's political organization, the National Council of Negro Women, and she joined Roosevelt's "Black Cabinet" in 1936.[76]

Furthermore, the once-positive relationship between the Republican Party and black women's political voices had come undone with the election of Herbert Hoover. A general defection from the Republican Party had begun around 1928, as the GOP appeared increasingly out of touch with economic issues, such as the growing poverty rate and labor disputes, and racial issues, such as black disenfranchisement and the spread of segregation in the nation's capital. After he was elected president, Hoover and the GOP made an additional blunder, authorizing the War Department to segregate the Gold Star Mothers on their trip to France to visit the graves of their sons and husbands on the Western Front. In "providing for [the Negro mothers] a different sort of accommodation in hotels and on shipboard," the segregation of the Gold Star Mothers evoked the memory of the World War, when black soldiers endured similar racial restrictions, causing an uproar within the army and in the United States. Fifty-five black women canceled their registrations and sent a letter of protest to Hoover. The decision regarding the Gold Star Mothers was just the last in a string of missteps and false promises between the GOP and black women. As Evelyn Brooks Higginbotham has argued, by 1932, the honeymoon between the Republican Party and black women's politics was over.[77]

Bethune's most significant accomplishment in the private and public leadership of the NACW, however, was to usher in a period of institutionalization of middle-class black women's politics. Bethune's political acumen guided black clubwomen as they abandoned the Republican Party and took up a new association with their former adversaries, the Democratic Party, this time led by Roosevelt and the New Dealers. Institutionalization, in the eyes of black politics' earliest female luminaries—Mary Church Terrell, Mary B. Talbert, Fannie Barrier Williams, Margaret Murray Washington, Hallie Q. Brown, and Mary McLeod Bethune—assumed recognition. Promoting a greater awareness of the interwoven oppressions of race, class, and gender had always motivated black women's politics. Bethune's close relationship with Eleanor Roosevelt, as well as the power Bethune carried as the Director of Negro Affairs in the National Youth Administration, furthered signaled the arrival of black women's politics on a fundamental level. However, black clubwomen had not foreseen that their form of social welfare could be bureaucratized and hidden away from public eyes, and that federal bureaucracy could quiet their independent voices and vision in black social welfare. Still, occupying a seat at the federal table signified a critical watershed, particularly when black women's organizations, nearly two decades earlier, were barely granted federal recognition of their war work and patriotic activity during World War I. Though black women's politics faced greater challenges leading up to World War II, the institutionalization of black women's political activism bore witness to the organizational, social, and political trails that were blazed and would remain accessible for future generations of black women leaders to follow.

Finally, the headline in the 7 May 1927, edition of the *Pittsburgh Courier* read, "Opinion From All Classes Indicate Chief Benefit From Great Upheaval Was Chance For Race To Find Itself." Culled from several interviews of middle-class African Americans, the article remarked that the Great War had brought about measurable transformation in black life, including increased economic opportunities and vibrant political movements. But in the ten years since the United States declared war on Germany, few American racial practices had changed. Jim Crow ruled the South. The Congress had repeatedly scuttled an anti-lynch law. Blacks continued to be legally disenfranchised. And though the migration of southern blacks to northern urban areas redrew political lines and led to new political allegiances, discrimination in employment, housing, and education, still constricted black advancement. The numbers of poor black people grew across the country throughout the decade.

Yet, the awakening in black consciousness after the war was evoked by a reframing, or rather a new way of examining, white supremacy. Mrs. Geradlyn Dismond, a journalist and society matron in New York, explained, "We got a clearer understanding as to the attitude of white America toward us [African Americans]. . . . Intelligent Negroes were made more dissatisfied when they compared the treatment they received abroad with that which they were surrounded at home, and intelligent dissatisfaction tends toward improvement. The masses were given a broader viewpoint. For many it afforded the first experience outside their native communities. Industrially the war offered new fields for Negro Labor. It also gave us a lot of husbands."[78]

Indeed, World War I had set into motion a series of transformative events that eventually granted black women's politics a chance for exploration and definition. Despite the exclusion from the suffrage movement, black women's politics flourished in the 1920s around the core, unifying issues—voting registration, challenging disenfranchisement, increased involvement in holding office, and national party politics. That black women were assigned a narrow political space in the New Negro Movement led to the reform of organizational politics, as well as a sophisticated and ambitious approach to electoral politics. Middle-class black women utilized race, gender, and class to persuade the GOP and the Democratic Party that they could best represent all black women and their electoral choices. And throughout the social and cultural upheaval, the NACW served as the political umbrella for black women's politics. The most important consequence of black women's organizational politics prior to World War I was that they made politics accessible to black women after World War I and through the 1920s. Even after organizational politics found it hard to keep up with the postwar political allegiances and social upheavals, they produced future black women leaders who would help to initiate a civil rights movement after another World War. But between World War I and World War II, middle-class black women empowered their political lives and visions, and in the process, created an institutional foundation for the unfolding narrative of twentieth-century black consciousness and civic advancement.

# Notes

## Abbreviations

ADN                                Alice Dunbar-Nelson Papers, Box 6, Special Collections, University of Delaware Library, Newark, Del.

ALC/JWJC                           James Weldon Johnson Collection, Series II, Grace Nail Johnson Collection, Beinecke Rare Book and Manuscript Library, Yale University, New Haven, Conn.

MCT Papers                         Mary Church Terrell Papers, Library of Congress, Washington, D.C.

NAACP Administrative Files         *Papers of NAACP, Part 1, Meetings of the Board of Directors, Records of Annual Conferences, Major Speeches, and Special Reports, 1909–1950* (Frederick, Md.: University Publications of America, 1981), microfilm

NAACP/NWP                          *Papers of the NAACP, Part 11, Special Subject Files, 1912–1939, Series B, Harding, Warren G. through YWCA Editorial Advisor* (Frederick, Md.: University Publications of America, 1990), microfilm

NACW Papers                        *Records of the National Association of Colored Women's Clubs, 1895–1992,* ed. Lillian Serece Williams (Bethesda, Md.: University Publications of America, 1993), microfilm

Records of the YMCA and USA        Records of the YMCA and USA Armed Services Division,
Armed Services Division            Kautz Family YMCA Archives, Special Collections, Elmer L. Anderson Library, University of Minnesota, Minneapolis, Minn.

SLR                                Schlesinger Library, Radcliffe College, Cambridge, Mass.

TNCF                               Tuskegee Institute News Clipping Files

WC Central Correspondence          Box 512, Folder 131, Records of the Committee of Women's Defense Work, Records of the Council of National Defense, Record Group 62, National Archives Records Administration II, College Park, Md.

WC Monthly Reports                 Committee on Women's Defense Work of the Council of National Defense, Weekly and Monthly Reports, Records of the Committee on Women's Defense Work, Records of the Council of National Defense, Record Group 62, National Archives Records Administration II, College Park, Md.

WC Minutes                         Committee on Women's Defense Work of the Council of National Defense, Minutes, Box 570, Records of the Committee on Women's Defense Work, Records of the Council of National Defense, Record Group 62, National Archives Record Administration II, College Park, Md.

YWCA Colored Work        Records of the YMCA Colored Work Department, Kautz
    Department           Kautz Family YMCA Archives, Elmer L. Anderson Li-
                         brary, University of Minnesota, Minneapolis, Minn.

YWCA Papers, SSC         YWCA National Board Records, Sophia Smith Collec-
                         tion, Smith College Library, Smith College, Northamp-
                         ton, Mass.

## 1. Patriotism and Jim Crow

1. Mary B. Talbert, "Concerning the Frederick Douglass Memorial," *The Crisis* 14 (August 1917): 167–168; National Association of Colored Women, 11th Biennial Convention Minutes, July 1918, *Records of the National Association of Colored Women's Clubs, 1895–1992,* ed. Lillian Serece Williams (Bethesda, Md.: University Publications of America, 1993), 7 (hereafter cited as NACW Papers); Elizabeth Lindsay Davis, *Lifting as They Climb* (Washington, D.C.: National Association of Colored Women, 1933), 60–61, 78–82, 87; Tulia Brown Hamilton, "The National Association of Colored Women, 1896–1920" (Ph.D. diss., Emory University, 1978), 63–64.

2. Francis J. Grimke to the National Association of Colored Women, Washington, D.C., 1 July 1918, Talbert Family Papers, Erie County Historical Society, Buffalo, N.Y.

3. "Nearly Ten Thousand Take Part in Big Silent Protest Parade Down Fifth Avenue," *New York Age,* 2 August 1917, in Tuskegee Institute News Clipping Files, reel 6, heading "Riots" (hereafter cited as TNCF, with reel number and heading title).

4. "Negroes in Parade to Protest Riots," *Brooklyn Eagle,* 29 July 1917, in TNCF, reel 6, heading "Riots"; Ida B. Wells-Barnett, "The East St. Louis Massacre: The Greatest Outrage of the Century" (Chicago: Negro Fellowship Herald Press, n.d. [probably 1917]), in *Federal Surveillance of Afro-Americans 1917–1925,* ed. Theodore Kornweibel (Frederick, Md.: University Microfilms of America, 1985), reel 10, subject heading "East St. Louis"; *Federal Surveillance of Afro-Americans,* reel 19, subject heading "Ida B. Wells Barnett," 6; James Waldon Johnson, *Black Manhattan* (New York: Alfred A. Knopf, 1940; reprint New York: Arno Press, 1969), 236–239.

5. "Federal Surveillance of Northeastern Federation of Colored Women's Clubs," 20 January 1918, in *Federal Surveillance of Afro-Americans,* reel 10, subject heading "East St. Louis" (italics in original).

6. "Women's Club Notes," *Half-Century Magazine,* August 1917, 10.

7. Theodore Kornweibel, *Investigate Everything: Federal Efforts to Compel Black Loyalty during World War I* (Bloomington: Indiana University Press, 2004), 5, 1–6; Mark Ellis, "'Closing Ranks' and 'Seeking Honors': W.E.B. Du Bois in World War I," *Journal of American History* 79, no. 1 (June 1992): 98, 96–124. See also: William Jordan, "'The Damnable Dilemma' African-American Accommodation and Protest during World War I," *Journal of American History* 81, no. 4 (March 1995): 1562–1583; Theodore Kornweibel, *No Crystal Stair: Black Life and The Messenger, 1917–1928* (Westport, Conn.: Greenwood Press, 1975); Mark Ellis, *Race, War, and Surveillance: African Americans and the United States Government during World War I* (Bloomington: Indiana University Press, 2001).

8. Deborah Gray White, *Too Heavy a Load: Black Women in Defense of Themselves, 1894–1994* (New York: W. W. Norton, 1999), 63, 60–65.

9. Stephanie J. Shaw, *What a Woman Ought to Be and to Do: Black Professional Women Workers during the Jim Crow Era* (Chicago: University of Chicago Press, 1996), 112, 111–134.

10. Glenda Elizabeth Gilmore, *Gender and Jim Crow: Women and the Politics of White Supremacy in North Carolina, 1896–1920* (Chapel Hill: University of North Carolina Press, 1996), 101, 61–89.

11. "Federal Surveillance of Northeastern Federation of Colored Women's Clubs" and "Federal Surveillance of the Negro Fellowship League," in *Federal Surveillance of Afro-Americans,* reel 10, subject headings "East St. Louis" and "Ida B. Wells-Barnett."

12. Ralph Tyler, "Who Wouldn't Love a Mother?" *Cleveland Advocate,* reprinted in *Washington Bee,* 22 December 1917, in TNCF, reel 7, heading "Soldiers."

13. "We Are in the War," *Half-Century Magazine* 3 (December 1917): 18.

14. "Economic Opportunity," *New York Age,* 5 September 1916.

15. "Shall the Negro Fight?" *New York Age,* 15 February 1917.

16. "The Great Responsibility," *New York Age,* 28 December 1916. Johnson wrote several editorials that held the same perspective on the war and on the war's impact on men. See the articles in the *New York Age:* "More about Employment," 30 September 1915; "The Spring Exodus," 1 March 1917; "The Duty of Hour," 5 April 1917.

17. "The Letter from the Colored Wife and Mother," *New York Age,* 20 April 1916, 4.

18. Ibid.

19. Addie Hunton, "The Colored Woman as an Economic Factor," *New York Call,* February 1916, in TNCF, reel 7, heading "Women's Work."

20. "Our Woman Wage-Earners," *Norfolk Journal and Guide,* 8 March 1917, in TNCF, reel 6, heading "Labor."

21. Mary B. Talbert, "President's Address," in National Association of Colored Women, 11th Biennial Convention Minutes, July 1918, NACW Papers, 7.

22. Lillian S. Williams, "Mary Morris Talbert," in *Notable Black American Women,* ed. Jessie Carney Smith (Detroit: Gale Research, 1992), 1095–1100.

23. Martha E. Williams, "President's Address" (speech given before the Kentucky Federation of Colored Women's Clubs on 1 December 1917), in National Association of Colored Women, Holograph Reports, 1897–1952. *The Papers of Mary Church Terrell* (Washington, D.C.: Library of Congress Photoduplication Service, 1977).

24. Georgia A. Nugent, "Report of the Corresponding Secretary for 1917 and 1918," in National Association of Colored Women, 11th Biennial Convention Minutes, July 1918, NACW Papers, 7.

25. Mary Waring, "Health, Hygiene, and War Foods," in National Association of Colored Women, 11th Biennial Convention Minutes, July 1918, NACW Papers, 37.

26. "War Work of Colored Women," National Association of Colored Women folder, box 607, Committee on Women's Work, Council of National Defense, National Archives II, College Park, Md., n.d. [1918].

27. Ibid., 50.

28. Ibid., 54; Davis, *Lifting as They Climb,* 62.

29. Elnora Manson, "War Activities among the Colored Women of Chicago," *The (Chicago) Broad Ax,* 21 December 1918; *New York Age,* 5 April 1917.

30. Melnea Cass, interview by Tahi Lani Mottl, 9 February 1977, transcript, Black Women Oral History Project, Schlesinger Library, Radcliffe College, Cambridge, Mass., 20–21; *Minutes of League of Women for Community Service,* 21 May 1918, Schlesinger Library, Radcliffe College, Cambridge, Mass., 6 (hereafter cited as SLR); Gerald W. Patton, *War and Race: The Black Officer in the American Military, 1915–1941* (Westport, Conn.: Greenwood Press, 1981), 80.

31. Hallie Q. Brown, *Homespun Heroines and Other Women of Distinction* (Xenia, Ohio: Aldine Publishing, 1926), 222–224.

32. *New York Age,* 12, 26 April 1917; 17, 24 May 1917.

33. *New York Age,* 24 May 1917.

34. *New York Age,* 26 April 1917.

35. Bessie R. James, *For God, For Country, For Home: The National League for Women's Service* (New York: G. P. Putnam's Sons, 1920); *New York Age,* 26 April 1917.

36. "Praise Negro Race for Patriotism in Present Crisis," *Wilkes-Barre* (unknown title), 24 August 1917, in TNCF, reel 7, heading "Women's Work."

37. *New York Age,* 26 April 1917.

38. *New York Age,* 20 July 1918, 5. See also Evelyn Brooks Higginbotham, *Righteous Discontent: The Women's Movement in the Black Baptist Church, 1880–1920* (Cambridge, Mass.: Harvard University Press, 1993); Opal Easter, *Nannie Helen Burroughs* (Garden City, N.J.: Garland Publishing, 1995).

39. "The Negro and the Present Crisis," *Boston Transcript,* 13 October 1917, in TNCF, reel 6, heading "War Conditions and Results."

40. "Negro Women in War Work," *Beaumont Journal,* 12 January 1918, in TNCF, reel 9, heading "War Conditions and Results."

41. "The Welfare League" (unknown newspaper, unknown date, probably March 1918), in TNCF, reel 9, heading "War Conditions and Results."

42. "The Women's Patriotic League," *Baltimore Daily Herald,* 19 October 1917, in TNCF, reel 7, heading "Soldiers."

43. "Lad of 4 Wants to Fight Kaiser," *Portland Evening Telegram,* 3 January 1918, in TNCF, reel 9, heading "War Conditions and Results."

44. Alice Dunbar-Nelson, "Mine Eyes Have Seen," in *Black Theater U.S.A.: Forty-Five Plays by Black Americans, 1847–1974,* ed. James V. Hatch (New York: The Free Press, 1974), 173–177.

45. Ibid., 176, 177.

46. August Meier and Elliot Rudwick, "The Rise of Segregation in the Federal Bureaucracy, 1900–1930," *Phylon* 28 (Summer 1967): 178–184, 179, 181. The Departments of Navy and War retracted the policy a month later, but the War Trade Commission maintained its position. See also Kathleen Wolgemuth, "Woodrow Wilson and Federal Segregation," *Journal of Negro History* 44 (April 1959): 158–173.

47. Nicholas Patler, *Jim Crow and the Wilson Administration: Protesting Federal Segregation in the Early Twentieth Century* (Boulder: University Press of Colorado, 2004), 169, 154–173.

48. "Forced to Give Up Seat to White Woman, Says Negress Seeking $5000," *Atlanta Constitution,* 7 July 1917, in TNCF, reel 6, heading "Discrimination."

49. "Another Big Store Draws the Color Line," *Louisville News,* 23 December 1917, in TNCF, reel 6, heading "Discrimination."

50. "Women Win Suit against 5 & 10c Store," *Chicago Defender,* 8 December 1917, in TNCF, reel 6, heading "Discrimination."

51. "Colored Women Lose in Civil Rights Fight," *New York News,* 11 June 1916, in TNCF, reel 5, heading "Discrimination."

52. "Urge McCall to Remove Medfield Hospital Head," *Boston Traveler and Evening Herald,* 21 April 1916, in TNCF, reel 5, heading "Discrimination."

53. "A Colored Working Girl and Race Prejudice," *New York Age,* 2 April 1916, in TNCF, reel 5, heading "Discrimination."

54. Ibid.

55. "Jane Bosfield Going Back to Work in Medfield Hospital," *Boston Traveler and Evening Herald,* 27 April 1916, in TNCF, reel 5, heading "Discrimination."

56. "Chicago Soldiers Stop Mob Rule," *Chicago Defender,* 6 July 1917.

57. "Murder and Arson in High Carnival at East St. Louis For Day and Night," *Atlanta Constitution,* 3 July 1917, in TNCF, reel 6, heading "Riots."

58. "Negroes Started, but White Men Finished It, Is Callous Opinion of East St. Louisians," *St. Louis Democrat,* 4 July 1917, in TNCF, reel 6, heading "Riots."

59. "North Doesn't Know Negroes," *Wilmington (Delaware) News,* 22 August 1917, in TNCF, reel 6, heading "Riots."

60. "Race Rioters Fire on East St. Louis and Shoot or Hang Many Negroes; Dead Estimated at from 20 to 75," *New York Times,* 3 July 1917, in TNCF, reel 6, heading "Riots."

61. W. E. B. Du Bois and Martha Gruening, "The Massacre of East St. Louis," *The Crisis* (September 1917): 219–238.

62. "Negro Child Cast into Burning House," *Atlanta Constitution,* 23 October 1917, in TNCF, reel 6, heading "Riots."

63. Linda O. McMurray, *To Keep the Waters Troubled: The Life of Ida B. Wells* (New York: Oxford University Press, 1998), 315, 314–317.

64. Wells-Barnett, "The East St. Louis Massacre: The Greatest Outrage of the Century," 4.

65. College Alumnae Club, "Extract from an Open Letter to the President," *The Crisis* 14 (August 1917): 165.

66. "Ask Wilson to Stop Acts of Lawlessness," *New York Age,* 12 July 1917.

67. Wells-Barnett, "The East St. Louis Massacre: The Greatest Outrage of the Century," 20.

68. "Federation of Women's Clubs Elects Officers," *Chicago Defender,* 1 September 1917.

69. "Woman's Call to Prayer," *New York Age,* 2 August 1917.

70. "Prayer Meeting," *Chicago Defender,* 11 August 1917.

71. "Auxiliary Notes," *New York Age,* 9 August 1917.

72. Robert V. Haynes, *A Night of Violence: The Houston Riot of 1917* (Baton Rouge: Louisiana State University Press, 1976).

73. "America and Democracy?" *New York Age,* 22 December 1917.

74. Ibid.

75. See Gerald R. Patton, *War and Race: The Black Officer in the American Military, 1915–1941* (Westport, Conn.: Greenwood Press, 1981); and Arthur Barbeau and Florette Henri, *Unknown Soldiers: Black American Troops in World War I* (Philadelphia: Temple University Press, 1974).

76. Elliot Rudwick, *Race Riot at East St. Louis, July 2, 1917* (Urbana: University of Illinois Press, 1982), 140–141.

77. "The Negro and the Socialists," *New York Call,* 22 July 1917, in TNCF, reel 6, heading "Riots."

78. "Wartime Contributions of Madam C. J. Walker and her daughter Lelia Walker," n.d. [1918], folder "National Association of Colored Women," box 607: Publications, September 1916 to October 1918, Records of the Committee of Women's Defense Work, Records of the Council of National Defense, Record Group 62, National Archives and Records Administration II, College Park, Md.

79. *New York Age,* 2, 9 February 1918, 4.

80. National Association of Colored Women, Convention Minutes, July 1918, in NACW Papers, 54.

## 2. Investigations of the Southern Black Working Class

1. Alice Dunbar-Nelson, Jacksonville, Fla., to Hannah Patterson, Washington, D.C., 30 August 1918, box 512, folder 131. Records of the Committee of Women's Defense Work, Records of the Council of National Defense, Record Group 62 (National Archives Records Administration II, College Park, Md.) (hereafter cited as the description of the communication, followed by the date and WC Central Correspondence).

2. Alice Dunbar-Nelson, Jacksonville, Fla., to Hannah Patterson, Washington, D.C., 1 September 1918, WC Central Correspondence.

3. Hannah Patterson, Washington, D.C., to Alice Dunbar-Nelson, Wilmington, Del., Washington, D.C., 12 August 1918, Alice Dunbar-Nelson Papers, box 6, Special Collections, University of Delaware Library, Newark, Del. (hereafter cited as author and recipient of the communication, followed by date and ADN).

4. Alice Dunbar-Nelson, "Things That Have to be Explained to Colored Audiences and Committees," September 1918, ADN.

5. The best contemporary accounts of these organizations are: Bessie R. James, *For God, For Country, For Home: The National League of Women's Service* (New York: G. P. Putnam's Sons, 1920); National Woman's Liberty Loan Committee, *Report of National Woman's Liberty Loan Committee for the First through Fourth and Victory Loan Campaigns* (Washington, D.C.: Government Printing Office, 1920); Ida C. Clark, *American Women and the World War* (New York: D. Appleton, 1918); and Emily N. Blair, *The Woman's Committee: United States Council of National Defense, An Interpretative Report: April 21, 1917 to February 27, 1919* (Washington, D.C.: Government Printing Office, 1920).

6. William J. Breen, "Black Women and the Great War: Mobilization and Reform in the South," in *Our American Sisters: Women in American Life and Thought,* ed. Jean E. Friedman (Lexington, Mass.: D.C. Heath, 1982), 411–431. For further discussions of social reform and its war stimulus, please see Allen F. Davis, "Welfare, Reform, and World War I," *American Quarterly* 19 (Fall 1967): 516–533.

7. "Colored Women Find Places in Industry," *Cleveland Advocate,* 31 August 1918, TNCF, reel 8, heading "Labor."

8. Alice Dunbar-Nelson, personal memorandum, January 1918, ADN.

9. Ibid.

10. Ibid.

11. "$1,000,000 War Aid Sought by Negroes," *Philadelphia Inquirer,* 26 May 1918, in TNCF, reel 7, heading "Nurse Training Schools."

12. Committee on Women's Defense Work of the Council of National Defense, Minutes, Meeting of 8 July 1918, box 570, Records of the Committee on Women's Defense Work, Records of the Council of National Defense, record group 62, National Archives Record Administration II, College Park, Md. (hereafter cited as WC Minutes with date and box number).

13. Ibid.

14. Hannah J. Patterson, Resident Director of the Committee on Women's Defense Work, Washington, D.C., to Alice Dunbar-Nelson, Wilmington, Del., 5 July 1918, ADN; Patterson to Dunbar-Nelson, 12 August 1918, ADN.

15. For further biographical details see "Alice Ruth Dunbar Nelson," in *Who's Who in Colored America,* vol. 1, (New York: Who's Who in Colored America Corp. Publishers, 1927), 148–149; Rosalie Murphy Baum, "Alice Dunbar-Nelson," in *African American Women: A Biographical Dictionary,* ed. Dorothy Salem (New York: Garland Publishing, 1993), 165–167.

16. For a compelling study of the relationship between Paul Laurence Dunbar and Alice Ruth Moore, see Eleanor Alexander, *Lyrics of Sunshine and Shadow: The Tragic Courtship and Marriage of Paul Laurence Dunbar and Alice Ruth Moore* (New York: New York University Press, 2002).

17. Alice Dunbar-Nelson's two sets of diaries, 29 July to December 1921, and November 1926 to December 1931, offer remarkable insight into a thriving, African American feminist community, one that interwove sexuality, class, race, and gender into a multilayered consciousness of African American womanhood. Akasha Gloria Hull has edited these diaries as *Give Us Each Day: The Diary of Alice Dunbar-Nelson* (New York: W. W. Norton, 1984). See also Hull's article, "Researching Alice Dunbar-Nelson: A Personal and Literary Perspective," in Patricia Scott Hull and Barbara Smith, eds., *All the Women Are White, All the Blacks Are Men, But Some of Us Are Brave* (Old Westbury, N.Y.: Feminist Press, 1982).

18. Ernest L. Jones, Fort Thomas, Ky., to Alice Dunbar-Nelson, Wilmington, Del., 25 January, 1, 7 February 1918, ADN.

19. "For Families of Negro Soldiers," *New York Times,* 30 September 1917, in TNCF, reel 7, heading "Soldiers."

20. The Circle for Negro War Relief, Inc., Pamphlet and Subscription Cards, January 1918, ADN.

21. Caroline S. Bond, New York, N.Y., to Alice Dunbar-Nelson, Wilmington, Del., 18 January 1918, ADN.

22. Ibid.; Uriah J. Robinson, Chaplain for the 365th Infantry, Rockford, Ill., to The Circle for Negro War Relief, Inc., New York, N.Y., 13 January 1918, Arthur Springarn Papers, Library of Congress, Washington, D.C.

23. Bond to Dunbar-Nelson, 18 February 1918, ADN.

24. "Urge War Relief for Negro Soldiers," *Wilmington News,* 20 August 1917, in TNCF, reel 7, heading "Soldiers."

25. *New York Age,* 5 January 1918, 1.

26. *The Crisis* 16 (June 1918): 83.

27. *The Crisis* 16 (August 1918): 188.

28. Bond to Dunbar-Nelson, 18 March 1918, ADN.

29. Dunbar-Nelson's best-known war poems, "I Sit and Sew" and "Let Me Live," were published in the *A.M.E. Church Review* in July 1918. Another poem, "The Song of the Land," a patriotic anthem, remains unpublished, but it is available in her personal papers at the Alice Dunbar-Nelson Collection, Morris Library, University of Delaware.

30. Blair, *The Woman's Committee,* 21.

31. Ibid., 19–20.

32. Mary B. Talbert, Buffalo, N.Y., to State Presidents and Heads of Departments of the NACW, 4 August 1917, WC Central Correspondence.

33. Mary B. Talbert, Buffalo, N.Y., to Clarinda Lamar, Washington, D.C., 18 January 1918, WC Central Correspondence; Mary B. Talbert, Buffalo, N.Y., to Anna Howard Shaw, Washington, D.C., 19 September 1918, WC Central Correspondence.

34. Anne Meis Knupfer, *Towards a Tenderer Humanity and Nobler Womanhood: African American Women's Clubs in Turn-of-the-Century Chicago* (New York: New York University Press, 1996), 21.

35. Elizabeth Lindsay Davis, *Lifting as They Climb* (New York: G. K. Hall, 1984), 60–62.

36. Mary B. Talbert, Fort Smith, Ark., to Anna Howard Shaw, Washington, D.C., 25 October 1918, WC Central Correspondence; Hannah Patterson, Washington, D.C., to Mary B. Talbert, Buffalo, N.Y., 29 October 1918, WC Central Correspondence.

37. Committee on Women's Defense Work of the Council of National Defense, Weekly and Monthly Reports, May 1917 to October 1918. Monthly Report, Work Accomplished: 15 October to 15 November 1917; 19 April 1918. Records of the Committee on Women's Defense Work, Records of the Council of National Defense, Record Group 62, National Archives Records Administration, College Park, Md. (hereafter cited as WC Monthly Reports with date).

38. WC Monthly Reports, 19 April 1918; 20 June 1918.

39. WC Monthly Reports, 20 August 1918.

40. Alice Dunbar-Nelson, New Orleans, La., to Hannah Patterson, Washington, D.C., 14 August 1918, WC Central Correspondence.

41. "New Orleans Colored Women Told Part They Must Play in War," *New Orleans Item,* 16 August 1918, WC Central Correspondence.

42. "To Treat with Servants: Woman Suggests League to Require References from Negro Help," *New Orleans Times-Picayune,* 12 May 1918, in TNCF reel 8, heading "Labor and Unions." For more on pan-toting see Mia Bay, *The White Image in the Black Mind: African American Ideas about White People, 1830–1925* (New York: Oxford University Press, 2000).

43. Robin D. G. Kelley, *Hammer and Hoe: Alabama Communists during the Great Depression* (Chapel Hill: University of North Carolina Press, 1990).

44. Dunbar-Nelson to Patterson, 14 August 1918, WC Central Correspondence.

45. "Negro Workers Organize," *New Orleans Picayune,* 23 May 1918; "Not Spies, Says Servant Union Leader Here," *New Orleans States,* 23 July 1918, in TNCF reel 8, heading "Labor and Unions."

46. Hannah Patterson, Washington, D.C., to Alice Dunbar-Nelson, New Orleans, La., 19 August 1918, ADN. An affiliation between the Woman's Committee and NAWSA was also strengthened by the presence of the former and current presidents of NAWSA on the Woman's Committee executive board, Anna Howard Shaw and Carrie Chapman Catt.

47. Dunbar-Nelson to Patterson, 14 August 1918.

48. Ibid.

49. Alice Dunbar-Nelson, Como, Miss., to Hannah Patterson, Washington, D.C., 19 August 1918, WC Central Correspondence.

50. Alice Dunbar-Nelson, Sardis, Miss., to Hannah Patterson, Washington, D.C., 20 August 1918, WC Central Correspondence.

51. Alice Dunbar-Nelson, Sardis, Miss., to Hannah Patterson, Washington, D.C., 21 August 1918, WC Central Correspondence.

52. *Vicksburg Evening Post,* 31 July 1918, 24–27, 29.

53. Alice Dunbar-Nelson, Jackson, Miss., to Hannah Patterson, Washington, D.C., 23 August 1918, WC Central Correspondence.

54. Alice Dunbar-Nelson, Selma, Ala., to Hannah Patterson, Washington, D.C., 25 August 1918, WC Central Correspondence.

55. Ibid.

56. Dunbar-Nelson, "Things That Have to be Explained to Colored Audiences and Committees."

57. "Negro Women Adopt Rule of Strike Pickets," *Mobile Advertiser,* 26 April 1918, TNCF reel 8, heading "Labor and Unions."

58. Alice Dunbar-Nelson, Mobile, Ala., to Hannah Patterson, Washington, D.C., 29 August 1918, WC Central Correspondence.

59. Alice Dunbar-Nelson, Birmingham, Ala., to Hannah Patterson, Washington, D.C., 28 August 1918, WC Central Correspondence.

60. Ibid.

61. Ibid.

62. Alice Dunbar-Nelson, Birmingham, Ala., to Hannah Patterson, Washington, D.C., 26 August 1918, WC Central Correspondence

63. Alice Dunbar-Nelson, Jacksonville, Fla., to Hannah Patterson, Washington, D.C., 30 August 1918, WC Central Correspondence.

64. Ibid.

65. Hannah Patterson, Washington, D.C., to Hannah Jackson, 28 August 1918, ADN.

66. Ibid.; Alice Dunbar-Nelson, Jacksonville, Fla., to Hannah Patterson, 31 August, 1 September 1918, WC Central Correspondence.

67. Dunbar-Nelson to Patterson, 28 August 1918, WC Central Correspondence.

68. Dunbar-Nelson to Patterson, 22 August 1918, WC Central Correspondence.

69. "Madam Cary Appointed," *Atlanta Constitution,* 9 August 1918; "Work among Colored Women," *Atlanta Constitution* [n.d.], September 1918, in TNCF, reel 8, heading "Labor, Welfare Work during War."

70. Alice Dunbar-Nelson, Atlanta, Ga., to Hannah Patterson, Washington, D.C., 3 September 1918, WC Central Correspondence.

71. Alice Dunbar-Nelson, Atlanta, Ga., to Hannah Patterson, Washington, D.C., 4 September 1918, WC Central Correspondence.

72. Ibid.

73. Ibid.

74. "Woman Suffrage," *Christian Recorder,* 8 August 1918, in TNCF, reel 8, heading "Politics."

75. Rosalyn Terborg-Penn, *African American Women and the Struggle for the Vote, 1850–1920* (Bloomington: Indiana University Press, 1998).

76. Alice Dunbar-Nelson, Columbia, S.C., to Hannah Patterson, Washington, D.C., 5 September 1918, WC Central Correspondence.

77. Alice Dunbar-Nelson, Charlotte, N.C., to Hannah Patterson, Washington, D.C., 7 September 1918, WC Central Correspondence.

78. Ibid.

79. "Negro Women in War Work," *Beaumont Texas Journal,* 12 January 1918, in TNCF, reel 9, heading "War Conditions and Results."

80. Alice Dunbar-Nelson, Knoxville, Tenn., to Hannah Patterson, Washington, D.C., 10 September 1918, WC Central Correspondence.

81. "Appeal to Servants," *Nashville Banner,* 31 March 1918, in TNCF, reel 9, heading "War Conditions and Results."

82. Council of National Defense, State Council Section, News Bulletin and Press Release, 18 September, 1918, ADN; Blair, *The Woman's Committee,* 125–126.

83. Hannah Patterson, Washington, D.C., to Alice Dunbar-Nelson, Wilmington, Del., 11 October 1918, ADN.

84. Ibid.

85. Irene Goins, Springfield, Ill., to Alice Dunbar-Nelson, December 1918, ADN.

86. Emmett J. Scott, Washington, D.C., to War Camp Community Service Headquarters, New York, N.Y., 2 December 1918, ADN; Rosalie Murphy Baum, "Alice Dunbar-Nelson," in *African American Women: A Biographical Dictionary,* ed. Dorothy Salem (New York: Garland Publishing, 1993), 165–167.

87. Dunbar-Nelson, "Negro Women in War Work," in *The Official History of the American Negro in the World War,* ed. Emmett J. Scott (Chicago: Homewood Press, 1914; reprint New York: Arno Press, 1969), 374–397.

88. Ibid., 376.

89. Ibid., 376–77, 383–84.

90. Breen, "Black Women and the Great War," 424–425.

91. Ibid., 376.

92. *Handbook of War Camp Community Service: Policies, Fundamental Principles and Instructions* (New York: War Camp Community Service, Inc., 1918), 8.

93. Ibid., 7, 15–16.

94. Ibid., 13.

95. Ibid., 18–20.

96. Ibid., 4.

97. Ibid., 91.

98. *War Camp Community Service and the Negro Soldier* (New York: War Camp Community Service, Inc., 1920), 2–3.

99. Ibid., 3.

100. Mary Church Terrell, *A Colored Woman in a White World* (Washington, D.C.: Ransdell, 1940; reprint New York: G. K. Hall, 1996), 318–319 (page citations are to the reprint edition).

101. Mary Church Terrell, "Conditions and Recommendations for Biloxi," ca., 4 March 1919, box 26, folder 19, Mary Church Terrell Papers, Library of Congress, Washington, D.C. (hereafter cited as title and date, followed by MCT Papers); Terrell, *A Colored Woman in a White World,* 323–324. Terrell recounted the interview verbatim in her autobiography, but she declined to reveal Mr. Tonsmire by name, as were most of the reluctant WCCS workers in her autobiography. Consult the unpublished interviews in the Mary Church Terrell Papers for a fuller representation of the discussions.

102. Ibid.

103. Mary Church Terrell, "Conditions and Recommendation for Gulfport, Mississippi," ca., 6 March 1919, MCT Papers.

104. Ibid.

105. Mary Church Terrell, "Interview With Mr. Stacy A. Bowing, Community Organizer of Chattanooga, Tennessee," 13 February 1919, MCT Papers.

106. Mary Church Terrell, "Attitude of Eight Representative Cities of Tennessee, Alabama, Mississippi and Florida Toward Having a Colored Worker Sent Down from Headquarters to Work in the Colored District," 12 March 1919, MCT Papers.

107. Ibid.

108. Mary Church Terrell, "Conditions and Recommendations in Pensacola," 8 March 1919, MCT Papers.

109. Ibid.

110. Mary Church Terrell, "Interview with Mr. Wm. T. Elges, Community Organizer in Montgomery, Alabama," 21 February 1919, MCT Papers.

111. Mary Church Terrell, "Conditions and Recommendations in Pensacola," 8 March 1919, "Conditions and Recommendations for Atlanta, Ga." [n.d.], "Interview with Mrs. Gibson, and Mr. Stearns, Macon, Ga.," 12 March 1919, MCT Papers.

112. Mary Church Terrell, "Report of Conference with Mrs. Aime Regarding Need for Work with Colored Girls in New York City," 12 March 1919, MCT Papers, 2; Terrell, *A Colored Woman in a White World,* 327.

113. Ibid.

114. Mary Church Terrell to Robert Terrell, 24 March 1919, MCT Papers.

115. Terrell, *A Colored Woman in a White World,* 327–328.

116. Dunbar-Nelson, "Negro Women and War Work," 376.

117. Ibid.

## 3. Volunteering with the Red Cross and the YWCA

1. Aileen Cole Stewart, "Ready to Serve," *American Journal of Nursing* 63, no. 9 (September 1963): 85–87.

2. Eva Perry Moore, "Report of the Department of the Maintenance of Existing Social Service Agencies," 26 March 1918, in *Minutes of Meetings of the Committee on Women's Defense Work, May 2, 1917 to February 12, 1919 and Weekly and Monthly Reports of the Committee on Women's Defense Work, May 12, 1917–October 15, 1918,* Council of National Defense, Woman's Committee (Washington, D.C.: National Archives and Records Service, 1978), 438.

3. Darlene Clark Hine, "The Call That Never Came: Black Women Nurses and World War I, an Historical Note," *Indiana Military History Journal* 15 (January 1983); reprint, *Black Women in US History* (Brooklyn, N.Y.: Carlson Publishing, 1990), 650–653 (page citations are to the reprint edition).

4. Lavinia L. Dock and Sarah Elizabeth Pickett, "Mobilization," in *History of American Red Cross Nursing,* eds. Lavinia L. Dock et al. (New York: Macmillan, 1922), 289, 291–292; Connie L. Reeves, "Invisible Soldiers: Military Nurses," in *Gender Camouflage: Women and the U.S. Military,* ed. Francine D'Amico and Laurie Weinstein (New York: New York University Press, 1999), 17–18.

5. "Comment Here and There," *New York Age,* 15 June 1918, 4; "The First Six Months," *New York Age,* 13 July 1918, 4, Adah Thoms, comp., *Pathfinders: A History of the Progress of Colored Graduate Nurses* (New York: Kay Printing House, 1929), 155–156; Monroe N. Work, *Negro Yearbook and Annual Encyclopedia of the Negro* (Tuskegee, Ala.: Negro Yearbook Publishing Co., 1918), 90; Hine, "The Call That Never Came," 650–651.

6. "Negro Nurses: A Complaint That 600 Who Are Ready Are Not Wanted," *New York Sun,* 6 June 1918, in TNCF, reel 8, heading "Nurses."

7. "Minutes of the National Committee on Red Cross Nursing Service," 5 December 1911, 20 June 1917, cited in Thoms, *Pathfinders,* 155–156.

8. "Colored Nurses Seek War Service," *Philadelphia Telegraph,* 6 June 1918, in TNCF, reel 8, heading "Nurses."

9. Thoms, *Pathfinders,* vii–ix.

10. Adah Thoms, "Greetings to the National Medical Association—Delivered by Mrs. Adah Bell Thoms, R.N., at Philadelphia, August 30, 1917," *Journal of the National Medical Association* (n.d.) 1918, in TNCF, reel 8, heading "Nurses." For more on the battle to integrate

the nursing corps, see Darlene Clark Hine, *Black Women in White: Racial Conflict and Cooperation in the Nursing Profession, 1890–1950* (Bloomington: Indiana University Press, 1989).

11. "Colored Women Sail for France," 25 May 1918, *New York Post,* in TNCF, reel 9, heading "YMCA and YWCA."

12. "Negro Nurses," *New York Sun,* 6 June 1918, in TNCF, reel 8, heading "Nurses."

13. "Start Big Movement to Send Colored Nurses to Europe; Women Hold Patriotic Meeting," *New York Age,* 18 May 1918, TNCF, reel 8, heading "Nurses."

14. "The First Six Months," *New York Age,* 13 July 1918, 4.

15. "Colored Nurses Seek War Service," *Philadelphia Telegraph,* 6 June 1918, TNCF, reel 8, heading "Nurses."

16. Stewart, "Ready to Serve," 85.

17. "2,000 Colored Nurses Enroll in the Red Cross: Congratulatory Letter Read from Theodore Roosevelt at Convention of Nurses," *New York Age,* 7 September 1918, TNCF, reel 8, heading "Nurses."

18. Ibid.

19. Thoms, *Pathfinders,* 166; Mabel K. Staupers, *No Time for Prejudice: A Story of the Integration of Negroes in Nursing in the United States* (New York: Macmillan, 1961), 97–98.

20. Stewart, "Ready to Serve," 86.

21. "No More Nurses Are Needed Overseas," 28 December 1917, *New York Age,* in TNCF, reel 8, heading "Nurses."

22. Stewart, "Ready to Serve," 87.

23. "Prejudice and the Color Line Are Paradox Even in the Y.W.C.A. Shown by Miss Bowles Visit," 15 July 1918, *Denver Post,* in TNCF, reel 9, heading "YWCA."

24. Ibid.

25. Judith Weisenfeld, *African American Women and Christian Activism: New York's Black YWCA, 1905–1945* (Cambridge, Mass.: Harvard University Press, 1997), 9–14, 124.

26. Cynthia Neverdon-Morton, *Afro-American Women of the South and the Advancement of the Race, 1895–1935* (Knoxville: University of Tennessee Press, 1989), 222.

27. Addie W. Hunton, comp., *Beginnings among Colored Women* (New York: Young Wom-en's Christian Association, 1913), 5–6, YWCA National Board Records, Sophia Smith Collection, Smith College Library, Smith College, Northampton, Mass. (hereafter cited as YWCA Papers, SSC, with folder number and description); Jane Olcott Walters, comp., "History of Colored Work, 1907–1920" (n.p., November–December 1920), 24, 26–60, Young Women's Christian Association Papers, SLR.

28. Lucille O'Connell, "Eva D. Bowles," in *African American Women: A Biographical Dictionary,* ed. Dorothy Salem (New York: Garland Publishing, 1993), 54–56; Committee on Colored Work, "Minutes," 13 November 1918, cited in Walters, "History of Colored Work," 68, Young Women's Christian Association Papers, SLR.

29. Scott, "The Negro in the World War," 611; "$400,000 to be Spent for Work among Colored Girls," November 1918 (unknown newspaper), in TNCF, reel 9, heading "YWCA."

30. Eva Bowles, "Negro Women and the War," *Southern Workman* 47 (September 1918): 425.

31. "Officers Stop Riot at Camp Upton," 14 September 1917, *New York Times;* "Negro Troops Clash with White Men; Clash at Yaphank," 13 September 1917, *Brooklyn Eagle,* in TNCF, reel 7, heading "Soldiers."

32. "Negro Women Warned Not to Go Camp Dodge," 23 November 1917, *Birmingham Advertisement,* in TNCF, reel 7, heading "Soldiers."

33. Alice Dunbar-Nelson, "Negro Women in War Work," in *The Official History of the American Negro in the World War,* ed. Emmett J. Scott (Chicago: Homewood Press, 1914; reprint New York: Arno Press, 1969), 386.

34. Patty B. Semple, "War Work at Home," *Southern Workman* 48 (January 1919): 7.

35. Jane Olcott, *The Work of Colored Women* (New York: National Board of the Young Women's Christian Association, 1919), 15; Dunbar-Nelson, "Negro Women in War Work," 380.

36. Olcott, *The Work of Colored Women,* 15.

37. Ibid., 16.

38. Ibid., 16–20. Other base camps with Hostess Houses were: Camp Gordon, Ga.; Camp Grant, Ill.; Camp Dodge, Iowa; Camp Funston, Kan.; Camp Taylor, Ky.; Camp Devens, Mass.; Camp Custer, Mich.; Camp Green, N.C.; Camp Travis, Tex.; Camps Jackson and Wadsworth, S.C.; and Camps Alexander and Lee, Va.

39. Lugenia Burns Hope, "Mission of the Hostess House," *New York Age,* 6 July 1918, 6.

40. Jacqueline Anne Rouse, *Lugenia Burns Hope, Black Southern Reformer* (Athens: University of Georgia Press, 1989), 108–110.

41. Ibid.

42. Olcott, *The Work of Colored Women,* 15.

43. Ibid.

44. Eva Bowles, Executive Director of Colored Work, "Report for the Commission on Morale," box 42-B, folder 12, YWCA Papers, SSC.

45. Eva Bowles, "Negro Women and the Y.W.C.A. of the United States," box 41, folder 2, YWCA Papers, SSC.

46. Committee on Colored Work, "Minutes," 9 August 1918, quoted in "History of Colored Work," 67.

47. Ibid.

48. Ibid., 20.

49. Olcott, *Work of Colored Women,* 7–8. Please see Adrienne Lash Jones, "Struggle among the Saints: Black Women in the YWCA," in *Men and Women Adrift: The YMCA and YWCA in the City* (New York: New York University Press, 1997); Adrienne Lash Jones, *Jane Edna Hunter: A Case Study of Black Leadership, 1920–1950* (Brooklyn: Carlson Publishing, 1990); Evelyn Brooks Higginbotham, *Righteous Discontent: The Women's Movement in the Black Baptist Church* (Cambridge, Mass.: Harvard University Press, 1993).

50. "Open Colored Branch of Y.W.C.A. in Germantown," *Philadelphia Press,* 19 November 1918; "Colored Women to Form Branch of Local 'Y,'" *Dayton News,* 29 October 1918; "Colored Girls Will Have Club," *Detroit Times,* 7 October 1918, all in TNCF, reel 9, heading "YWCA."

51. Committee on War Work among Colored Girls and Women, "War Work among Colored Girls and Women," box 428, folder 12, YWCA Papers, SSC.

52. Dunbar-Nelson, "Negro Women in War Work," 376.

53. "War Opportunities for Colored Women," *New York Post,* 27 March 1918, in TNCF, reel 9, heading "YWCA."

54. National Association of Colored Women, 11th Biennial Convention Minutes, 12–16 July 1920, 18–19, in NACW Papers.

55. Bureau of Colored Work, "Conference of Outstanding Colored Women," 24 September 1920, in box 41, folder 2, "Interracial-Negro-History, 1913–1943," YWCA Papers, SSC.

56. Gilmore, *Gender and Jim Crow,* 194–195.

57. Olcott, *The Work of Colored Women,* 122.

58. "Report of Eva Bowles, Secretary for Colored Work Convention, 1915–1920," in box 42B, folder 6, YWCA Papers, SSC.

## 4. Supporting Black Doughboys in France

1. "Entertained at the Home of the President," 26 October, *New York Age,* in TNCF, reel 9, heading "YWCA."

2. Darlene Clark Hine, "Rape and the Inner Lives of Black Women in the Middle West," in *Unequal Sisters: A Multi-Cultural Reader in U.S. Women's History,* eds. Vicki L. Ruiz and Ellen Carol DuBois, 2d ed. (New York: Routledge, 1994), 342–347. Deborah Gray White found the same pattern in the memoirs of black professional women, particularly Mary Church Terrell. See White, *Too Heavy a Load.*

3. Addie W. Hunton and Kathryn Johnson, *Two Colored Women with the American Expeditionary Forces* (New York: Brooklyn Eagle Press, 1920), 7.

4. Ibid., 11–12.

5. The four most prominent African Americans to discuss American race relations at international conferences and forums prior to 1920 were Frederick Douglass, William Wells Brown, Ida B. Wells-Barnett, and Mary Church Terrell. See Frederick Douglass, *Narrative of the Life of Frederick Douglass, An American Slave, Written by Himself* (Boston: Anti-Slavery Office, 1845; reprint Cambridge, Mass.: Belknap Press, 1960); William Wells Brown, *Narrative of William W. Brown, A Fugitive Slave, Written by Himself* (London: C. Gilpin, 1849; reprint New York: Mentor Book, 1993); William Wells Brown, *Three Years in Europe: Or, Places I Have Seen and People I Have Met* (London: Charles Gilpin, 1852); Ida B. Wells-Barnett, *Crusade for Justice: The Autobiography of Ida B. Wells* (Chicago: University of Chicago Press, 1970); Mary Church Terrell, *A Colored Woman in a White World* (New York: G. K. Hall, 1996).

6. Nina Mjagkij, *Light in the Darkness: African Americans and the YMCA: 1852–1946* (Lexington: University Press of Kentucky, 1994), 8–52. Addie D. Waites Hunton, William Hunton's wife, wrote the most complete biography of the director of the Colored Work Department of the YMCA. See Addie W. Hunton, *William Alphaeus Hunton: A Pioneer Prophet of Young Men* (New York: Association Press, 1938).

7. Charles H. Williams, "Negro Y.M.C.A. Secretaries Overseas," *Southern Workman* 49 (January 1920): 24–35, 24.

8. Ibid., 24.

9. Hunton and Johnson, *Two Colored Women,* 7.

10. *Who's Who in Colored America, 1927* (New York: Who's Who in Colored America Corporation Publishing, 1927), 50; *Who's Who in Colored America,* 2d ed., 1928–1929 (New York: Who's Who in Colored America, 1929), 94; W. Allison Sweeney, *The History of the American Negro in the Great World War: His Splendid Record in the Battle Zones of Europe* (Chicago: Cuneo-Henneberry, 1919), 251–252.

11. Addie W. Hunton, "The National Association of Colored Women," *The Crisis* 2 (May 1911): 17.

12. Sylvia Dannett, *Profiles of Negro Womanhood,* vol. 2 (New York: M. W. Lads, 1964), 118–120; Faye E. Chadwell, "Addie Waites Hunton," in *African American Women: A Biographical Dictionary,* ed. Dorothy Salem (New York: Garland Publishing, 1993), 263–266; Jean Blackwell Hutson, "Addie D. Waites Hunton," in *Dictionary of American Negro*

*Biography,* ed. Rayford Logan and Michael R. Winston (New York: Norton, 1982), 337–338.

13. Dorothy Salem, *To Better Our World: Black Women in Organized Reform, 1890–1920* (Brooklyn, N.Y.: Carlson Publishing, 1990), 172–174.

14. Kathryn Johnson, "The Negro and the World War," *Half-Century Magazine,* no. 6 (June 1917): 13.

15. Kathryn Johnson, "The Colored Soldiers at Camp Dodge," *Half-Century Magazine* 4, no. 2 (February 1918): 8.

16. *Who's Who in Colored America,* 1st ed., 108.

17. Hunton and Johnson, *Two Colored Women,* 41–42.

18. Ibid., 139.

19. Ridgely Torrence, *The Story of John Hope* (New York: Macmillan, 1948), 221; Hunton and Johnson, *Two Colored Women,* 34.

20. Hunton and Johnson, *Two Colored Women,* 32–33.

21. Mjagkij, *Light in the Darkness,* 86–90.

22. Hunton and Johnson, *Two Colored Women,* 214, 202–210.

23. "Report to the Committee on Colored Work of the Sub-Committee Appointed to Investigate the Charges against Dr. Moorland" [n.d., probably 1919], box 2, folder "Correspondence and Reports, 1918–1920," Records of the YMCA Colored Work Department, Kautz Family YMCA Archives, Elmer L. Anderson Library, University of Minnesota (hereafter cited as document, box number, folder, and YMCA Colored Work Department).

24. Matthew Bullock, Paris, France, to Jesse Moorland, Washington, D.C., 10 August 1918, box 2, "WWI Letters: Correspondence with Soldiers and Secretaries in France," YMCA Colored Work Department.

25. Hunton and Johnson, *Two Colored Women,* 23–24.

26. G. W. Moore (n.p., probably Washington, D.C.) to R. B. DeFrantz (n.p., probably Washington, D.C.), 30 August 1918, box 2, "WWI Correspondence and Reports," YMCA Colored Work Department.

27. A. L. James, Florida, to R. B. DeFrantz (n.p., probably Washington, D.C.), 16 July 1919, box 2, "WWI Correspondence and Reports," YMCA Colored Work Department.

28. Frank Nichols (n.p., probably Washington, D.C.) to Jesse Moorland, Washington, D.C., 22 July 1919, box 2, "World War I Correspondence and Reports," YMCA Colored Work Department.

29. Kathryn Johnson, Paris, France, to Jesse Moorland, Washington, D.C., 29 September 1918, box 2, "WWI Letters," YMCA Colored Work Department.

30. Ibid.

31. Hunton and Johnson, *Two Colored Women,* 191.

32. "Report to the Committee on Colored Work of the Sub-Committee Appointed to Investigate the Charges against Dr. Moorland," YMCA Colored Work Department.

33. Nichols to Moorland, 22 July 1919.

34. Hunton and Johnson, *Two Colored Women,* 26.

35. Ibid., 38.

36. Ibid., 102–103.

37. Guidebooks and other touring information for white American soldiers can be found in boxes 50 and 51, "Leave Area Publications, 1918–1922," Records of the YMCA and USA Armed Services Division, Kautz Family YMCA Archives, Special Collections, Elmer L. Anderson Library, University of Minnesota, Minneapolis, Minn. (hereafter cited as "Leave Area Publications" and Records of the YMCA and USA Armed Services Division).

38. Hunton and Johnson, *Two Colored Women,* 102, 182–183.

39. "Documents of the War," *The Crisis* (May 1919): 16–17.

40. Ibid.

41. Reprinted in *Two Colored Women,* 53–54.

42. Emmett J. Scott, *The Official History of the American Negro in the World War* (New York: Arno Press, 1969), 139.

43. Hunton and Johnson, *Two Colored Women,* 23–24, 41.

44. Reprinted in Hunton and Johnson, *Two Colored Women,* 46–47.

45. See Haynes, *A Night of Violence: The Houston Riot of 1917.*

46. Hunton and Johnson, *Two Colored Women,* 146.

47. Ibid., 144.

48. Ibid., 142.

49. Ibid., 157; Williams, "Negro Y.M.C.A. Secretaries Overseas," 33–34.

50. Williams, "Negro Y.M.C.A. Secretaries Overseas," 34.

51. Hunton and Johnson, *Two Colored Women,* 156.

52. Ibid., 156–157.

53. Ibid., 22.

54. Bullock to Moorland, YMCA Colored Work Department.

55. Hunton and Johnson, *Two Colored Women,* 155–156.

56. Williams, "Negro Y.M.C.A. Secretaries Overseas," 35.

57. Ibid.; Hunton and Johnson, *Two Colored Women,* 20.

58. Ibid.

59. Ibid., 141.

60. "Entertained at the Home of the President," 26 October, *New York Age,* in TNCF, reel 9, heading "YWCA."

61. Ibid., 139.

62. "United States Army and Navy YMCA in France Saint-Nazaire: Soldiers and Sailors Handbook, 1917," in "Leave Area Publications," Records of the YMCA and USA Armed Services Division.

63. Ibid., 26.

64. Ibid., 143.

65. Hunton and Johnson, *Two Colored Women,* 234–235, 239.

66. Barry Stentiford, "Historical Controversies: Performances of U.S. Black Troops," in *Encyclopedia of World War I, 1914–1918* (Denver: ABC-CLIO, 2005); Robert Edgerton, *Hidden Heroism: Black Soldiers in America's Wars* (Boulder, Col.: Westview Press, 2001), 85, 83–90.

67. Robert R. Moton, "Negro Troops in France," *Southern Workman* 48 (May 1919): 219.

68. Ibid.; "Robert R. Moton," *The Crisis* 18 (May 1919): 9.

69. Moton, "Negro Troops in France," 219–220. A brief history of the Service of Supplies Unit is outlined in Scott, *The Official History of the American Negro in the World War;* and Charles H. Williams, *Sidelight on Negro Soldiers* (Boston: B. J. Brimmer Company, 1923).

70. Moton, "Negro Troops in France," 223–224.

71. Ibid., 223; "With Negro Troops," *Southern Workman* 48 (February 1919): 87.

72. "Robert R. Moton," 9–10.

73. Hunton and Johnson, *Two Colored Women,* 230–231.

74. Ibid., 253–254.

75. Hunton and Johnson, *Two Colored Women,* 152; Williams, "Negro YMCA Secretaries Overseas," 33–34.

76. Ibid., 253.

77. "No More Nurses Needed Overseas," *New York Age,* 28 December 1918, in TNCF, reel 8, heading "Nurses."

78. J. E. Blanton, St. Helena, S.C., to R. B. DeFrantz, Washington, D.C., 9 September 1919, box 2, "World War I Correspondence and Reports," YMCA Colored Work Department.

79. Hunton and Johnson, *Two Colored Women,* 28–29.

80. Ibid., 157.

## 5. Gender Relations and the New Negro

1. "The Lynching Industry, 1919," *The Crisis* 19, no. 4 (February 1920): 183–186; National Association for the Advancement of Colored People, *Thirty Years of Lynching in the United States, 1889–1918* (New York: National Association For the Advancement of Colored People, 1919; reprint New York: Negro Universities Press, 1969), 29.

2. Johnson, *Black Manhattan,* 246, 231–259.

3. "Riot Trouble Is Followed by Quiet Sunday," *Charleston Evening Post,* 12 May 1919, in TNCF, reel 11, heading "Race Riots."

4. Chicago Commission on Race Relations, *The Negro in Chicago: A Study of Race Relations and a Race Riot* (Chicago: University of Chicago Press, 1922), 17, 1–52, passim.

5. George E. Haynes, "What Negroes Think of the Race Riots," *Daily Herald* (unknown city), 14 August 1919, in TNCF, reel 10, heading "Race Riots."

6. Clayton D. Laurie, "U.S. Army and the Omaha Race Riot," *Nebraska History* 72 (Fall 1991): 135–143. For a further exploration of the vice underworld operating in Omaha in the 1910s, as well as a graphic description of the lynching, see "The Real Causes of Two Race Riots," *The Crisis* 19 (December 1919): 56–62.

7. "The Riot at Longview, Texas," *The Crisis* 18 (October 1919): 297–298.

8. "Asks a Riot Inquiry," *Washington Post,* 23 July 1919, in TNCF, reel 10, heading "Race Riots."

9. "The Rights of the Black Man," *Washington Bee,* 2 August 1919.

10. James Weldon Johnson, "The Riots: An N.A.A.C.P. Investigation," *The Crisis* 18 (September 1919): 241–243.

11. "Defend Negro in Race Riots," *Newark Star,* 25 July 1919, in TNCF, reel 10, heading "Race Riots."

12. Bay, *The White Image in the Black Mind,* 204.

13. As quoted in Chicago Commission on Race Relations, *The Negro in Chicago,* 30.

14. Ibid., 31.

15. Walter F. White, "Chicago and Its Eight Reasons," *The Crisis* 18 (October 1919): 293–297.

16. McMurry, *To Keep the Waters Troubled,* 325.

17. "Urges Joint Committee to Solve Race Problem," *Chicago Journal,* 29 July 1919, in TNCF, reel 10, heading "Race Riots."

18. Margaret Higonnet and Patrice L. R., "The Double Helix," in *Behind the Lines, Gender and the Two World Wars,* ed. Margaret Higonnet (New Haven, Conn.: Yale University Press, 1987), 35, 31–47.

19. "Defend Negro in Race Riots," *Newark Star,* 25 July 1919, in TNCF, reel 10, heading "Race Riots."

20. Claude McCay, "If We Must Die," in *Cornerstones: An Anthology of African American Literature,* ed. Melvin Donaldson (New York: St. Martin's Press, 1996), 134.

21. "Delaware State Federation of Colored Women's Clubs Holds Annual Session," 28 October 1922, in TNCF, reel 17, heading "Women's Work."

22. Mary Church Terrell, "The Race Worm Turns" (n.d., probably 1920), in MCT Papers, 1.

23. "Honorable Mrs. Talbert Returns from Abroad," *National Notes* (October–December 1920): 12, reel 23, NACW Papers.

24. Wanda Hendricks, *Gender, Race, and Politics in the Midwest: Black Club Women in Illinois* (Bloomington: Indiana University Press, 1998), 126–128.

25. "National Association of Colored Women's Clubs," *Woman's Forum* (September–October 1922): 5, in MCT Papers, LOC, container 26, heading "Terrell, Mary Church: Biographical and Testimonial."

26. "National Association of Colored Women Outline Progressive Program," *Dallas Express,* 12 February 1921, in TNCF, reel 15, heading "Women's Work."

27. White, *Too Heavy a Load,* 120.

28. "The New Negro Vs. the Old-*Age* Readers Discuss the Subject," *New York Age,* 20 March 1920, in TNCF, reel 12, heading "Race Consciousness."

29. "A Great Racial Awakening," *Atlanta Independent* (n.d., 1920), in TNCF, reel 12, heading "Race Consciousness."

30. Alain Locke, "The New Negro," in *The New Negro: An Interpretation,* ed. Alain Locke, with new Introduction by Allan H. Spear (New York: Albert & Charles Boni, 1925; reprint New York: Johnson Reprint Corporation, 1968), 11, 14; David Levering Lewis, *W.E.B. Du Bois: The Fight for Equality in the American Century, 1919–1963* (New York: Henry Holt, 2000), 165.

31. Beverly Guy-Sheftall, *Words of Fire: An Anthology of African-American Feminist Thought* (New York: New Press, 1995), 79.

32. Elise Johnson McDougald, "The Task of Negro Womanhood," in *The New Negro: An Interpretation,* ed. Alain Locke (New York: Albert & Charles Boni, 1925; reprint New York: Johnson Reprint Corporation, 1968), 370, 371, 369–382. See also Elise Johnson McDougald, "The Struggle of Negro Women for Sex and Race Emancipation," *Survey Graphic* (October 1924–March 1925); reprinted in Guy-Sheftall, *Words of Fire: An Anthology of African-American Feminist Thought.*

33. Ibid., 371, 378, 380–382.

34. Bay, *The White Image in the Black Mind,* 216.

35. "Women Voters Hold Meeting," *Savannah Tribune,* 16 March 1922, in TNCF, reel 16, heading "Politics."

36. See Robert Zangrando, *The NAACP Crusade against Lynching* (Philadelphia: Temple University Press, 1980).

37. Minutes of the Board of Directors, 12 June 1922, National Association for the Advancement of Colored People, Part I, 1909–1950, "Meetings of the Board of Directors, Records of Annual Conferences, Major Speeches, and Special reports," University Microfilm of America, reel 1.

38. Ida B. Wells, *Crusade for Justice, The Autobiography of Ida B. Wells,* ed. Alfreda M. Duster (Chicago: University of Chicago Press, 1970), 397–404.

39. "Has Spent $35,000 Fighting Lynching," *Baltimore Afro-American,* 9 December 1921, in TNCF, reel 14, heading "NAACP."

40. McMurry, *To Keep the Waters Troubled,* 327.

41. "Tulsa's Terrible Tale Is Told," *Chicago Whip,* 11 June 1921, in TNCF, reel 14, heading "Riots."

42. Alfred L. Brophy, *Reconstructing the Dreamland: The Tulsa Race Riot of 1921* (New York: Oxford University Press, 2002), 24–25, 60–70, 77–78.

43. Anti-Lynching Crusaders, "Foreign Press Service Release" (October 1922), James Weldon Johnson Collection, Series II, Grace Nail Johnson Collection, Beinecke Rare Book and Manuscript Library, Yale University, New Haven, Conn. (hereafter cited as ALC/JWJC).

44. Chairman of the Publicity Committee of the Anti-Lynching Crusaders, "Statement to Mrs. Nahum D. Brascher, The Associated Press," 16 November 1922, ALC/JWJC.

45. Mary B. Talbert and Mary E. Jackson, "A Million Women United to Suppress Lynching," ALC/JWJC, 3.

46. Mary Jane Brown, *Eradicating This Evil: Women in the American Anti-Lynching Movement, 1892–1940* (New York: Garland Publishing, 2000), 171–222; Rosalyn Terborg-Penn, "African-American Women's Networks in the Anti-Lynching Crusade," in *Gender, Class, Race, and Reform in the Progressive Era,* ed. Noralee Frankel and Nancy S. Dye (Lexington, Ky.: The University Press of Lexington, 1991), 157–158.

47. Ibid.

48. Mary B. Talbert to Grace Nail Johnson, 25 June 1922, ALC/JWJC.

49. Salem, *To Better Our World,* 233, 232–234.

50. Reprint in "Encouraging Signs of Race Progress," *A.M.E. Church Review* 35 (July 1918): 38–39.

51. Chairman of the Publicity Committee of the Anti-Lynching Crusaders to Mrs. Nahum D. Brascher, Associated Negro Press.

52. *New York Times,* 5, 18, 26, 27 January 1922.

53. *New York Times,* 24, 30 May 1922.

54. Mary B. Talbert to Grace Nail Johnson, 13 October 1922, ALC/JWJC.

55. "The Anti-Lynching Crusaders," *Woman's Forum* (September and October, 1922): 1.

56. Anti-Lynching Crusaders, Printed Index Cards for Distribution, October 1922, ALC/JWJC.

57. Anti-Lynching Crusaders, "Directions for Buffalo Key Women," October 1922, ALC/JWJC.

58. Mary B. Talbert to John Shillady, 29 September 1919, in *Papers of NAACP, Part 1, Meetings of the Board of Directors, Records of Annual Conferences, Major Speeches, and Special Reports, 1909–1950* (Frederick, Md.: University Publications of America, 1981), microfilm (hereafter cited as NAACP Administrative Files).

59. Mary B. Talbert to James Weldon Johnson, 28 June 1922, in NAACP Administrative Files.

60. Terborg-Penn, "African-American Women's Networks in the Anti-Lynching Crusade," 154.

61. Emma Wold to Harriet Stanton Blatch, 29 December 1920; Mary White Ovington to Mary Talbert, 20 December 1920, TL; Mary White Ovington to Alice Paul, 4 January 1921, TL; all in *Papers of the NAACP, Part 11, Special Subject Files, 1912–1939, Series B, Harding, Warren G. through YWCA Editorial Advisor* (Frederick, Md.: University Publications of America, 1990), microfilm (hereafter cited as NAACP/NWP File). Blatch attached

a side-note to the letter for a colleague's view stating, "This is the reply to my letter urging the inclusion of Mrs. Talbert. It makes the point obviously. Whenever Miss Paul does not wish to face an issue, she always manages to be so busy or absent, so that she delegates the answer to a subordinate."

62. Mary B. Talbert to Mary White Ovington, 5 January 1921, NAACP/NWP File.

63. Hall, *Revolt against Chivalry,* 167, 165–166.

64. "Georgia Women Will Make Fight on Mob Violence," *Atlanta Constitution,* 11 September 1921, in TNCF, reel 14, heading "Race Relations."

65. "Southern White Women Speak Again," *New York Age,* 8 October 1921, in TNCF, reel 14, heading "Race Relations."

66. Neverdon-Morton, *Afro-American Women of the South,* 227, 226–233.

67. Mary B. Talbert to White Women for Affiliation, 11 October 1922, ALC/JWJC.

68. Mary B. Talbert to Executive Board and State Directors of the Anti-Lynching Crusaders, n.d. (1922), ALC/JWJC.

69. Mary B. Talbert to Executive Board and State Directors of the Anti-Lynching Crusaders, October 1922, ALC/JWJC.

70. Mary B. Talbert to Grace Nail Johnson, 13 October 1922, ALC/JWJC.

71. Mary B. Talbert to Grace Nail Johnson, 19 October 1922, ALC/JWJC.

72. Mary B. Talbert to Grace Nail Johnson, 22 November 1922, ALC/JWJC.

73. Paul Kennaday to Grace Nail Johnson, 7 December 1922, ALC/JWJC.

74. Foreign Press Service, Inc., "The Shame of America, Serial #6598," ALC/JWJC.

75. See Ida B. Wells, *Southern Horrors: Lynch Law in All Its Phases* (New York: New York Age Print, 1892); reprinted in Ida B. Wells-Barnett, *On Lynchings, Southern Horrors, A Red Record, Mob Rule in New Orleans* (New York: Arno Press, 1969).

76. Ida B. Wells-Barnett, "Anti-Lynching Crusaders," *Woman's Forum* (September–October 1922): 2.

77. Ibid.

78. Ibid.

79. Wells-Barnett, *Crusade for Justice,* 75.

80. Chairman of the Publicity Committee of the Anti-Lynching Crusaders, "Statement to Mrs. Nahum D. Brascher, The Associated Press."

81. Patricia Schechter has offered an incisive analysis on the roots of Wells-Barnett's troubles with the NAACP and the NACW. See Patricia Schechter, *Ida B. Wells-Barnett and American Reform, 1880–1930* (Chapel Hill: University of North Carolina Press, 2001), chaps. 4, 6.

82. "The National Association of Colored Women's Clubs," 2.

83. Rayford Logan and Michael R. Winston, *Dictionary of American Negro Biography* (New York: W. W. Norton, 1982), 576–577.

84. *New York Times,* 29–20 November, 1–3 December 1922; Mary B. Talbert to Executive Board Members and State Directors, 5 December 1922, ALC/JWJC.

85. Ibid.

86. Ibid.

87. *Buffalo Evening Times,* 16 October 1923.

88. Nannie H. Burroughs, "A Great Woman," Nannie Helen Burroughs Collection, LOC.

89. Mary White Ovington to Mary Talbert, 9 October 1923, TL, in *Papers of the NAACP, Part 7, The Anti-Lynching Campaign, 1912–1955, Series B, Anti-Lynching Legisla-*

*tive and Publicity Files, 1916–1955* (Frederick, Md.: University Publications of America, 1987), microfilm.

90. See the National Association for the Advancement of Colored People, *Thirty Years of Lynching in the United States, 1889–1918*; Walter F. White, *Rope and Faggot* (New York: Arno Press, 1969); Zangrando, *The N.A.A.C.P. Crusade.*

91. "A Citizenship Call Sounded to Race Women," *Norfolk Journal and Guide,* 4 October 1924, in TNCF, reel 22, heading "Women's Work."

92. "Serious Questions for Club Women," *National Notes* 26 (July 1924): 11.

93. Rebecca Stiles Taylor, "Four Sectional Federations," *National Notes* 26 (July 1924): 5–6.

94. White, *Too Heavy a Load,* 124–128, 129–130.

95. Gertrude E. Hall, "Forces Contributing to the Delinquency of Our Girls," *National Notes* 26 (July 1924): 11.

96. Ula Taylor, *The Veiled Garvey: The Life and Times of Amy Jacques Garvey* (Chapel Hill: University of North Carolina Press, 2002), 70.

97. "Twelve Thousand Dollars Is Raised at Women's Meeting; Mrs. Bethune Made President," *Birmingham Reporter,* 16 August 1924, in TNCF, reel 22, heading "Women's Work"; Davis, *Lifting as We Climb,* 68.

98. "The National Association of Colored Women—Attention," *Christian Recorder* (Philadelphia), 22 February 1923, in TNCF, reel 19, heading "Women's Work."

99. "The Black Mammy Statue," *National Notes* 25 (April 1923): 3.

100. Stephanie Shaw, *What a Woman Ought to Be and to Do,* 209.

101. Christia Adair, interview by Dorothy R. Robinson, 25 April 1977, transcript, *Black Women Oral History Project,* SLR, 33–34.

## 6. National Party Politics through the Depression

1. "Assails Lynching Plank," *Indianapolis* (unknown title), 15 July 1920; "Colored Women's Clubs Fail to Endorse G.O.P.," *Peoria Transcript,* 17 July 1920; both in TNCF, reel 12, heading "Women's Work."

2. John W. Dean, *Warren G. Harding* (New York: Henry Holt), 67, 123.

3. See Nancy J. Weiss, "The Negro and the New Freedom: Fighting Wilsonian Segregation," *Political Science Quarterly* 84 (March 1969): 61–79; Karen Wolgemuth, "Woodrow Wilson and Federal Segregation," *Journal of Negro History* 44 (April 1959): 158–173; August Meier and Elliot Rudwick, "The Rise of Segregation in the Federal Bureaucracy, 1900–1930," *Phylon* 28 (Summer 1967): 178–184.

4. Warren G. Harding to R. R. Moton, Tuskegee, Ala., in "Minutes of the 1920 Tuskegee Convention," 54, NACW Papers, reel 1.

5. "Georgia Plans Moving to Washington after March 4," *New York Dispatch,* 12 November 1920, in TNCF, reel 11, heading "Labor."

6. "Clubwoman Protests to Harding on Segregation," *Chicago Defender,* 23 April 1921, in TNCF, reel 13, heading "Discrimination."

7. Dean, *Warren G. Harding,* 124; Robert Murray, *The Harding Era: Warren G. Harding and His Administration* (Minneapolis: University of Minnesota Press, 1969), 401.

8. Evelyn Brooks Higginbotham, "Clubwomen and Electoral Politics in the 1920s," in *African American Women and the Vote, 1837–1920,* ed. Ann D. Gordon (Amherst: University of Massachusetts Press, 1997), 135.

9. "The National Association of Women's Clubs," *Birmingham Reporter,* 24 July 1920, in TNCF, reel 12, heading "Women's Work."

10. "Would Frighten White Women Voters with a 'Black Menace,'" *Norfolk Journal and Guide,* 25 September 1920, in TNCF, reel 12, heading "Politics, Women in."

11. "The Woman of the South," *Montgomery Advertiser,* 15 August 1919, in TNCF, reel 10, heading "Suffrage."

12. Terborg-Penn, *African American Women and the Struggle for the Vote, 1850–1920,* 134.

13. "Miss Alice Paul's Pronunciamento," *Daily Herald,* 22 February 1919, in TNCF, reel 10, heading "Suffrage"; Terborg-Penn, *African American Women and the Struggle for the Vote,* 130.

14. "Secretary Shillady Rebukes Miss Paul," *Daily Herald,* 21 February 1919, in TNCF, reel 10, heading "Suffrage."

15. Terborg-Penn, *African American Women and the Struggle for the Vote,* 107–135.

16. "The Negro and Suffrage," *Waco Tribune,* 23 May 1919, in TNCF, reel 10, heading "Suffrage."

17. "Men of Atlanta, Wake Up and Register: No Slackers Wanted," *Atlanta Independent,* 12 March 1919, in TNCF, reel 9, heading "Politics, Women in."

18. "Woman Suffrage," *The Crisis* 19 (March 1920): 234.

19. *New York Post,* 24 April 1919, in TNCF, reel 10, heading "Suffrage."

20. "Grandmother's Clause," *Atlanta Independent,* 21 June 1919, in TNCF, reel 10, heading "Suffrage."

21. "Willing to Sacrifice Colored Women," *Baltimore Afro-American,* 19 February 1919, in TNCF, reel 10, heading "Suffrage."

22. "Grandmother Clause," *New York Age,* 19 February 1921, in TNCF, reel 14, heading "Politics."

23. "944 Oklahoma Negroes Called Illegal Voters," *New York Tribune,* 3 August 1924, in TNCF, reel 21, heading "Politics."

24. "First Colored Woman of Alabama Seeks Right to Vote," *Louisville News,* 8 March 1924, in TNCF, reel 21, heading "Politics."

25. Tera Hunter, *To 'Joy My Freedom: Southern Black Women's Lives and Labors after the Civil War* (Cambridge, Mass.: Harvard University Press, 1996), 219–222.

26. "Hoodlums Put Honest White Man on Carpet," *Cleveland Advocate,* 16 October 1920, in TNCF, reel 12, heading "Politics, Elections and Suffrage Rights."

27. "Florida White Would Prevent Blacks Voting," *Baltimore Afro-American,* 24 March 1922, in TNCF, reel 16, heading "Politics, Suffrage."

28. Walter White, "Election by Terror in Florida," *Cayton's Monthly* (February 1921), in TNCF, reel 14, heading "Politics."

29. "Negro Women Seek Franchise Probe," *Atlanta Constitution,* 13 February 1921; "Aftermath of Women's Convention," *Wilmington* (Del.) *Advocate,* 26 February 1921; both in TNCF, reel 14, heading "Politics."

30. George Fredrickson, *The Black Image in the White Mind: The Debate on Afro-America Character and Destiny, 1817–1914* (New York: Harper & Row, 1971).

31. "Ollie James Gives Keynote to Southern Opposition to Woman Suffrage," *Louisville News,* 27 January 1917, in TNCF, reel 6, heading "Politics."

32. *St. Louis Argus,* 1 March 1918, in TNCF, reel 8, heading "Politics, Women in."

33. [no title], *Christian Recorder,* 8 August 1918, in TNCF, reel 8, heading "Politics, Women in."

34. Kelly Miller, "Negro Vote A Puzzle in North," *New York Times*, 24 August 1924, in TNCF, reel 21, heading "Politics."

35. "Progressives Name First Negro Elector In Ill.; Mrs. Nelson To Organize Women," *Washington Tribune*, 23 August 1924, in TNCF, reel 21, heading "Politics."

36. "Director of Organization Speaks to Federation of Colored Women's Clubs Urging Education of Masses," *Dallas Express*, 26 August 1922, in TNCF, reel 17, heading "Women's Work."

37. "To the Negro Women of Georgia," *Savannah Journal*, 4 September 1920, in TNCF, reel 12, heading "Politics, Women in."

38. "The Women—God Bless Them!" *Houston Informer*, 6 November 1920, in TNCF, reel 12, heading "Politics, Women in."

39. "It Is Time for Men and Women of Our Group to Register," *Atlanta Independent*, 24 April 1924, in TNCF, reel 21, heading "Politics, Suffrage."

40. "Suffrage Has Stirred Negro People of B'ham; Negro Women Refused Right to Register; Threaten Protest," *Birmingham Reporter*, 9 September 1920, in TNCF, reel 12, heading "Politics, Women in"; "The Colored Women's Voters' League," *Birmingham Reporter*, 14 April 1921; "The Women Voters' Club," *Birmingham Reporter*, 4 June 1921; both in TNCF, reel 14, heading "Politics."

41. "The Woman Voter Hits the Color Line," *The Nation*, 6 October 1920, in TNCF, reel 12, heading "Politics, Women in."

42. "Suffrage Meeting," *Savannah Tribune*, 27 March 1920, in TNCF, reel 12, heading "Politics, Women in."

43. "Registration Office Gets Assistance; Women Swamp Place; Race Segregation," *Richmond Leader*, 17 September 1920, in TNCF, reel 12, heading "Politics, Women in."

44. "Denies South Carolina Women Want to Vote," *Negro World*, 18 February 1919, in TNCF, reel 10, heading "Politics."

45. "'Negroes Lack Interest," *Southwestern Christian Advocate*, 7 October 1920, in TNCF, reel 12, heading "Politics."

46. "A Word to Women Voters" (unknown title, probably *Baltimore Afro-American*) [n.d., probably 1920]), in TNCF, reel 12, heading "Suffrage, Women in."

47. "YOU ARE NO MAN!!" *Houston Observer*, 3 November 1917, in TNCF, reel 6, heading "Politics and Suffrage."

48. "Women Organize Voters League," *Dallas Express*, 18 October 1919, in TNCF, reel 10, heading "Politics."

49. "Houston Judge Rules Recent Act of Texas Legislature Unconstitutional; Colored Men and Women Must Vote," *Houston Informer*, 31 October 1920, in TNCF, reel 12, heading "Politics, Elections and Voting Rights."

50. "Woman of Interest," *Competition Magazine*, October–November 1920, in TNCF, reel 16, heading "Suffrage."

51. "Mrs. Williams Is Appointed to Library Board," *Chicago Defender*, 26 July 1924, in TNCF, reel 21, heading "Politics."

52. "Colored Woman First Woman to Hold Office in Arkansas," *Wilmington* (Del.) *Advocate*, 16 April 1921, in TNCF, reel 14, heading "Politics."

53. Terborg-Penn, *African-American Women and the Struggle for the Vote*, 148–149.

54. "Running for Legislative Seat," *Pittsburgh American*, 17 March 1922, in TNCF, reel 16, heading "Suffrage."

55. "Negress Gets Most Votes," *Federated Press Bulletin*, 16 December 1920; "Colored Woman Leads in Connecticut Voting," *Pittsburgh American*, 22 December 1920; "Able-

Minded Negress Running for Congress on Farmer-Labor Ticket in First District; Mrs. Mary Townsend Seymore [*sic*] Career," *Bridgeport* (Conn.) *Herald*, 10 October 1920, all in TNCF, reel 16, heading "Suffrage."

56. "Annual National Meeting of Colored Women," *Wilmington* (Del.) *Advocate*, 12 March 1921, in TNCF, reel 14, heading "Politics."

57. "The Women's Republican Advisory Committee Recently Appointed at a Meeting of the Republican State Central Committee," *Atlanta Independent*, 3 March 1921, in TNCF, reel 14, heading "Politics."

58. "Negro Woman Gets High Post," *Kansas City* (Mo.) *Sun*, 14 July 1923, in TNCF, reel 19, heading "Politics." See also, on the same reel and under same heading: "Link Johnson Wants Women on Auxiliary," *Baltimore Afro-American*, 6 July 1923; "Henry Johnson Names Negro Clubwoman as His Associate," *Pittsburgh American*, 17 August 1923.

59. "G.O.P. Balks Naming of Negro Committee Woman from Georgia" (no title, no city), 3 December 1923.

60. "Negro Woman Wins New Distinction for Her Race," *New York World*, 23 April 1924, in TNCF, reel 21, heading "Politics."

61. "Negro Woman Is Elected to National Committee," *New York Times*, 13 June 1924, in TNCF, reel 21, heading "Politics."

62. Higginbotham, "Clubwomen and Electoral Politics in the 1920s," 141, 144.

63. Hallie Q. Brown, "Republican Colored Women of America," *National Notes* 27 (December 1924): 2, in NACW Papers.

64. "Hallie Q. Brown to Direct Republican Women's Activities," *New York Age*, 6 September 1924, in TNCF, reel 21, heading "Politics."

65. "Women's Political Study Club Praised G.O.P. Stand," *Chicago Defender*, 20 September 1924, in TNCF, reel 21, heading "Politics."

66. "Leading Colored Women Form National Republican League," *New York Amsterdam News*, 22 October 1924, in TNCF, reel 21, heading "Politics."

67. Higginbotham, "Clubwomen and Electoral Politics in the 1920s," 143–147.

68. Audrey Thomas McCluskey and Elaine M. Smith, eds., *Mary McCleod Bethune: Building a Better World: Essays and Selected Documents* (Bloomington: Indiana University Press, 1999), 4–7; Joyce Ann Hanson, *Mary McLeod Bethune and Black Women's Political Activism* (Columbia: University of Missouri Press, 2003), 11–55.

69. "Southern Negro Women and Race Co-operation," in Mary McLeod Bethune Papers, Mary McLeod Bethune Foundation, Bethune-Cookman College, Daytona Beach, Fla.; reprinted in *Building a Better World*, 145.

70. Ibid., 148.

71. Ibid., 132.

72. Mary McLeod Bethune, "Great Designs: President's Address to the Fifteenth Biennial Convention of the National Association of Colored Women," in *Building a Better World*, 158, 161.

73. Mary McLeod Bethune, interview by Charles S. Johnson, undated oral history, transcript, Mary McLeod Bethune Papers, Amistad Research Center, Tulane University, New Orleans, La., microfilm, 27–28.

74. "President's Monthly Message," *National Notes* ( January 1927): 3, in NACW Papers, reel 23.

75. Bethune, "Great Designs," 161.

76. Hanson, *Mary McLeod Bethune and Black Women's Political Activism*, 113–117.

77. "Black and Gold Stars," *The Nation,* 23 July 1930, in Schomburg Center Clipping File, 1925–1974, New York Public Library, N.Y., heading "World War I"; Evelyn Brooks Higginbotham, "Clubwomen and Electoral Politics in the 1920s," 146–147; Nancy J. Weiss, *Farewell to the Party of Lincoln: Black Politics in the Age of FDR* (Princeton, N.J.: Princeton University Press, 1983), 3–33.

78. "Opinion from All Classes Indicate Chief Benefit from Great Upheaval Was Chance for Race to Find Itself," *Pittsburgh Courier,* 7 May 1927, in Schomburg Center Clipping File, 1925–1974, New York Public Library, New York, heading "World War I."

# Index

NIKKI BROWN is Chair of the History Department at Grambling State University in Grambling, Louisiana.